# Meryl Jean
# Another Whirlwind

Noel Barton

Copyright © 2019 Noel Barton
Print Edition

ISBN: 978-1-7330134-0-6

All rights reserved. No part of this book may be reproduced, transmitted downloaded, distributed, stored in or introduced into any information storage and retrieval system, in any form or by any means, whether electronic or mechanical, without express permission of the author, except by a reviewer who may quote brief passages for review purposes.

This book is a work of fiction and any resemblance to any person, living or dead, or any events or occurrences, is purely coincidental. The characters and story lines are created from the author's imagination or are used fictitiously. Any trademarks, service marks, product names, or named features are assumed to be the property of their respective owners and are used only for reference. There is no implied endorsement if any of these terms are used. Except for review purposes, the reproduction of this book in whole or part, electronically or mechanically, constitutes a copyright violation.

Cover design by Robin Kinser
Editing and formatting Ruth Nickolich
Special final editing and formatting Bobbie Falin

# Dedication

I dedicate this book to Mrs. Ruby Turner and Mrs. Marjorie Scott. These two excellent high school English teachers saw my potential and encouraged me to use it. I only wish I could share my stories with them today. And I hope they would be proud.

# Table of Contents

Praise for Meryl Jean Another Whirlwind ................................. ix
Map ........................................................................................ xi
Foreword ............................................................................. xiii
Prologue ............................................................................... xv
Chapter One ........................................................................... 1
Chapter Two .......................................................................... 5
Chapter Three ...................................................................... 12
Chapter Four ....................................................................... 17
Chapter Five ........................................................................ 22
Chapter Six .......................................................................... 31
Chapter Seven ...................................................................... 35
Chapter Eight ...................................................................... 40
Chapter Nine ....................................................................... 46
Chapter Ten ......................................................................... 52
Chapter Eleven .................................................................... 60
Chapter Twelve .................................................................... 66
Chapter Thirteen ................................................................. 73
Chapter Fourteen ................................................................ 83
Chapter Fifteen .................................................................... 88
Chapter Sixteen ................................................................... 93
Chapter Seventeen ............................................................... 97
Chapter Eighteen ............................................................... 103
Chapter Nineteen .............................................................. 106
Chapter Twenty ................................................................. 111
Chapter Twenty-One ......................................................... 116
Chapter Twenty-Two ......................................................... 121
Chapter Twenty-Three ....................................................... 126
Chapter Twenty-Four ........................................................ 129
Chapter Twenty-Five ......................................................... 138
Chapter Twenty-Six ........................................................... 144
Chapter Twenty-Seven ....................................................... 153
Chapter Twenty-Eight ....................................................... 160

| | |
|---|---|
| Chapter Twenty-Nine | 165 |
| Chapter Thirty | 171 |
| Chapter Thirty-One | 178 |
| Chapter Thirty-Two | 185 |
| Chapter Thirty-Three | 189 |
| Chapter Thirty-Four | 194 |
| Chapter Thirty-Five | 200 |
| Chapter Thirty-Six | 204 |
| Chapter Thirty-Seven | 214 |
| Chapter Thirty-Eight | 218 |
| Chapter Thirty-Nine | 226 |
| Chapter Forty | 234 |
| Chapter Forty-One | 239 |
| Chapter Forty-Two | 244 |
| Chapter Forty-Three | 250 |
| Chapter Forty-Four | 254 |
| Chapter Forty-Five | 258 |
| Chapter Forty-Six | 264 |
| Chapter Forty-Seven | 274 |
| Chapter Forty-Eight | 282 |
| Chapter Forty-Nine | 289 |
| Chapter Fifty | 298 |
| Chapter Fifty-One | 304 |
| Chapter Fifty-Two | 309 |
| Chapter Fifty-Three | 315 |
| Chapter Fifty-Four | 326 |
| Chapter Fifty-Five | 332 |
| Chapter Fifty-Six | 341 |
| Chapter Fifty-Seven | 347 |
| Chapter Fifty-Eight | 357 |
| Chapter Fifty-Nine | 367 |
| Chapter Sixty | 376 |
| Chapter Sixty-One | 381 |
| Chapter Sixty-Two | 387 |
| Chapter Sixty-Three | 396 |
| Chapter Sixty-Four | 405 |
| Chapter Sixty-Five | 411 |
| Chapter Sixty-Six | 422 |
| Chapter Sixty-Seven | 431 |
| Chapter Sixty-Eight | 437 |

Chapter Sixty-Nine ..................................................................445
Chapter Seventy .......................................................................453
Chapter Seventy-One ...............................................................460
Chapter Seventy-Two ...............................................................467
Chapter Seventy-Three .............................................................472
Chapter Seventy-Four...............................................................478
Acknowledgments ...................................................................483
About the Author.....................................................................485

## Praise for Meryl Jean Another Whirlwind

Noel has written another enchanting story about days gone by. Bad breaks and bad choices can't break an indomitable spirit. This story shows our past helps to form us but it doesn't dictate our future.
—Mr. Rudy's boy, Jeff Pylant

MERYL JEAN ANOTHER WHIRLWIND is a richly imagined and thoughtful coming-of-age story that is sure to entertain readers of all ages."
—David Bell, author of LAYOVER

"First of all, let me admit that I am biased. I absolutely loved "Watch for the Whirlwinds," Noel Barton's first foray into a bygone era that is still very familiar to those of us of a certain age. I am happy to report that her sophomore effort, "Another Whirlwind" picks up where her first book left off and extends the story even further. There were times I laughed out loud, and there were times I felt my eyes getting misty. Once again, Barton has managed to elicit the full spectrum of possible emotional reactions in "Another Whirlwind." As was the case with her previous book, you won't be able to put this one down either. Again, I believe her stories should be made into a miniseries or a major motion picture. I look forward to her next installment."

—Aaron Hughey

Noel Barton has managed to once again weave moral (and religious lessons) into a wonderful story without being "preachy."…The book has great examples of growing through obstacles, recognizing true friendship, and meeting the challenges of tragedy with faith and courage. Like her first book, this is one I look forward to reading (and learning from) a second time.

—Joe Causey,
Retired Pastor,
Hospital Chaplain

Noel Barton skillfully navigates readers through the perilous adolescence of a motherless girl growing up in rural (Bootheel) Missouri. Readers will be enraptured by Meryl Jean's difficult but entertaining, heartwarming, and at times humorous journey!

—Kimberly Bartley,
author of Until Death Parts and Go Forth and Multiply

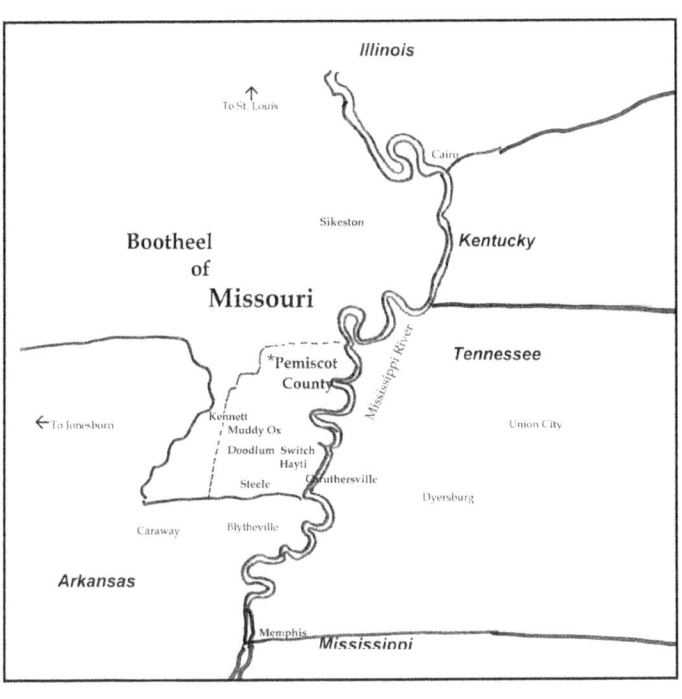

# Foreword

The dictionary defines a parable as a simple story illustrating a moral or religious lesson. Noel Barton has managed to weave once again moral (and religious lessons) into a wonderful story without being "preachy." Woven into this wonderful story of the high school years of a young lady being raised by her grandmother, are lessons about God answering prayer and watching over his children. Jean Strom, the young high school student, somewhat abandoned by her father after her mother died, was brought to her "God fearing" grandmother in the first story and is now facing her high school years with its trials by fire, "friends," and the growing pains of adolescence. Throughout the story, Jean discovers a number of "spiritual lessons" as evidenced through phrases such as; "people can't out give God," "things are things," "don't give up praying," and a reference that "education goes beyond the textbook."

This book (and her first one, "Watch for the Whirlwinds') are wonderful; not just for the story but for the lessons learned from the challenges life brings. If it were possible, I would strongly suggest (or require) their reading by all children and adolescents as they travel through their school years. The book has great examples of growing through obstacles, recognizing true friendship, and meeting the challenges of tragedy with faith and courage. Like her first book, this is one I look forward to reading (and learning from) a second time. It is a book for parents (learn from grandmother) and youth (learn from Meryl Jean).

Joe Causey
Retired Pastor
Hospital Chaplain

# The First Whirlwind…

Although it seemed much longer, we'd been chopping cotton for only two hours. Waves of heat, from the scorching sun, flowed across the field. My bonnet worked well for keeping the sun from my face, but didn't allow me to feel any breeze, had there been one.

My feet burned from the baking ground and my shoulders ached from continuously swinging the hoe. Despite my gloves, there was a small blister rising between my thumb and forefinger. My tender hands that had never experienced work before were not standing up to the challenge very well. I was already in trouble. It was four hours before noon and all I could think about was washing my face in a pan of cold water and resting in the swing on Grandma's back porch. While stopping to examine my blister, I heard Tara yell in excitement.

"Jean, look up! "Push your bonnet back. It's headed your way." Tara was pointing to a whirlwind only a few rows over from me.

Whirlwinds, also called dust-devils were common occurrences out in the hot, flat, cotton fields. My whirlwind didn't last long, but it cooled me off a bit and dried my sweating face. Anything that offered relief from the parching hot sun out in the cotton field was appreciated. I'd never been in the midst of a whirlwind before, but from then on, I made it a practice to look long and hard for one that might be headed my direction. I later learned there are many kinds of whirlwinds. Some refreshed you; some almost sucked the life out of you.

## Another Whirlwind…

It had been three years since Meryl came to live with Grandma in the Bootheel of Missouri in Muddy Ox, a tiny community where everybody knew everybody and everybody's dog.

At age sixteen, she'd evolved from a pampered child who hadn't been made to pick her socks off the floor to one who could skillfully hoe a field row and pick two hundred and fifty pounds of cotton in a twelve-hour day.

Her motivation came when Grandma told her she could keep all the money she made to buy her books and school clothes. She quickly calculated she'd never have to wear the boy shoes her dad had made her wear because of her wide feet causing ridicule and embarrassment by her peers. Sending a little fat girl to school wearing boy's shoes only guaranteed she'll be tormented.

Meryl brought a list of 'nevers' with her after she and her father moved to Muddy Ox from Brooksville, Illinois. First of all, never wear those boy shoes again. Second, never be the butt of jokes because she cast a larger shadow than some other children. And last, never be belt whipped by an alcoholic father again. How Meryl found ways to cross off those and other 'nevers' later added to her list is the heart of this novel but there is so much more.

My first novel, Watch for the Whirlwinds ended with Meryl at the tender age of fifteen years old. This second one takes her from age sixteen and launches her out into the world.

There are several plots and subplots to this story, but it begins with a dream that Meryl had about her mother. This dream significantly follows her through her young life. There is a firebug running amuck in Muddy Ox. The twist in discovering its identity will surprise you. Be with Meryl as she experiences her first date, first kiss and first heartbreak. Follow her journey into adulthood and feel the pain of some of the events that left scars from her childhood.

God bless you if you've experienced the sudden death of someone who balanced your world or have been abruptly ripped away from all things familiar to you. A special blessing to the reader whose been bullied—for any reason. May you find encouragement within Meryl Jean's story.

*A Love Song*

*The moon is bright, and it shines on me.*
*Down through the leaves of our willow tree*
*Please let the moon that shines on me,*
*Shine on the one I love.*

*I hear a bird, diddle dum dee dee.*
*Singing a song for my love and me*
*Please let the bird that sings to me,*
*Sing to the one I love.*

What a sweet song…

# Chapter One

FEAR GRIPPED MY throat. I could barely breathe as my feet found and splashed in nearly every puddle in the dark, winding, cave. Escaping from whomever or whatever was chasing me was virtually impossible. Yet I pressed on, fearful to continue down the tunneled path—and fearful to not.

"Meryl, Meryl, stop," a distorted, yet vaguely familiar voice called. They surely know me. They called my name.

"Meryl, Meryl, stop," the voice echoed again.

The harder I ran, the heavier my feet became. Finally, exhaustion forced me to stop. I'd have to face my fears as I'd done that day in the high school gym. The sounds of approaching footsteps echoed throughout the tunnel, much as the insults seemed to echo off the gym walls when I was called fat during a noon hour basketball game after blocking the winning shot.

When I turned to the voice behind me, I saw my pursuer was not an enemy at all—it was my mother. How could this be? She'd been dead three years.

This couldn't be real. Rubbing my eyes for clarity only made the vision more vivid. I reached toward her and wanted to run and feel Mama's warm embrace, but my feet felt frozen to the cave floor. Why wasn't she reaching for me? Where was her warmth? Her trembling voice seemed to be captured within a thick vapor that bounced off the walls and filled the cave's cavity, as the insults had filled the gym.

"Meryl, I—I am ashamed of you—ashamed of you—ashamed of you," it echoed.

The void in my heart that only a mother could fill remained empty. My eyes welled with tears, as when I stood by the shell of Mama lying in the casket. Her vision slowly faded, and I found myself looking at—me.

Then I awoke.

I'D HAD DAYDREAMS but never an actual night dream of Mama since she died. This dream left me nearly as emotionally wounded as I was wounded physically by my dad's belt whippings. I needed to hear Mama say she loved me, missed me, and was sorry she died and left me—not that she was ashamed of me. Why was my mother ashamed of me? Nothing I'd done could be labeled shameful. I'd bravely approached my forced adult role, worked like a slave in the cotton fields, obeyed every one of Grandma's rules, and reckoned with Daddy as best I could.

The dream momentarily made me forget the events of the day and why I was sleeping on Simp and Katty's couch and not in my bed—in my own room. My eyes welled again with tears to remember our tragedy. Our house had burned along with the school clothes, shoes, and other things I'd labored for in the cotton field all fall.

"You and Meryl Jean can stay with us as long as you need to Mrs. Strom," Katty Simpson had said. Katty, John, and daughter Sadie were Grandma's lifelong friends and closest neighbors.

Katty respectfully addressed Grandma as Mrs. Strom because she was her elder. Grandma often said their bond with us was as close as if we'd been blood kin. She hated to impose on them now, but it wasn't like we had other options. We surely didn't have money to buy more clothes, restore the house, or rent a place until we could figure out what to do. Of course, Grandma didn't have insurance.

The screens on their open windows held the mosquitoes at bay but not the stench of smoldering wood and melting asphalt siding. After all, a strong arm could have thrown a rock from the Simpson's house to ours. If John Simpson, known to all as Simp, and Obadiah McDougal, a volunteer fireman, hadn't held me back, I would have foolishly braved the fire in an effort to rescue my clothes and…Mama's trunk.

Sickness gripped my stomach to again think of our loss. Poor Grandma was so beside herself. All she could do was wring her hands and cry.

Remnants of the dream again overpowered reality. Ashamed of me—my mother is ashamed of me? Exhaustion from the day's events and the dream drew me back into restless slumber. Thankfully, the remainder of the night offered no more dreams.

## Chapter Two

"THIS IS MR. Rudy Pylant... and that's it for Old Camp Meetin' Time this morning. Everyone have a blessed day and join us again at five a.m. tomorrow morning on KBOA, 830 on your dial for more Old Camp Meetin' Time. Now I sure hope y'all got your cotton picked because I'm going to leave you now with Lester Flatt and Earl Scruggs singing, *He Will Set Your Fields on Fire*."

I could envision dancing legs on Miss Katty's kitchen radio as Flatt and Scruggs' blue-grass gospel twang bounced through its speakers. Once the song was over, Katty switched off the radio.

"Mrs. Strom, Simp's gone to the field, and I'm gonna feed my cats and go work in the garden 'fore the heat of the day sets in. You and Meryl Jean go on and sleep as long as you want. Here kitty, kitty, kitty!"

The nerves in my face flinched with each of Katty's booming words. She was louder than usual this morning to be heard over the blare of her kitchen radio. The screened door slammed and banged behind her and she proceeded to the garden, hoe in hand. The nearly deaf Katty failed to realize how loud she and her radio were, especially at that hour of the morning. What was a whisper to her was a scream to everyone else. Sadie was so accustomed to her mother's tone she never made a stir.

*He Will Set Your Fields on Fire*—well it wasn't our fields that had been on fire—it was our house. Because of the comfortless couch and my disturbing dream, I hardly felt rested at all. I was in a semi-awaken state when Grandma appeared from her sleeping quarters. She twisted her braid into its familiar knot on the back of her head and stuck hairpins in all the right places from memory, as she passed on her way to the kitchen.

"How'd you sleep?" she asked once I joined her but didn't wait for my reply. "I guess I rested okay, after I finally got the fire kinda' out of my head," she continued.

"I—I managed all right," answering her already forgotten question and not wanting to complain about the Simpson's lumpy couch.

"Katty left us some gravy and a plate of her 'cat-head' biscuits. Let's eat a bite and then go look at the house. Maybe it won't look so bad today since the fire's out and the smoke's gone." Sweet Grandma, reassuring me while her own heart was so heavy.

Grandma referred to Miss Katty's biscuits as 'cat-head biscuits' because they were big, round, and lumpy. Katty didn't invent cat-head biscuits, but hers were probably tom-cat-size, while others' were merely kitten-size.

She didn't roll her biscuit dough onto a board as Grandma did. With well-floured hands, she pinched the dough between her thumb and forefinger to form giant, imperfect, balls. The size of her hands made her biscuits huge. Katty's biscuits were truly about the size of a big old tom cat's head.

I loved Katty's cake and chocolate icing that she bragged was perfected by holding her mouth just right while she made it, and her white beans and cornbread that she made a pot and pone of every day of her life. But when it came to biscuits, I preferred Grandma's thinner, crustier, not so doughy ones.

I dissected a cathead biscuit, slicing the crusts from the top and bottom. I placed the buttered crusts on the edge of my plate for later and spooned a little milk gravy over a portion of the crumbled inside. Grandma did a similar ritual, and between the two of us, there still remained the insides of almost an entire tom-cat-head biscuit.

"Grandma, what are we going to do? We love the Simpsons but staying with them is nerve-racking. Did you hear Old Camp Meeting Time this morning?"

I then realized it was likely that most of Silver Leaf had heard Old Camp Meeting Time this morning. Neighbors could save electricity by merely listening to Katty's radio.

"We'll do somethin'. Right now I am not sure what.

But we'll do somethin'." Grandma's tone and expression didn't offer a great sense of assurance.

I hoped she had a plan. Grandma usually had a plan. But it was sounding as though we'd be staying with our neighbors as long as they'd have us, or until we lost our hearing or sanity.

"Meryl, we'll pray and just see what happens. God's been takin' care of you and me all our lives. I can't see Him forgettin' us now."

There it was. Grandma's plan was to trust God. I wanted to have that same trusting feeling, but honestly, it wasn't there. I had heard and seen enough in the short time I'd lived with her to know when Grandma prayed—God listened. Nevertheless, I had to ask.

"I wonder. And I don't want to be disrespectful. But…if God is taking care of us, then why did our house burn? Why if God knows how much you trust Him, and He saw how hard I worked to get my school clothes, then why did He let this fire happen?

I waited to see if lightning was going to strike or if the ground would rumble beneath us, for Grandma's response. It took a while, which only added to my uneasiness. Then, choosing her words carefully, she slowly began.

"Meryl, it's easy to trust in somethin' you can see. If the end of a tunnel is in sight, then it's not hard to trust what's there. But, if you enter somethin' blind, then trust becomes more—it becomes faith."

If not for the dream about my mother, I wouldn't have understood. Ironically, Grandma's reference to the tunnel was all too real.

"I had a dream about Mama last night," I began softly. "It's the first real dream I've had about her since—she died."

"Oh, I've had dreams of your grandpa Omar, too. Sometimes I feel as though we had a nice visit," Grandma rambled. She obviously considered my dream a good thing.

The pain in my face and the tears with a mind of their own, quickly told her differently. "Grandma, Mama was chasing me. Only it turned out I was chasing myself. But it was Mama chasing me at first, down this wet, stinky, tunnel. I had to stop because I couldn't run any longer and…she…spoke to me. She said she was ashamed of me." My voice had trailed to a whisper.

After a few seconds, I angrily continued. "How could Mama be ashamed of me? What have I done to be ashamed of? After three long years, what does she tell me? That she's ashamed of me? She's the one who should be ashamed. She left me, a thirteen year old in the hands of an alcoholic father. How many times had she seen Daddy take his belt to me? My mother was the one who disappeared. Okay…she died, but it doesn't matter, death or desertion have the same result—abandonment." I caught my breath, wiped my wet cheeks and continued.

"I've been brave, worked hard, and battled sweat, blisters, and even stinging worms in the cotton patch. I've crossed off most of the 'nevers' I brought with me after Daddy dumped me on your porch. I survived every whirlwind so far that's come my way." Nevers were things I *never* wanted to experience again. Whirlwinds were present day experiences.

"Mama should be proud of me—not ashamed. I wanted her to hold me and say she loved me. The last thing I needed to hear was she's ashamed of me."

Had I been a six year old and reacted in such a manner, one could have said I had a tantrum. Momentarily, the only sounds that could be heard were chickens clucking and scratching in the yard and the steady slicing of Katty's garden hoe. Again, I waited for lightning or the earth to move. I'd questioned God and blamed my mother for dying—all before breakfast.

The tongue lashing response I had feared never came. Instead, for the second time that morning, Grandma chose her words carefully. She'd never before witnessed such an outburst from me.

"I hadn't realized until now Meryl, but I guess I've been mad at your Grandpa for leavin' me too, after some of the dreams I've had of him. Here's all I know. The Bible says a man's days are numbered. Omar didn't die 'cause he wanted to. I know your mother didn't want to go and leave you neither. If it wasn't their choice, then we can't blame 'em. And we should never allow ourselves to be mad at or blame God. We can question as Job did, but not blame. We're not promised forever here on this earth. There's a time to be born and a time to die. For reasons yet unknown, it was their time to go. If it wasn't, they'd still be here." Grandma cupped her hand over mine and continued.

"Honey, it was just a dream. Your mama wasn't chasin' you, and you sure wasn't chasin' yourself. Sometimes dreams mean somethin' and sometimes they are about how we react to life. Since you stopped before the end of the tunnel in your dream, then you don't know what was waitin' for you there. Now, it's about trust and faith again. You need enough faith to believe God has a purpose for you at the end of your tunnel and trust He will guide you through it.

"Meryl, God's ways are not our ways. I don't know everything. What I do know is there was never a time before or since your precious mother's death that she had one ounce of shame for you. Where you were concerned, the only things that could ever be seen in her eyes was pride and love."

## Chapter Three

Katty stomped onto the porch. Sadie appeared from her bedroom and crouched into the chair beside me. Red-faced and dripping with sweat, Katty burst into the kitchen, poured a dipper of water from the bucket into the wash pan, washed her face and hands, and directed Sadie to do the same.

Grandma, not wanting Katty to think we were wasteful, had already crumbled our remaining biscuit middles onto a plate and asked Sadie if she was ready to eat. Sadie agreed, and Grandma quickly covered the crumbles with gravy for her.

I spooned a little strawberry jelly over my pre-buttered crusts to enjoy them with coffee. Of course, Sadie wanted the same, minus the coffee, so Katty copied my dissecting procedure for her. Grandma had the kitchen cleaned and orderly, except for Sadie's plate before Katty realized.

"Mrs. Strom, you don't have to do that," Katty protested once she noticed Grandma's tidying.

"Well, it's the least I can do after you and Simp were so kind to let Meryl Jean and me stay here 'til we can get settled again. We're goin' over to the house in a bit and see what can be salvaged. Darby said the fire only reached the bedrooms. The rest of the rooms just had smoke damage. They're of the opinion it started in my closet."

"That don't make no sense a'tall. There ain't no wirin' or anythin' in that closet that could start a fire. Surely, they're wrong about that," Katty challenged.

"Maybe the smolderin' will be stopped by the time we get there," Grandma said.

"I didn't see but very little smoke on my way to the garden this mornin', and didn't notice any a'tall just now," Katty reported.

There was a peck on the door.

"Mornin' Darby. Come on in. Want some coffee? There's a few biscuits left too if yer hungry," Katty said as she got up to give him a chair. Now, when Katty gives you a chair—you take it. She practically knocked Darby's feet from under him as she slid the chair to him.

"Thanks Katty. Mornin' Mrs. Strom. I'll take a jelly biscuit to go if it's okay with y'all," Darby said but fell back into the chair anyway. "Obe and a couple of his crew from the cotton gin came too. They're waitin' out in the yard. We thought we'd help you sort through your house Mrs. Strom if you need us."

"That's so good of y'all, Darby. I can use all the help I can get. How many are out there? Three did you say? Katty, let's fix them a jelly biscuit too." Grandma hardly ever missed an opportunity to feed someone.

Katty swirled a heaping tablespoon of strawberry jelly with a matching spoonful of butter into a saucer to make soppins' for the men's breakfast treats. After she doled out the biscuits, she ordered Sadie to stay on the porch and play with her jacks. "You don't need to get over there in that mess." Sadie didn't put up a fuss since tagging along would call for wearing shoes and that was hardly ever her wish.

Other than the smell of smoke, you wouldn't have known there'd been a fire. The table remained set for Grandma's arrival from church. The food, now inedible, would eventually become chicken scraps. Darby led the way. Grandma, Katty, and I followed.

"Oh," Grandma gasped, lifting her hand to her mouth. She wasn't as prepared as she thought. The lacquer finish on her dresser had peeled from the heat, but the wood wasn't damaged. The two beds in her room, along with my bed were cast iron so the frames survived. Everything else in both bedrooms was either damaged by fire or water.

"Mrs. Strom, don't you worry about your dresser. I'll help you clean it up. It's been a while since we've used that old iron wash kettle out in the shed. I'll drag it into the yard and fill it with water. We'll get a good hot fire a goin' under it and boil the smoke right out of yer curtains and whatever else survived in 'em dresser drawers."

"You're a blessin' Katty." Grandma fought more tears.

"I'm goin' to get Sadie, and we'll walk to the Big Store and get you some vinegar, a couple boxes of bakin' soda, and an extra box of salt. I might get another bundle of onion sets, too, while I'm there. By the time we get back, Darby and the men should have the salvage pulled out of the house and we'll know what else we're workin' with."

Grandma barely had time to agree and slip her some money before Katty was out the door to gather Sadie for their brisk mile walk to town. No one doubted it would be a brisk walk. Katty was not one to drag her feet at anything, and she was now on a mission.

My heart sank as I walked into my room. The wallpaper and curtains were a complete loss. The broken mirror remained hanging on the wall. It could be cleaned up, but the heavy corrugated box that doubled as a dressing table and everything on it was only a pile of ashes. What wasn't burned, water soaked, or shattered in my closet was covered with fruit, tomatoes and other canned goods Grandma had stored there. The glass canning jars had exploded from the heat.

"Hey, what's this?" Obe asked. He was Obadiah or Mr. McDougal to everyone else. But he was Obe to me ever since he'd rescued me from my first stinging worm in the cotton patch. I would have addressed him as Mr. McDougal in the presence of others, but here in our burned bedrooms, digging in the ruins for us, he was—Obe.

I caught a glimpse of Mama's trunk as Obe pulled it from beneath a stack of heavy, singed, Army blankets and dragged it onto the front porch. Once opened, I was met with the familiar aromas inside before finding its contents safe. I remembered opening that lid one last time before we packed it in its place of priority in the car for our move to Muddy Ox from Brooksville, Illinois, after Mama died.

Dear Obe. He had now rescued me from a stinging worm, probable death or injury the day before when I tried to run into our burning house, and now he'd rescued Mama's trunk. I wished Daddy had been there. He'd thank him as he did in the cotton patch the day Obe put that spittle of chewed tobacco on my sting after the worm got me. Then Daddy stomped the thing into the ground because it hurt me. Had I been given a choice, I'm not sure I would have chosen a glob of chewed tobacco smeared on my hand, until I noticed it drew the pain from my welt.

Obe's helpers pitched the pile of Army blankets into the yard. When they landed, the remains of a charred Saucy Walker doll rolled out of them. She was the only item from my childhood that I'd brought with me from Illinois. Wrapped in only a single blanket, she couldn't withstand the fire. Oh well, the rest of my childhood was gone, minus the memories. I was sixteen now, not six. She was just a doll.

## Chapter Four

OBE AND DARBY would have saved our things—even Saucy—had it been possible. But the fire was too fierce. Plus, they couldn't help what happened with the fire truck. If it hadn't been so tragic, the fire truck fiasco that day could have been comical.

Amid the chaos, some men pumped buckets of water while others dipped more from the rain barrel and wildly hurled it onto the blaze. Finally, the fire truck arrived. Orders were shouted, "Get back, we're comin' through. Grab that hose. Y'all go to the other side of the house." Several strong men scurried around yelling various commands to one another while unwinding the heavy hose and stretching it toward the flames.

"Okay, let her rip," one man bellowed.

Four of them, two on each side, gripped the hose. Another held the nozzle, pointed toward the blaze. For about five minutes, water gushed freely, and it looked as though the fire would be squelched. That is, until the huge stream was reduced to a ripple, then drops, then—nothing.

People speculated that whoever was in charge of filling the truck's water tank after the last fire, failed to follow through. Or, maybe since fires were rare in Muddy Ox, the water had evaporated. For whatever reason, the Muddy Ox fire truck that day didn't have enough water to put out a big bonfire, much less a burning house.

By that time, however, Simp, Asa, Obe, and Jake joined several other townsfolk to form a human chain to pump and pass buckets of water until the fire was reduced to smoldering timbers—then to only smoke. They had to break the windows and knock down my bedroom door to get in, but at least the fire was out.

Poor us—poor Grandma. The house she'd shared with Grandpa Omar until he died would never be the same. However, thanks to quick thinking, only our bedrooms and closets were gutted, leaving the rest of the house intact. I walked into the front room in time to hear Darby's disturbing conclusion.

"Mrs. Strom, I hate to say it but, it looks like this fire was intentionally set. The girl's room took the worst of the damage. Who would do this? Y'all have anyone who'd want to do you harm?"

"Darby, I don't know a soul who'd do this to me or Meryl. If either of us have any enemies, it's a mystery to me. Meryl was home alone when it started. She had an earache and didn't go to church. I went on with Jake and Effie Walby. Meryl said she decided to surprise me with dinner once she felt better. But like you said, the kitchen wasn't harmed; so we know it didn't start there." Grandma looked at me to corroborate.

"I was here alone. I'd just put dinner on the table once my earache got better. As I was scooping the mashed potatoes into a bowl, Sadie called from the yard for me to go to the toilet with her. I told her to wait until I could get the potatoes scooped because Grandma was due home any minute, and dinner was a surprise. Sadie was so insistent. She kept rushing me. Grandma, you know how she is." Grandma nodded, and I continued.

"Not having to go myself, I waited outside the toilet door. After getting a whiff of smoke, I saw the fire. I told Sadie to run to Mrs. McCrady's to call for the fire truck. Instead, she ran screaming for Katty. I don't know who called the fire house. That's really all I know. As soon as I got to the porch, I saw Jake's car pull down the lane, and I knew Grandma was home. Grandma, you know the rest."

"Mrs. Strom, could I talk to you alone for another minute?" Darby Talbot opened the door for Grandma to join him in the other room. I passed the well-set kitchen table again on my way to the porch swing. The reality of our ordeal rolled over in my head.

Oh, how I wish I'd gone to church, even if I had been sick with an earache. Grandma often said how people easily found excuses to miss church. It was just an earache. It got better. Shame on me—I'd picked cotton and had worse pain.

If Sadie hadn't come for me to go to the toilet with her, I might have stopped the fire before it got so bad. Or maybe…what if I'd gotten burned up in it before Sadie called me out of the house? Guess her insisting was a good thing. Sadie sure came at the right time. It wasn't uncommon for us girls to go to the toilet together. Most outhouses conveniently had two and three holes for that purpose. Spiders or even snakes could crawl into those outhouses. Also, sometimes mischievous boys found it funny to tip a toilet over with a body inside. Having a toilet partner and a guard at the door was smart.

But why did Sadie come past her own outhouse to get me to go with her to ours? And where was Katty? Why didn't Sadie get her mother to be her toilet partner? I told her how busy I was fixing dinner for Grandma—but she insisted. Sadie was usually Katty's shadow. Why did she need me and not Katty this time?

Grandma, Darby, and his helpers were still trying to piece together what Darby had decided was a probable case of arson as they arrived onto the porch.

"Meryl, do you promise no one else was here?" Grandma knew the answer but had to ask, at least for Darby's sake.

"Grandma, I promise. I fell back to sleep after you put sweet oil in my ear and laid the warm wash cloth on it. Sadie was the only other person I saw, heard, or talked to, after you left for church. That's the honest truth."

Suddenly, we heard the bell and siren from the fire house. There was another fire. Darby, Obe, and the others went running.

"Well, I hope this time the tank's been filled," I spouted.

"Yes, and I pray to God it's only things that get burned and no one gets hurt," said Grandma. Her eyes were closed. I knew she was praying. I had no doubt God was listening.

## Chapter Five

OUR HELPERS EXCHANGED their Good Samaritan hats for their Volunteer Fireman helmets, leaving Grandma and me to deal with our own fire scene. We couldn't do much with the two burned bedrooms, but we could do our best to put the front room and kitchen back in order. Despite the lack of fire damage, those two rooms reeked of smoke, things were scattered, and the floors were covered with muddy footprints.

I grabbed the curtains, scarves, and doilies, to toss them into a pile with the contents from Grandma's dresser drawers. She appeared with a pan of hot water and a clean rag from her ragbag for each of us. Had her bag of rags not hung on the back porch, they too would have reeked of smoke.

"Let's get to cleaning with what vinegar, salt and bakin' soda we already have, until Katty gets back with more." Grandma cleaned every possible surface, including the couch and both arm chairs, with a rag dampened with vinegar and salt water. I followed with a cloth moistened with water and baking soda. We opened the windows and turned on the box fan to circulate air through the room. Then, we worked our way into the kitchen.

I made a couple of trips to the pump to fill the dishpan and for a fresh bucket of drinking water. The curtains were added to the kettle pile and the rest of the kitchen was also given a vinegar, salt, and baking soda bath. To use her vernacular, we were *'liken to a team of oxen. We both pulled our yokes in the same direction to get the job done.'* When I first heard that term from Grandma, I had no idea what an oxen's yoke was or looked like. The only *yolk* I'd ever known about had been attached to an egg.

"I see Jesse Peterson out by her hog pen. I'll take her the food we can't use for chicken scraps. It'll make her some good slop." Grandma had both hands full of yesterday's ruins as she left for Jess and her hog pen.

I'd mopped my way out of the kitchen and onto the porch when I heard Katty and Sadie coming from the far end of the lane. You could always hear Katty before you saw her. Grandma returned about the same time they reached the edge of our yard.

"Mrs. Strom, did you hear the fire whistle over in Muddy Ox?" The winded pair dropped to the porch edge.

"The Green Fly was on fire," announced an excited Sadie. The Green Fly was the small diner attached to the Big Store. I had always thought it took someone with a strange sense of humor to name a diner The Green Fly and expect people to eat there. However, it was the only diner in Muddy Ox and the food was tasty and reasonably priced.

"It was not the diner itself. The porch behind the diner was on fire," Katty clarified.

"The porch was on fire? Not the diner? Do they think it was electrical? Isn't the wirin' old like in most of the other buildings around here?" Grandma asked.

"There was only one light bulb that dangled from the porch ceilin'. The ceilin' wasn't where the fire was. The water hose was pointed 'neath the porch. Besides, if it'd been an electrical fire, wouldn't it have worked its way into the diner and the Big Store? They was all wired at the same time don't you reckon? We didn't stick around to see a lot, but I did notice where they were pointin' the hose as we was leavin'," Katty accounted.

"Well if the smoke got into the diner like it did our kitchen and front room, they're in for a big cleaning job too."

"No, Darby and his crew got it put out before it reached that far. And, just like your house, Mrs. Strom, they couldn't tell how it started. It scared me to death. I'm still shakin' to think about it. I was lookin' at onion sets after I got your cleanin' stuff when I heard the fire whistle. I reached for Sadie, but she was gone. I found her a few feet from the porch. She said she saw a mama dog and her puppies in the yard and went to pet 'em. Well, I grabbed Sadie as soon as I could, and we got out of the way. You know how people are at a fire. They're all nearly runnin' over each other. Darby caught me as we were leavin' and said to tell you he and the men would be back tomorrow to finish gettin' the things out of the bedrooms for you."

Katty set the cleaning supplies on the porch next to the receipt and said she was going to round up the wash kettle.

"Meryl, you and Sadie get some wood from Simp's wood pile to put under the kettle? I'll get a little coal oil to douse on it to get it started real good. It takes a real hot fire and a good while for water to get to boilin' in an iron kettle," Grandma said as she grabbed an old empty coffee can and headed for the oil barrel. Sadie and I went for wood.

"Let's get some big pieces of wood so we can make a big fire," Sadie exclaimed.

"Okay, but we'll need some smaller pieces too for kindling," I replied.

Sadie busied herself gathering more wood. Katty rolled the kettle to the middle of the yard, onto a spot bare of grass. I helped her pull the kettle upright. Grandma, Sadie, and I began positioning the wood around its base.

Katty appeared with two buckets, one in each hand, from her rain barrel. I helped her with a couple more trips to finish filling the kettle.

"Meryl, go rip a few pages out of that old Sears catalog from the toilet so we can stuff 'em under and around the kindlin'," Grandma said.

"Sadie, you and Meryl Jean stand way back," Katty instructed after I returned with the catalog pages. Grandma doused the coal oil and threw a match onto the pile. *Whoosh!* Surely that big fire would heat the water in that iron kettle in record time. The flames licked high before they settled down to a hot, glowing blaze.

"Sadie and Meryl, y'all go fetch a few more pieces of wood so we'll have 'em handy if the fire starts to die down," Katty said while digging a small trench around the kettle, leaving piles of loose dirt to throw on any unruly flames.

After we returned with the wood, Sadie found what she perceived as a safe place and sat cross legged—far away enough for safety but near enough to poke at the fire with a long stick.

"Sadie, haven't you heard a child who plays with fire will wet the bed?" Grandma teased.

A scowl flew across Sadie's face as she grumbled, "I don't wet my bed."

"Scoot farther back, Sadie. Sparks might jump out on you."

"But Mama, then my stick won't reach the flames," Sadie argued and stayed put. Katty, accustomed to picking battles with her strong-willed child, continued to stoke the fire but kept Sadie in full view.

After the water started to simmer, Grandma appeared with an arm full of stinky linens along with the curtains, dish rags, wash rags, and towels from her kitchen. The load was thrown into the kettle with a cup of vinegar and a half box of salt then stirred and poked with her broom handle. "We'll let 'em boil a while and give 'em a good washin' in the machine later," she promised.

I rolled a stump over by Sadie to join her. Despite her mother's wishes, she continued to play in the fire with her stick. Grandma poked the contents of the kettle again before leaving to ready the washer. Katty watched Sadie closely while still minding the fire.

"I'm surprised you didn't come home with a new puppy, Sadie. What kind of puppies were they?" I asked, trying to draw Sadie's attention from her obsession.

"Umm…wasn't puppies—was kittens," Sadie hesitated.

"I thought you said it was a mama dog and her puppies you were pettin', Sadie. Was it puppies or kittens?" Katty challenged as she overheard our exchange.

"Uh… it was kittens. Yeah, it was a mama cat and her kittens. They ran from under the porch, and I petted 'em."

"Well… how did you see 'em run from under the porch if…?" Katty was about to quiz Sadie more but was interrupted by Darby and Grandma. Both appeared troubled.

"Mrs. Strom, the men and I are coming back to work on your place tomorrow. But I wanted to come and talk to you now. It appears the porch of the Green Fly was a deliberately set fire—same as your house."

"I been sayin' there's a firebug 'round here. We'd better keep watch 'til they ketch 'em," Katty butted in.

"Katty, did you see anyone suspicious today while you were at the Big Store or maybe around The Green Fly?" Darby questioned.

"No, I was lookin' at onion sets after I got Mrs. Strom's cleanin' stuff. When I heard the fire whistle and all the racket goin' on, I reached for Sadie, but she was gone. I went to look for her, and I met her runnin' toward me from 'round the back of the diner. She said she'd been pettin' a litter of puppies... uh kittens... well, one or the other, not far from the Green Fly's porch."

"Oh, so you were behind the diner and close to the porch? Did you see anybody that looked like they shouldn't a been there, Sadie?" Darby probed.

"No, I just saw the puppies and kittens, and I was pettin' 'em. They ran out from under the bushes 'cause they were scared."

"How long were you there Sadie? You couldn't a been gone more than a couple a minutes. So it was puppies and kittens? Thought it was kittens, and they came from under the porch? So they come from the bushes?" Katty's confusion mounted.

"It was both. I'm not sure if they come from the porch or the bushes, but they were scared." Sadie had changed her story more than a few times by then. Darby was one breath short of interrogating her a little deeper when Katty came to her rescue.

"She was a scared little girl, Darby. She probably can't remember what she was pettin' or where they come from. Surely there was others that saw or heard somethin' besides Sadie." Katty clearly wanted Darby to gather his facts other than questioning Sadie when she saw the frustration on her child's face.

"Well, I'll ask around. Someone had to have seen somethin'," Darby decided to rest his interrogation of Sadie for the time being.

"Mrs. Strom, I'm gonna pull Sadie and her stick away from that fire and head to the house. Got to check on my pot a beans. They should be done. I put 'em on this mornin' before y'all got up. I'll pick us some tomatoes and fry up a few cornbread cakes and call it dinner."

This time, Katty had no intention of losing the battle with Sadie as she grabbed her up and headed home. Sadie had no choice but to oblige her mother's forceful tug, but defiantly dragged her poking-stick behind her all the way.

"Sadie, leave that stick out in the yard and go wash your hands. I'll let you help stir up a cake when I get back from the garden." Katty marched to the garden.

Sadie pitched her stick and went inside.

"I got to get back to the Green Fly right now, Mrs. Strom. Like I said, we'll be here in the mornin'; that is if we don't have to run to another fire."

"Thanks, Darby. Meryl and me got started on the front room and kitchen today while y'all was gone. See you in the mornin'."

Got started? I felt like we had finished with the kitchen and front room. I should have known better. Oh well…that was Grandma.

## Chapter Six

GRANDMA SENT ME to Katty's with some unsalvageable garments and instructions to cut the buttons off before they were discarded for good. She said Katty probably needed the buttons more than we did with a hard-working man and a child to mend for. Once there, I grabbed Katty's button jar and a razor blade and pulled up to the far end of the kitchen table. Sadie willingly obeyed her mother this time in anticipation of helping her make one of her special cakes.

The screen door slammed behind her as Katty arrived with an apron full of red and green tomatoes, a few cucumbers, a couple of bell peppers and a hand full of green onions. She dumped her goods into a pan in her dry sink for later.

"Okay Sadie, did you wash your hands real good?"

Sadie nodded and Katty tied an apron around Sadie's skinny middle wrapping the string around her twice and tying it with a bow in front. Sadie was poised on her knees in a chair and holding an egg beater.

I'd witnessed Katty making her cakes many times but never grew tired of watching the production. She sifted a generous amount of flour into a large crock bowl and added a pinch of salt, a sprinkle each of baking soda and baking powder, a dash of vanilla flavoring, a heaping spoon of lard, two large eggs, a rounded cup of sugar, and some milk. After a few stirs she turned it over to Sadie who moved the beater in a circular motion around the bowl while slowly cranking the blades.

"Keep mixing while I get the vegetables ready," Katty instructed. By the time the vegetables were washed and drying, Sadie had the batter blended and ready to pour into their largest, generously greased, iron skillet. With the cake in the oven, Katty prepared her signature icing.

Because she never measured anything, Katty's recipes were hard to duplicate. Regardless, her cake icing was always the same and always delicious. Using a heavy iron saucepan, she mixed part evaporated milk and part water, sugar, vanilla flavoring, cocoa powder, and a dollop of butter. If there was ever anything else, I never knew. She told Sadie to fix her mouth just right and stir continuously over the burner until she saw bubbles. It was then removed from the burner and set aside.

Katty insisted it was the fixing of one's mouth just right that was the secret to her icing. I figured years later it made Sadie feel like a bigger part of the procedure and helped her stay more focused during the process. At any rate, it was the icing that made Katty's cakes exceptional. After poking holes into the hot cake with a butter knife, she poured on the bubbling icing. Once cooled, a crusty glaze formed that tasted like a marriage of chocolate candy and cake icing. Katty's cakes were just—special.

Watching mother and daughter that day, I was amazed how Katty, who was typically rough and gruff with most everything was so gentle and patient with her child. How Sadie stayed on task and didn't balk at all also amazed me.

They were so involved, I'm not sure they noticed my leaving.

Grandma was inspecting more clothing remnants and reluctantly threw them into the trash as I arrived. It wasn't her wish to ever throw anything away but as hard as she tried, she couldn't find use for some things.

It wasn't long until our noses told us dinner was ready and it was going to be good. We left the washer agitating while we made our way toward Katty's kitchen. She'd decided fried green tomatoes would make our meal complete and was taking the last one out of the skillet as we arrived. After washing our hands, we pulled up to the feast. It was a totally meatless meal, but no one noticed or cared. White beans, fried potatoes, fried cornbread cakes, and fried green tomatoes. The only things not fried were the white beans. Not to fear, they'd probably show up on the table as fried bean cakes either the next day or maybe the next. That wasn't a complaint—it was a matter of fact.

Our dinner meal was so filling we agreed to wait until after supper for our cake. Katty declined our help afterward and dismissed us to our own task at hand.

## Chapter Seven

GRANDMA AND I were draining the rinse tubs and had just gotten the last item pinned on the line when we heard a commotion next door. We went to see what was going on.

"Sadie, you have to come inside now. I need your help in the kitchen." Katty's voice was even louder than usual and sounded a bit shaky.

"But Mama, I just helped you in the kitchen," Sadie argued.

"And you—you need to go on home now. Sadie's got to come inside," Katty barked to a young boy making his way out of their yard.

The boy didn't seem to fear Katty, although he did as she asked. Moving in a slow gait, he looked back, never taking his eyes off Sadie. Once beyond their yard, he leaned against a ditch willow tree across the gravel road from their house. Sliding a can of Prince Edward tobacco and a slip of paper from his pocket, he skillfully rolled a cigarette. After methodically licking the edge of the paper to make it hold together, he placed it between his lips, lit it, dropped the match, and ground it into the gravel with his boot. Nodding to Sadie, he strolled away.

Smoke trailed behind him. It certainly must have riled Katty that he wasn't intimidated by her in the least. For him to ogle Sadie as he did and nod as he left, probably made Katty's blood boil.

Grandma and I recognized him, having seen him with his family around town. Carl Chaffin had let them live in one of his tenant houses to work on his farms. Mr. Chaffin owed a corner store in Silver Leaf and several farms in and around Muddy Ox.

It was rumored this strange family migrated to our parts from the mountains of Eastern Kentucky. Their last name was Boone. It was also rumored that they claimed to be descendants of Daniel Boone. Mr. Chaffin put them in his shotgun house beside Seldom Seen Ditch along the gravel road leading to 84 Highway. No one really knew how many were in their family. The loud and unruly children were hardly still long enough in one place to be counted.

All that people knew for sure was there was a house full of them and the children were very close in age. It was hard to distinguish the boys from the girls because every one of them wore britches and work shirts all of the time and the boys and girls alike had long hair.

The mother wore a dress over her britches. Her braided hair was partially hidden neath a wide brimmed hat, usually pulled down past the middle of her forehead.

The dad was never seen in anything but bib-overalls,

most of the time shirtless, wearing a matching hat to his wife's, and shouldering his shotgun. Carl Chaffin's shotgun house was definitely appropriate for them. It was said one could stand at the front door, shoot a gun straight through a shotgun house and out the back door and never hit a wall since the rooms were built in a straight line with no halls.

"Katty, what did that young man want?" Grandma asked as we reached the porch.

"I don't know. He was standin' there talkin' to Sadie as I walked up after pickin' the garden. I couldn't hear nothin' he said."

"Well, he was bold to come right up in your yard like that," Grandma said.

"Sadie, it looked like he was showin' you somethin'. What was it? And what was he talkin' to you about? What made him want to stop by here?" Katty shot one question after another to Sadie.

"He didn't want nothin'. He just came up to the porch. He never sat down. He was showin' me a knife. Said it was called a Bowie knife, and it once belonged to his great, great grandpa. He didn't do nothin' wrong. He was just walkin' by our house on his way home. When he was at the Big Store today, he was showin' that knife to some other kids out by the store porch."

"You seen him at the Big Store today? Did he talk to you there? Why didn't you tell Darby about him? He asked you if you saw anyone who looked strange, hangin' 'round the diner." By this time, Sadie gave up answering her mother until she was sure the questioning was done.

"No, you come and got me 'fore he said anythin' to me there. We just looked at each other. That was all. I figured he had a right to be at the store like the rest of us."

"Well, I don't want him or any of that family comin' around here. They're different. How did he even know where you lived?" Katty's voice had reached a higher pitch.

"Mrs. Strom, when Simp drove by their house the other day on his way to pay our light bill, he saw some of those kids playin' and crawlin' all over the roof of that house. And of all things, the mother was sittin' on the front porch smokin' a pipe. They can brag about being related to Daniel Boone all they want, but I bet if he was still alive he wouldn't be claimin' kin to them. Why, I do believe I can still smell that kid, and he was only standin' in the yard." Katty didn't hide her feelings when she didn't like someone.

"And Sadie, what do you mean he was just walkin' by on his way home? He'd have to circle a whole block out of his way to be just walkin' by our house." Katty was right to ask. He had to have purposely turned down our lane. He wasn't just casually passing by.

Only a few families in Muddy Ox fit into the category of well off. The rest of us were either existing or struggling. However, I guess as in most communities, there was a kind of *pecking order*. Those of us existing and struggling still didn't fall into the category of low class. We had values, convictions, morals and manners—just not finery or money. How we took care of ourselves, and our homes said a lot about us. Katty wasn't usually one to throw a rock at others or look down her nose at them, but she had no qualms about not wanting to rub elbows with this Boone family.

Grandma's reaction to them seemed more out of fear of the unknown. The Boones had no intentions of letting themselves really be known. This boy, Army Boone, was the first of them who had attempted to interact with people other than their immediate family. His lack of social skills was evident to think waving a knife around would open any doors for him or make him any friends.

"We'll see what Simp has to say about that boy comin' around here when he gets home. Bet he won't like it neither," Katty huffed.

"Maybe that'll be the last you'll see of him, Katty. I'm sure he could tell he wasn't welcome in your yard today, much less to come back again. That family didn't come here to stay. When the crops are gone, they'll be gone too." Grandma tried to ease Katty's mind, but Grandma's face didn't reveal she had succeeded by the way she rustled Sadie into her kitchen. Katty's actions proved she wasn't convinced that hoodlum wasn't still lurking around the corner somewhere. We guardedly returned to our cleaning quest.

## Chapter Eight

THE REST OF the afternoon, Grandma and I worked hard to do what we could do with the house. "You don't realize how smoke can get into every little nook and cranny until something like this happens," Grandma said finding yet another spot needing attention.

A ball of heat burned in the upper middle of my back sending painful impulses across my shoulder blades and down my arms. I wondered if we'd ever be done. But by the time we'd finished with the kitchen and front room for the second time, there was little evidence there'd ever been a fire in our house—until you stepped into the bedrooms.

"I hope Darby doesn't find the bedrooms in such a shape when he inspects them in the morning, that they can't fix them," I said.

"Oh, I feel pretty sure Darby will find a way to fix 'em. I just hope it won't be a long, drawn out, or too expensive job, to do it," Grandma looked tired and worried.

Simp arrived home, as we finished taking the wash off the line. We folded the linens and set the curtains aside to be ironed before hanging them back on the windows.

"We'll need to be up early in the morning before the workmen get here," Grandma noted on our way to the Simpson's. I knew there wasn't a chance of us oversleeping. Katty and her radio would determine when our day began, just as this morning. Supper was a repeat of dinner with a few more cornbread cakes, fried green tomatoes and fried potatoes added to it. Of course, the cake and a fresh pot of coffee would be waiting for after supper.

While sitting at the table, Katty told Simp about the Boone boy's visit. Simp was not any happier about him showing up at their house than she was. He agreed with Grandma that the family would be gone as soon as the crops were.

"The talk in the field today was the fire at The Green Fly was set on purpose," Simp said as he savored a bite of cake.

"It wasn't the diner that was on fire. It was only the porch. Me and Sadie was there getting some cleaning stuff for Mrs. Strom. You mean someone come to the field special to tell y'all about the fire?"

"No, Asa had to go get another water bucket and dipper."

"What was wrong with the bucket and dipper y'all had?" Katty asked since it wasn't common for a bucket and dipper to wear out in only one season.

"Seems the black folk and the Mexicans didn't want

the Boones drinking out of their buckets. Of course, Mrs. Bertram said none of us liked the idea of sharin' water and a dipper with that Boone bunch neither."

"What did the Boones have to say about it?" Katty asked.

"Evidently, they were used to stuff like that. They never said a word or didn't seem surprised when Asa handed the Pa the new bucket and dipper."

"I don't doubt they've had that problem before. I wouldn't want to drink after 'em neither, would you Mrs. Strom?" Katty snipped.

"I hate to admit it, but no, I wouldn't. I try not to be judgmental, but every one of the Boones it seems, uses some form of tobacco. No one wants to put their mouth where that's been. Almost every exposed part of them is dirty," Grandma replied.

"Soap's too cheap for that. People caint help bein' poor but there ain't no excuse for bein' dirty. The rim of a dipper ain't big enough around to find a different spot on it to drink from with that many of 'em sharin' it," Katty fussed.

"I've wiped the rim of a water dipper more than once with my shirt tail before drinking after another person. But I don't know if I could wipe hard enough behind all that tobacco juice and snuff drippings to feel like it was clean," Grandma added.

"When Asa got back to the field, he said the town was a buzzin' about the fire," Simp reported between chews. His eyes were still locked on Katty's face. I couldn't tell if he agreed with her or was astonished at her disregard toward the Boones. I think he might have even been surprised at Grandma's comments as well. But…fact was fact.

"So you and Sadie were there at the Big Store when the fire happened? Did they have water in the fire truck this time?" Simp couldn't resist the sarcasm, only to have it ignored. Enough was enough about the waterless fire truck.

Hearing Simp's account of how they were treated in Asa's field that day, I felt bad for that family. No wonder they never opened up to anyone and kept to themselves. They probably experienced cold shoulders and received cutting stares everywhere they'd been. However, feeling bad for them didn't remove my fear or dread of them.

"Asa said he'd be so glad when he saw the tail lights of their old truck heading toward Kentucky. He said the Ma and Pa and a few of the older ones ain't bad workers but those younger ones are wild as bucks."

"Bet it's hard to keep your mind on what your doin' with that ruckus a goin' on," Katty agreed.

"Yeah, they cause a commotion all over the field. Their parents don't say a word to 'em. They just let 'em rant and ramble. They calmed down pronto though, after Emmy Bertram scolded 'em for runnin' down the middles and trompin' all over her cotton. I have to say, I don't blame 'em. I'd stop, too, if Emmy scolded me," Simp smiled mischievously.

"I know firsthand how Mrs. Bertram can get. She really means business if she uses your whole name. She about scared me to death the day she yelled Meryl Jean Strom, from right behind me."

"I think I remember you telling me about that. What was it again that you done?" Grandma asked.

"I'd chopped down the cotton and left morning glories by mistake. I was just learning how to chop and couldn't tell the difference at the time. I learned real fast though after that day. If she knew you well enough to call you by your entire name you knew you had definitely crossed over—on the bad side of Emmy Bertram."

"I can see how she'd be upset at those children stompin' down her cotton. Also with you choppin' it down and leavin' all mornin' glories," Grandma agreed.

"Well, Emmy's fit with those kids didn't keep 'em from jawin' at one another the whole rest of the day. One thing it did for me, and few others was make us pull cotton faster so we could get on down the row away from 'em," Simp added.

"If the rest of that bunch goes to the field every day, wonder why the one they call Army was up at the Big Store and then came by our house like he did?" Katty. questioned.

"I overheard Asa ask the Pa where that boy was this

mornin'. I guess Asa has some idea of how many of 'em are supposed to be there workin', but the rest of us sure don't. The man thought that kid was there in the field somewhere. He didn't even know he was gone. Guess it's easy for one to go missin' when you got that many runnin' under foot. Anyway, he told Asa that Army gave him more trouble than the rest of 'em put together. He said Army didn't take to field work. For that matter, no other kind of work neither."

"Wonder where they come up with a name like Army? I never heard of anyone named that before," Katty asked.

"Asa and I were talkin' about that same notion today too. He said he brought that up to the Pa, in the beginnin' when he told him the boy's name.

"Accordin' to Asa, the Pa said, they named him Army, 'cause he seemed to be at war with his mom whilst he was bein' born into this world. Then he added his name even fits him more now, 'cause he's been at war with anythin' they ask him to do ever since."

"That tells me that woman had a hard time birthin' that child," Grandma said.

"Mrs. Strom, it tells me both them parents have had their hands full with that—child—since he's been in this world," spouted Katty.

Sadie had a few disgusted expressions during the conversation over supper but kept silent.

## Chapter Nine

"KATTY, LIKE ALWAYS, that was some good cake. I'm goin' to smoke now." Simp left for the porch. Grandma and I cleaned the kitchen while Katty ushered Sadie to bed since we'd had an unusually late supper. Then we joined Simp on the porch.

"Darby, Obe, and a few others are comin' again in the mornin' to see what they can do about fixin' my two burnt bedrooms," Grandma said as she began snapping the pan of green beans that Katty had gathered from the garden before supper.

"I wish pullin' time was over and I could help 'em," offered Simp.

"Simp, you've done more than enough. We appreciate you and Katty lettin' us stay here. I'm sure you know that." The Simpsons had reassured Grandma many times of how welcome we were, but she still felt bad to be crowding in on them.

"Mrs. Strom, you stop frettin' about that," Katty ordered as she banged the screen door shut and plopped a straight-back chair down next to Grandma to help with the snapping.

"Well, maybe after tomorrow we'll find out how

long it'll take to get us back to our own house," Grandma fretted regardless.

"Katty, I want you to keep an even closer eye on Sadie now that the Boone boy knows where we live and felt comfortable enough to come by here. He's probably not much older than Sadie but when kids, especially boys, are raised like those kids, it's not their age it's their experience that speaks for 'em. I'm like Asa. I'll be glad when they're gone," Simp cautioned.

"Oh, you know I'll have my eyes peeled. And I'll let you know for sure if he shows up 'round here anymore. I've already told Sadie she's not to talk to any of 'em and if that boy wanders by here again, she's to find me pronto."

"That's good," Simp agreed.

"You know this child, along with the rest of them children wern't born that way. All babies are born pure and innocent, even if it sounds like he about killed his mother durin' birth," Grandma sighed.

"I say it's the parents. They didn't do somethin' right raising 'em. That's for sure," Katty spouted.

"Katty, we can't know what those parents have or have not done," Grandma argued.

I imagined Grandma couldn't help but think about her own wayward son. It was common knowledge how she struggled to raise all five of her sons the same. Yet one, my dad, was always a greater challenge. Also, Katty was blind to the defiance of her own headstrong daughter. "You know, sometimes a child follows his own will, despite its parent's efforts." Grandma sighed.

"Mrs. Strom ain't you always sayin' God didn't think you knew how to raise a little girl 'til He gave you Meryl Jean? Well, God'll get 'em someday if they just let their children raise 'emselves." Katty added God to the equation to strengthen her point.

"Yes, I take the responsibility of havin' Meryl in my home very seriously. But parents, like anyone else, can make mistakes. We do what we think is right at the time. Then sometimes find out later we could have maybe done things differently. By then, it's too late to change it. In my case, I hope some of Larson's actions are not because of anythin' I did or didn't do." Then, Grandma quoted another of her common sayings, "After all, every tub's got to set on its own bottom."

"Mrs. Strom, I've heard you say that before. Just what in the world does that mean?" Simp couldn't hear Grandma use that quote one more time without clarification.

"It means every one of us will stand before God one day for our actions. The Bible says every knee will bow and every tongue will confess. Each of us has two knees and one tongue so it's surely meant for all. I can't bow or confess for you nor can you for me. Every tub's got to set on its own bottom," Grandma repeated, leaving no misunderstanding.

Hearing Grandma second guess herself concerning

my dad's raising and actions must have made Katty sorry for her criticism of the Boone's parental judgments. She started to say something to soften her words when Grandma stopped her.

"Speakin' of tubs Katty, are we sure there's no live sparks still under that kettle?" Our fire, along with that of the diner, made Grandma even more fire conscious.

"I'll go shovel a little dirt on it for good measure so we can go to bed without worryin'." Katty headed to the fire, shovel in hand.

"I've got to turn in. Four-thirty comes real early. Even earlier now that the days are gettin' shorter." Simp emptied his pipe then tapped it once more against the side of his pant leg to rid it of ashes and headed inside.

"I think we can finish up these beans in the mornin'. Don't you Katty?"

"Yes and we can go to bed with a clear mind about the fire. I covered the timbers with dirt and poured the water out of the kettle over it." Katty, too, left nothing for chance.

We made a final trip to the outhouse before bed. Then I got my pillow and headed to the couch. I couldn't believe it was only that morning that I'd had the terrible dream of my mother chasing and shaming me. I was humbly thankful that I wasn't struck by lightning, or the earth didn't part beneath me, when I blatantly blamed my mother for abandoning me and questioned God's love and understanding of us.

I was simply ranting out of anger. Given a choice, as Grandma had said, I realized Mama wouldn't have wanted to die and leave me. Thank God He gave me a Grandma willing to have a thirteen year old child dumped on her. If not for her, Daddy and I would still be in Brooksville, Illinois, in our shell of a home, minus a mother. Daddy would be taking me with him to the taverns on the weekends, and I'd be singing for drunks and getting rewarded with soft drinks.

After Mama died, Daddy ran out of places to leave me. I was too young to stay alone while he went drinking with his buddies. His solution was to take me with him. He'd give me a handful of coins to play the jukebox and kept me supplied in soft drinks. After he and his drinking buddies got tipsy, he'd begin his usual spiel.

"Have you fellas ever heard my little girl sing? She can sing as good as any of 'em on that there jukebox. Come on Baby, sing 'em a song."

As uncomfortable as I was to sing in a tavern for my dad's drunken friends, I was confident Daddy wouldn't let anything or anybody harm me.

"Yeah, come on, sing us a song. Hey fellas, unplug that noise box. Larson's little girl is gonna sing for us," one of his friends slurred.

I'd start off with *The Wayward Wind, How Much Was That Doggie in the Window,* and Brenda Lee's arrangement of *Jambalaya*. Then, I'd take requests. Some songs I knew entirely and only parts of others. It didn't matter as long as I sang. I could have made up the words for all they knew or cared—which I often did.

"Sing another one little girl," another one of Daddy's friends mumbled.

After I ran out of songs, I resorted to one of Mama's favorites. *How Far Is Heaven* was a well-known Kitty Wells hit of that era. There was nothing like a little girl who had just lost her mother singing *How Far Is Heaven* to a honky-tonk full of drunks to dampen the drinking mood. I was sure if haunting someone was possible; my mother surely haunted Daddy for taking me tavern hopping to sing for a bunch of guzzlers. By the time I was finished with that song, most of the patrons were crying in their beers and Daddy decided it was time for us to go.

I WONDERED WHERE Daddy was and if he'd heard about our fire. I was pretty sure he had friends around town that kept in touch with him occasionally. If they'd told him about our house burning, surely he would come home to check on us.

I tossed and turned on the Simpson's lumpy couch, trying to wallow into my usual sleep nest. The last thing I wished for before sleep came was a dreamless night.

## Chapter Ten

"THIS IS RUDY Pylant again signing off this morning on your Old Camp Meeting Time with Mama Maybelle Carter and the Carter Family singing, *I shall not be moved*."

My brain was jolted awake by Katty's blasting radio as I opened one eye and silently prayed, "Lord, I *want* to move. Please let us move back to Grandma's house soon." Bless her heart, Katty did everything loudly. I could hear pans banging and utensils rattling once The Carter Family sang their last line. When Katty flipped off her radio, I heard Grandma's voice, confirming it was time to get going. She wanted to be ready when Darby arrived. So did I.

"Morning," I said in a sleepy whisper as I stumbled into the kitchen. Making my way to the sink for a sip of water, I splashed some on my face and washed my hands. No one ever thought of sitting at Grandma's or Miss Katty's table without washing their hands. "It's Bible," Grandma would say. And she knew the scriptures to prove it.

"Mrs. Strom, I made some extra biscuits for the men when they come this mornin'. You can butter and jelly 'em if you want to while I'm puttin' on my pot of beans." Grandma made a pot of beans often, but not every single day as Katty did. If Katty's beans were not the main course—they were a side dish.

I pulled my chair to the table and Grandma quickly set my eggs before me. Learning to eat immediately upon rising in the mornings was an adjustment after coming to live with Grandma. She didn't tolerate finicky people saying they couldn't eat or didn't have an appetite when they first got up.

"People who don't eat breakfast will never last 'til noon out in the field. A body who thinks they cain't eat first thing in the mornin' never had to pick or chop cotton," Grandma spouted.

Picking season was over. At least it was for me since school would be starting in a few days. School—what was I going to do? All our clothes, with the exception of the jeans and a sweat shirt I had on and what Grandma wore to church that Sunday morning, had burned in the fire. Grandma could get by with borrowing some of Katty's house dresses, but I couldn't go to school wearing a house dress. Lord, what was I going to do?

"Morning Mrs. Strom, Katty, Meryl Jean," Darby said beyond the screen door.

"Come on in Darby," Katty said, again sliding a chair toward him.

This time, Darby didn't take the chair and Katty didn't insist. She knew this wasn't a visit. It was business.

"Cain't sit this morning, Katty. Just wanted to let y'all know we're here."

"Meryl, finish your breakfast then come on over, okay?" Grandma handed Darby his and his crew's biscuits and followed quickly on his heels.

"Okay, be right there," I was more than anxious to hear Darby's plans.

Sadie arrived at the table as I stepped off the porch. I heard Katty remind her to wash her hands before plopping a couple of eggs onto Sadie's plate.

Grandma and Darby were standing in the driveway by our shed when I arrived. Obe and his crew were unloading lumber and supplies from a flatbed trailer hitched to his truck.

"Mrs. Strom, the whole town pitched in to help. There's lumber, nails, paint, and almost everythin' we need to rebuild your rooms. I could tell the other day the fire had only gutted 'em. The foundation wasn't hurt. Barrin' any problems, we should have you back home by the first of next week." Darby smiled with pride as he told Grandma how the town showed up and of everyone's admiration for her.

"I don't know what to say Darby other than—thank you. And thanks to all of the town's people too." Grandma was visibly humbled.

"And that's not all Mrs. Strom," Obe stepped up holding an envelope. "The men at the cotton gin and the lumber mill pitched in with some money to help you get the things you need that maybe folks didn't or couldn't donate. We all saw how hard that little girl of yours worked to get her school clothes and how you've made her a home."

Then he whispered, "Not everybody knows, but Carl Chaffin matched what we collected. He said you're one of the nicest Christian ladies in Muddy Ox."

"This means more to us than you'll ever know. God will bless each one who gave to help us. People can't out-give God you know." Obe put the envelope in Grandma's hands, and she soaked his cheek with her tears.

My feet felt glued to the ground after hearing Obe tell Grandma of the town's gift to us. I felt ashamed to remember my tantrum of worrisome thoughts and doubtful words about God and His concern for us—me. Yes, God had seen how hard I worked through the eyes of those in Muddy Ox. Yes, He had taken care of Grandma and me all our lives and no—He was not about to fail us now. He'd answered my prayer this very morning. There might not have been anyone who could have shared their clothes with me, but God knew everything about me—including my dress size and the width of my feet.

"Look Meryl," Grandma said as she showed me the envelope and reiterated what she'd just been told. "There's money in here enough to buy you more school things—and…and… tennis shoes. God has done for us when He knew we couldn't do for ourselves. Darby says with all the wood and supplies they ought to get us back home in a week's time."

"It won't take much to rebuild this closet, Mrs. Strom," Darby said as we followed him into my bedroom. "We'll fix a row of shelves for your fruit jars and make the rest into a nice closet for Meryl. The door can go right here in the middle."

I couldn't believe my ears. I'd have a closet with a door. Not an old army blanket strung on a wire as a partition. It was my turn now to give them hugs.

As Darby continued to share his plan of rebirth to our bedrooms with Grandma, I slipped out on the front porch. Sitting on the edge, I recounted how fortunate I was that the money was donated to us. God truly was God and knew exactly how I needed to be helped. He was more of a reality to me now than ever before.

"Meryl, come see. Darby's going to make this whole end of the closet into shelves. You can stack your shoes and whatever else you want on the bottom. We can store the canned stuff over here on the higher shelves. Won't that be good?"

Grandma was beside herself. She didn't openly criticize Grandpa Omar's past efforts, but unlike Grandpa, Darby and his helpers actually had carpentry skills.

We left the crew to their work to tell Katty we

wouldn't be their house guests much longer. She'd just finished with cleaning the kitchen and was on her way to the garden. Sadie was on the porch snapping the beans we hadn't finished the night before. Grandma left me to help Sadie while she went with Katty to the garden.

"….and they're going to make Meryl some shelves in her closet and put sheetrock on the walls where there was bare wood before. We can paint instead of wallpaper." We could hear Grandma sharing Darby's plans with Katty all the way to the garden spot.

"You'll be in fifth grade this year won't you, Sadie?" I asked, pulling up a chair and digging into the pan of beans.

"Yes, but Mama says I only have to go another year after this one."

"So…you don't want to go to high school or graduate?" I couldn't imagine her not wanting to graduate high school.

"No. I don't like school like you do. Mama said she don't care if I quit after the sixth grade. I wish she'd let me quit now. Her or Daddy didn't even go to school this far."

Sadie's plan distressed me. Grandma hadn't gone to school a day in her life, but she wanted me to go. Neither she nor I ever considered me not finishing high school an option.

"Mama says you don't need an education to change baby diapers." After recognizing this as a direct quote from Katty and sort of taking it personally, I searched for a convincing argument. I of all people was almost without words. So I invented one.

"Well, I want to do more than just marry, have babies, and change diapers. But, if and when I do change diapers, at least I'll change them educational-wise." I knew I'd made up a new term for diaper changing but was trying to drive home a point.

"Mama, didn't you say I could quit school after the sixth grade?" Sadie wanted confirmation concerning her future in school as soon as Katty was in sight.

"Yes, I did. You don't need a high school diploma to change baby diapers."

Grandma and I looked at one another and both rolled our eyes. Her knowing mother and daughter so well, I figured Grandma also decided to let them have their way.

Sadie and I were dismayed as they refilled our pan, each having an apron filled with fresh beans.

"Mrs. Strom, we have a nice mess of beans here for cannin'. Don't you think?" Katty and Grandma pulled up chairs to help. "With four pairs of hands in the pan we can get done—lickety-split," Katty said.

"Yes, if we get these canned today, we can do the tomatoes and pickles tomorrow. I sure wish a fruit peddler would come by with some apples. I'd love to can some apples to make jelly and for some pies this winter—wouldn't you?" Grandma's wish fell upon silence, except for the snap, snap, snapping of beans.

## Chapter Eleven

THE NEXT MORNING, in addition to the radio and kitchen symphony offered by the clanging and banging of pots and pans, I woke to pounding hammers and grinding handsaws. Truthfully, those last two sounds were music to my ears. The thought of having a refurbished bedroom with a real closet was beyond exciting for me.

We skipped the doling out of breakfast biscuits this morning to our crew of carpenters. Grandma and Katty thought a dinner offering would be more appropriate since they were already hard at work. Plus they were anxious to get started on their canning.

Just for fun, I suggested Sadie and I walk to the school and back and time ourselves to see how long our walk would take, while Katty and Grandma did their canning. I'd walked that trek many times but had never thought of timing myself before. Katty was reluctant to let Sadie out of her sight, but Grandma convinced her that she was safe with me.

"Well, since you're goin' to town, can you stop in at the Big Store and get some sugar? I used mine makin' that cake yesterday." Katty handed me a few coins.

## MERYL JEAN ANOTHER WHIRLWIND

Wearing my mother's gold Bulova wrist watch, a treasure of hers I remembered to pack when Daddy and I made our move, I started off toward the school with Sadie.

Walking casually, we arrived at Sadie's elementary school in twenty minutes. I knew that on an extremely cold day, we could walk it in fifteen or less if we had to. The high school was minutes beyond the elementary. I could easily make it there before first bell.

"Jean," Tara McCrady shouted. Taking a pause from cheer practice, she walked over to greet me.

Tara was a model cheerleader, petite, blond, and bouncy. She was the youngest of the three McCrady sisters. She and her two older sisters, Scarlett and Melanie were my childhood friends for as long as I could remember. Their names were a result of their mother's fascination with *Gone with the Wind*. I'm sure had they been blessed with a brother; his name would have been Rhett. We loved playing together as children, during my visits to Grandma's in the years before Mama died. We once pricked our fingers and took turns holding them together and pledged to be blood-sisters for life. The McCrady's were now my neighbors. Tara and I were classmates.

"Watchadoin?" Tara asked. Being at school other than on a school day was a rarity for me since I didn't belong to any of the clubs or ever attend extracurricular activities. Tara was curious.

"Grandma and Miss Katty are canning. Sadie and I are timing ourselves to see how quickly we can make the walk to school."

"I'm sorry to hear your house burned. I'm glad no one got hurt though."

"Me too, I stayed home from church because of an earache. If Sadie hadn't yelled for me to go to the toilet with her, I would have been in the house after the fire started. It burned our bedrooms and all our clothes, but the front room and kitchen were only smoke damaged." To retell the tragedy sickened my stomach again.

"Oh, Jean, it burned your cute little room and all of your clothes? School's starting Monday. What are you going to do?" Tara knew how much my bedroom and new clothes meant to me. I'd invited her and her sisters that first summer to come and see the room Grandma and I'd created from a storage room. It paled in comparison to their bedrooms, but they could tell how proud I was to have a room of my own.

"What are you going to do about school starting Monday, Jean?"

"Darby Talbot formed a crew and people have donated lumber and supplies to rebuild our bedrooms—even better than before. Tara, I'm going to have a closet, not an old army blanket drawn on a wire across the end of the room. Y'all will have to come and see it once it is done. Also, he and some others took up money for us. Grandma and I are going to Kennett with the Simpsons this Saturday to try and replace as many of my clothes as we can. Isn't that wonderful? I think my guardian angel is at work again."

Tara knew what I meant about my guardian angel. I'd told her how I felt as though I had one looking out for me in times past. She didn't say, but probably knew I would have been at a loss for clothes without the divinely inspired generosity of the town's people.

"Oh Jean, that's wonderful. You know my sisters and I would have been glad to share some of our clothes with you if…well… you know we would have been glad," Tara said what we both knew without words. I could not have fit into their clothes.

"I know you would, Tara. But this is even better. Grandma doesn't know it, but I am going to insist she buy a few new church dresses too, since hers also burned. Miss Katty let her wear some of her house dresses. But of course, Katty's dresses wouldn't work for me. And Sadie's things are all too small."

"Sadie—where is Sadie?" I suddenly realized Sadie was gone.

In a panic, I said good-bye. Tara returned to the cheer group, and I rushed in search of Sadie. As I turned the corner by the elementary school, I spied her sitting in one of the playground swings. Someone was sitting in the swing next to hers. As I got closer, I recognized Army Boone. Their encounter looked innocent enough, but I could hear Miss Katty's disapproving voice in my head loud and clear. After all, she had trusted me with her pride and joy.

"Sadie, we better head home now. I thought you were standing beside me while I was talking with Tara McCrady. I never knew when you left."

"I got tired of standing there so I walked over to the swings. Army saw me and came to swing too," Sadie explained.

"Oh…hello, Army." His eyes met mine, but he made no response.

"Sadie, we need to go. Your mom and Grandma will be wondering about us."

"Bye Army," Sadie said without balking. I guessed she knew if she had balked and I told Miss Katty, she'd be in for certain trouble. Army continued his silent stare. As we walked away, he darted in the opposite direction, head down, and hands buried in his pockets.

"Sadie, did you know Army would be here?" Before I finished my question, I knew it was impossible she or Army could have planned a meeting. Our walk to school was my idea. It was strange; however, how Army just appeared. A chill ran through me. It was obvious. Army Boone had to be spying on us. How else would he have known to show up at the school when he did?

"No, I didn't know he'd be there. It was your idea to walk to school," Sadie grumbled.

I wanted to get us back home as quickly as possible. I had a real dilemma. Sadie would be mad if I told her mother about Army showing up. Miss Katty would be mad if I didn't tell her and she found out, which I was certain would somehow happen. Grandma would not be pleased either if I kept this to myself. I had to tell Grandma.

We were about half way home before I remembered Katty's sugar. I was trying to decide if we needed to go back when we heard the scream of the fire whistle. Within minutes, Darby and his crew whizzed by on their way to the fire truck.

Figuring Katty would rather have us home safely than take a chance on going back for sugar, I prompted Sadie to walk faster. Before long, we were sprinting.

Grandma and Miss Katty would be beside themselves knowing there was another fire in Muddy Ox—where we had gone. Sadie and I had barely escaped another fire scene, and she'd had another encounter with the dreaded Army Boone. Grandma's assurance to Katty that Sadie would be in good hands with me made me feel even worse. Sadie and Army sitting on the swings together seemed harmless—or was it? My dilemma about revealing mine and Sadie's run in with Army was growing.

## Chapter Twelve

AS WE TURNED down the lane to our houses, Katty and Grandma met us midway. Relief replaced worry on their faces after seeing us unharmed.

"Did y'all see what was on fire in Muddy Ox?" Katty asked, catching her breath.

"Meryl, did you see where the fire was?" Grandma echoed.

"No, we were halfway home when the alarm sounded. Also we forgot your sugar, Katty. Anyway, I figured you'd rather I get Sadie home than us go back for it."

"No, we didn't see anything," Sadie's reply trailed mine.

"Darby will be able to tell us when they get back. They left their tools to run to the fire truck. They'll be back—if not to work, to get their tools," Grandma said.

"Don't worry about the sugar, Meryl. You were right to high tail it back here with Sadie. That firebug's at it again, Mrs. Strom. Muddy Ox has never seen the like of fires that we've been having here of lately." Katty was more certain than ever that a firebug was terrorizing Muddy Ox.

"Katty, I think you're right. There's too many fires

too close together, no matter if they are accidental or on purpose."

"Mrs. Strom, Darby already told you your house and the big store were not accidents." Katty's eyes grew large and sharp. When we reached Grandma's porch, Katty and Grandma sat in the swing; Sadie and I on the porch edge.

"If it wasn't a bad fire, the men should be back soon. They may have time to do a little more work on your house depending on how soon they get done. I'll go throw some cornbread in the oven. My beans should be cooked by now. The men will be hungry for sure." Katty left quickly. Sadie followed but stopped to look over her shoulder at me before continuing on.

"My heart almost stopped when I heard that fire whistle. Katty tore across the yard so fast I feared she might have a heart attack. I had to run to keep up with her. I don't think a team of mules could have held her back."

"Grandma, I have something to tell you," I began.

"What's wrong?" she asked.

"When Sadie and I got to the school, I saw Tara McCrady practicing cheers. She was asking me about our fire when I realized Sadie had gone missing. I found her at the swings by the elementary school."

"Well, she didn't really get lost. You found her. She should have told you she was going to the swings, but that's Sadie. She does what comes to her mind without thinking. Katty won't be mad. It wasn't like she was really lost," Grandma dismissed my fault.

"That's not all. When I found her, Army was sitting in the swing next to her."

"Oh my," Grandma gasped.

"They weren't touching—just talking. It seemed innocent enough, except you know Miss Katty would be mad that she was even talking to Army."

"You didn't see him at all until you saw him sittin' next to Sadie in the swings, right? Did he say why he was there? How did he know y'all would be there?"

"No, he showed up unexpectedly. Grandma, he never said a word to me but when I got to them, he and Sadie stopped talking. I didn't ask him why he was there. I figured he could rightly be at the school swings as much as Sadie could." I realized I was echoing Sadie when she justified Army's being at the Big Store the day it caught fire.

"So, are you thinking he and Sadie had that planned?"

"That was my first thought, but the walk to school was my idea, not Sadie's. She couldn't have planned anything with him. I'm afraid Army was following us. If not us—he was following Sadie. I think he may like Sadie. As in…like her."

"You mean you think he's sweet on Sadie? She's too young to have a beau. Why Katty'd have a squealin' worm to think a boy had eyes for Sadie. She'd have an even bigger one if that boy was Army Boone." Grandma resorted to one of her old southern terms about Katty having a squealing worm. The mental picture of Katty's squealing worm might have been funny, had our discussion not been about Army's having designs on our Sadie.

Then, I pictured that if Katty did have a squealing worm, that worm, while squealing to the top of its lungs, would get stomped promptly by Katty's forceful foot. Now that mental picture did bring a smile to my face, in spite of the situation.

"Meryl, I hate for either one of us to be the one to tell them, but Katty and Simp need to know about this thing with Sadie and Army Boone."

"Not only will Katty be upset, but you know Sadie will be mad at me for telling. I'll be in trouble either way."

"We'll tell them all together. That way, Sadie can't say you went behind her back, and Simp can maybe calm Katty down if he needs to."

"I would love to act like it never happened."

"Think about it, Meryl, if you don't tell them and this boy was to harm Sadie in some way, you'd always feel like you could've stopped it. Sadie's gettin' mad now doesn't compare to her bein' protected from possible future harm."

"I know Grandma—you're right."

"Another thing," Grandma continued, "Army is too

young to be doing such things. Why, it's against the law to spy on people like that. If he gets found out, he may be a boy that's stopped now and won't be a man that does this or worse later on."

The longer Grandma reasoned why Army's actions should be exposed, the more I knew it was the right thing to do. I felt better knowing the account would be shared with everyone at the same time, and maybe Simp could console Katty if she went on a rampage. Grandma and I agreed that after supper, when everyone gathered on their porch before bed would be the best time to talk to the trio.

We stood to go help Katty with dinner when Darby Talbot's car turned down the lane, followed by Obe's work truck with his crew. We sat back down and waited.

"It was the bus barn at the school," Darby said walking to the porch.

"It would'a been worse if a group of cheerleaders hadn't been practicin' nearby and smelled the smoke," Obe added.

"Fortunately, the janitor heard the girls yell fire! He ran and stomped out the flames. Had Able Watson not been there, the barn and all the busses coulda been lost. Ain't no tellin' how far it would'a gone. We coulda lost the school and maybe even some of the houses nearby too," another crew member added with a bit of exaggeration.

"It's just good they acted fast, and we got there

before the fire completely got out of hand is all," Darby chimed in.

"How'd this one start?" No one noticed Katty had arrived.

"Looks like it was started by a pile a rags in the corner of the barn, Katty. If the rags had a been greasy, we might a blamed it on that, but I didn't smell any grease," Darby said.

"So you're sayin'…….?" Grandma started to ask.

"The rags were intentionally set Mrs. Strom, just like your house and the porch of the Green Fly," Darby interrupted.

"Like I been tellin' everbody—we got us a firebug runnin' around loose."

"Katty, I hate to agree. But it looks like you're right," Darby surrendered.

"Yep, you called it, Miss Katty. That's what we got here," Obe added.

"Well, there ain't nothin' we can do about that now, but I can feed you bunch of hungry carpenters or fire fighters, which ever one you want to hold claim to right now. Y'all come on over to my kitchen. I got a pone of cornbread and a big pot of white beans. And there's a plate of juicy, red, sliced tomatoes to go with it too." Katty liked nothing better than to serve a meal to a table of hungry people and see them enjoy it.

"You don't have to ask me twice Katty," said Obe.

"Me neither. Hey, you got onion to go with 'em

beans?" Another man asked.

"Yes, and a jar of chow-chow, too. It's got a little kick to it, but that's the way Simp likes it," Katty added, inspiring them to walk a little faster to get to her table.

"There's plenty of daylight left to get more done on your house after dinner, Mrs. Strom," Darby assured her on the way.

"Katty, that was so nice of you to feed those men like that," Grandma said after the crew had returned to work.

"Mrs. Strom, did you forget that arm load of food you brought over from your kitchen when y'all first come after the fire? It's only right to feed the ones who are helpin' you. They ain't askin' for no other kind of pay. The least I can do is feed 'em, especially if I'm feedin' 'em from your own supply of food." Katty outargued her again.

## Chapter Thirteen

"Apples! Got fresh apples for sale!" The chant of a fruit peddler echoed.

"Delight thyself in the things of the Lord and He will give you the desires of your heart." Grandma quoted Psalms 37:4, one of her favorite Bible verses.

"We'll take two bushels!" Katty yelled from the edge of her porch, stopping the peddler in his tracks.

"The Lord knew it was our hearts' desire to have some apples to can for pies and make jelly for this winter. I just wished for that very thing this mornin'." Grandma beamed.

"Mrs. Strom you're right. You know, it is a good day—even if there is a fire bug runnin' amuck out there somewhere." Katty had to throw in a little bitter with the sweet, just to keep things in perspective.

"The apples will keep til tomorrow so we can get these fresh pickins' dealt with first. Plus, they'll make your kitchen smell like a ripe apple orchard," Grandma said.

After admiring the many cans of vegetables, they could add to their other winter provisions, Katty and Grandma started supper before Simp arrived from the field. Darby and his group wouldn't be working much longer in the fading daylight, but the rooms were coming along fine.

"Mrs. Strom can you make a place for the cornbread there on the table?" Katty asked as Simp walked through the door. Sadie and I were placing silverware by the plates.

"Smells good y'all and this man's hungry," Simp said taking his place at the head of the table after washing up.

My food was being churned into a ball in the pit of my stomach during supper. I was anxious about having to share about mine, Sadie's, and Army's encounter once we gathered out on the porch. Her expression proved Grandma felt the same.

"Asa was talkin' about that fire they had in Muddy Ox today, after he got back from a run to town. Said it was the school's bus barn this time. These fires are gettin' real out a hand," Simp said between bites.

"You can say that again," Katty grunted.

"These fires are gettin' real out a hand," Simp teased. Katty whopped him on the arm as he continued. "They're sayin' this one was set on purpose too." Simp didn't know he was sharing old news.

"We know, Meryl Jean and Sadie had just left Muddy Ox and were on their way home when the fire whistle sounded," said Katty.

"Meryl 'bout made me run to get home," Sadie said

while smacking and chewing with her mouth full.

"Well, y'all still didn't get here soon enough to suit me. Sadie don't talk with your mouth full," Katty said, correcting her without taking a breath. Sadie wrinkled her nose in protest when her mother wasn't looking.

"I had to run to keep up with Katty, myself. I never saw a body move as fast as she can when she's bound for somewhere." Grandma laughed.

"We didn't know it was the bus barn that was on fire 'til Darby came back to work on Mrs. Strom's house, after they got it put out. All we knew was the fire whistle was going off in Muddy Ox and Sadie and Meryl went there," Katty added.

"That's twice now that Sadie's barely missed being right in the middle of a fire."

"Simp, the girls were on their way home and not really in the middle of the fire. But it scared me to death again for Sadie bein' out of my sight with fires a goin' on."

"Actually, we'd just left the school yard where we were talking to the cheerleaders who'd smelled the smoke and alerted the janitor," I said, puncturing the bubble of peace Katty had just claimed.

"Then y'all were close to it after all. The fire needed a little time after it got started to give off enough smoke for 'em girls to smell it," Katty calculated.

"Like I said, Sadie was almost in the middle of the fire again," Simp repeated.

"I sure hope they ketch that firebug soon." Katty sounded more anxious now than ever.

"Oh, he'll slip up 'fore long. Firebugs set fires either 'cause they have somethin' 'ginst the people whose property they set on fire or they're just plain sick enough that it gives 'em a thrill to see all the commotion goin' on," Simp said.

"I don't want it to be either case concernin' my house fire. I hope someone don't have anythin' against us to do such a thing to Meryl and me." Of the two evils, Grandma tried to pick the least threatening one, which was the firebug was satisfying his own thrills. That would have made it less personal at least.

"Well, I'm goin' to smoke my pipe 'fore bed. See y'all out on the porch in a bit?" Simp scraped the floor as he pushed his chair back and headed for his smoking spot.

Once the kitchen was put in order, we filed to the porch. After a few minutes of silence, Grandma began. "Y'all—Meryl and me have somethin' to talk to you about."

"Sounds serious Mrs. Strom," Simp said.

"Now, Mrs. Strom, if your plannin' to say how bad you feel that you and Meryl are havin' to stay with us again—just don't. We've told you and told you, and I thought we made it clear that we're glad to be a help. Y'all are like family," Katty quipped.

"Well, yes, we do feel bad, and we appreciate all you

done for us. And we have that same family feelin' about y'all, but that's not what we need to talk about right now."

"It's soundin' more serious by the minute, Mrs. Strom." Simp's suspicion grew.

"First of all, Sadie, don't be mad at Meryl. I am makin' her tell your mother and daddy about today. If you want to be mad at anybody, you can be mad at me." That was a smart move on Grandma's part. She knew Katty and Simp wouldn't tolerate Sadie holding a grudge toward her. Grandma had everyone's attention. Sadie began to squirm.

"Meryl told me that when she and Sadie went to the school today she lost sight of Sadie for a short time. When she found her, she was with Army at the swings." Grandma threw it out there for them to either catch it or let it hit them in the face.

"It seemed harmless enough. They were only talking and not touching. I just knew if you found out, Miss Katty, and I hadn't told you that you'd be upset with me. I know you don't like Army around Sadie." Next, I tried to smooth things with Sadie.

"I am not trying to get you in trouble, Sadie. I am trying to protect you." I was also protecting me too—from a pair of potentially angry parents.

"If anything ever happen to Sadie and we didn't tell, we'd never forgive ourselves," Grandma reasoned.

Up until this point neither of the trio had said a

word. It made me uncomfortable. I didn't know if it was the calm before the storm or what.

"Nothin's gonna happen to me. Army didn't do nothin'. He just set in the swing, and we talked," Sadie broke the silence.

"How did he know you were there in the first place? Why wasn't he workin' and pullin' cotton in the field with the rest of his family? Did you know he was goin' to be there Sadie?' Katty did her usual tactic of pelting Sadie with questions. Sadie did her usual thing of shutting down until her mother caught her breath.

"Answer your mother, Sadie," Simp demanded in a tone that shocked all of us, I think even him.

"I don't know how Army knowd we was there. It was Meryl's idea for us to walk to the school. I didn't tell him nothin'. He just showed up. Meryl was talkin' to her friends. I got tired and went to sit in the swings, and there he came." Sadie's tone was believable. I felt sorry for throwing her into the line of fire and came to her defense.

"True, it was my idea to walk to the school. It wasn't planned. We just did it."

"We're not accusin' you, Meryl," said Simp.

"I didn't know Tara would be there practicing cheers. When Tara saw me, she stopped to ask about our house fire. But we only talked for a few minutes. It scared me when I thought I'd lost Sadie."

"I know that feelin' for sure," Katty agreed.

"I don't blame you Sadie for going to sit in the swings. I only wish you'd told me you were going." Hopefully, I took a little heat off her.

"This brings us to the same question. How did that boy know y'all were goin' to the school, and why wasn't he in the field?" Katty couldn't let it go.

"Well, the only sensible answer is this boy's been keepin' his eyes on Sadie and none of us knew it." Simp said what Grandma and I had decided. But I was glad he said it first.

"Spyin' on Sadie, but why?" Katty wouldn't allow herself to think the obvious.

"He's probably sweet on her. I told you this boy might be Sadie's age, but life's made him older." Simp opened the door for the squealing worm to show its ugly head.

The blood slowly rose upward from Katty's neck until her face was blaze red. Her lips paled to a ghostly white. We couldn't tell if we were about to witness a stroke or a heart attack. Instead we saw a—squealing worm! Katty stood and began to pace. I do believe she would have exploded had she continued to sit. In a loud, high pitched, shaking, voice, she began. "Sweet—on—Sadie? That stinkin', work-dodgin', cigarette-rollin', knife-carryin', roof-hoppin', hillbilly, from the backwoods and hills of Kentucky is sweet on our Sadie?" Katty continued to pace while adding more. "Sadie's just a baby. Cain't nobody be sweet on her. Not as long as I have anythin' to say about it and I got plenty to say." She was still pacing when Simp cautiously intervened.

"Now Katty, jest calm down. He can think he's sweet on her all he wants as long as he doesn't let his thoughts be actions."

"Well, I don't even want him thinkin' it." Katty squealed as Simp finally convinced the pacing fireball to sit.

"I'm not comfortable that he is spyin' on her either. God knows, I'll be glad when pullin' is over, and they leave this place." Simp had no actual proof that Army Boone was spying or doing wrong toward his daughter. His only solution was—get the Boone bunch gone.

"We all cain't wait for 'em to go," Katty butted in.

"It ain't a crime to talk to a body unless they're sayin' somethin' out of the way or the body don't want to be talked to," Simp finished.

Simp came to Grandma's and my earlier conclusion. Sadie had defended this boy's right to talk to her, making it a welcomed conversation. If he'd said anything out of the way, it was unknown. Sadie was the only one who heard him. And she wasn't telling.

"My hands are tied to even say anythin' to his dad or him, 'cause I don't have proof. We just think it right now." Simp's expression screamed—helpless father.

"Well, then, what can we do?" Katty questioned.

"I cain't do nothin' with the boy. But I can do

somethin' with Sadie." Simp wasn't usually the disciplinarian. However, since he saw that he and Katty were of the same mind about this issue, he ran with it.

"Sadie, you're to tell us of any time that you see that boy around you, or if he even says as much as howdy to you. You hear me? Katty, she shouldn't be allowed to go anywhere without you until that bunch is out of here. Don't let her out of your sight."

Katty agreed and Simp looked proud like he'd settled the matter.

"So is school still goin' to start on Monday?" Sadie asked, not defying her father, but skirting the entire issue.

"Shouldn't be a problem. The buses didn't get hurt. Now, I am goin' to bed, or I'll never beat the sun up in the mornin'." Giving Sadie a long, questionable, look, Simp angrily shook out his pipe before going inside.

"Come on Sadie, let's go to bed too. Maybe my blood's cooled down enough now that I might be able to sleep." Sadie quietly followed her mother and father inside.

"Guess we oughta do the same, Meryl. Katty and me have another day's canning ahead of us tomorrow. It'll take most of the day to put up them apples along with whatever more pickens Katty finds in the garden come mornin'. Darby and the men have three more days to work on the bedrooms. It looks like they're going to get 'em done. If so, we can move back home the first of next week."

"Grandma, do you think Sadie will report to them if Army approaches her again?"

"Knowin' Sadie, it's hard to say. It didn't look to me like she was too shaken by their demands."

"Did you see how she quickly changed the subject, so she didn't have to agree to what Simp said? I asked.

"I've seen her pull that same thing on Katty. Sadie's a sly one, no doubt. You know if that boy is spyin' on Sadie, then he is spyin' on all of us."

I shivered to think there could be a pair of curious eyes peering at us that very moment. "Let's go inside too, okay?" I said nervously.

"Simp and Katty have their hands full with Sadie and she's only twelve years old. It's not goin' to get any easier the older she gets. Yes, I'm ready to call it a day. Surely those people will be headin' out of here soon," Grandma moaned.

## Chapter Fourteen

SILENCE, NOT A blasting radio or pounding hammers, greeted me the next morning. I lay quietly for a moment to gather my bearings. Yes, we were still at the Simpson's. The kink in my back from their lumpy couch confirmed that. After rising and stretching to get the blood moving, the feeling returned in my nearly numb hip. Why wasn't the kitchen buzzing with its usual morning sounds or tantalizing smells of breakfast? In fact, why was everything so quiet?

After stepping onto the porch, the sun's bright rays told me I'd slept later than usual. Poking my head back through the kitchen door, I saw the clock said seven o'clock. I never slept that late. What was going on? And where was Grandma?

I was actually relieved to see Katty's sun bonnet bobbing in her garden. Things were not completely amiss in my world. Following the soft hum of voices, I found Grandma and Darby sitting in our porch swing. They were so deep into conversation they didn't see or hear me approach.

"Mrs. Strom, it's too soon to actually accuse anyone, but she was at the scene of every one of the fires."

Darby was making some very serious but cautious presumptions.

"I can't imagine she would do any such thing," Grandma rejected.

"She who—she who would not do such a thing?" I asked. Surely, I wasn't the subject in Darby's suspicions. The two of them turned and met my startled face.

"Mornin' Meryl, I'm glad you're here. Let's keep this to ourselves, but Darby does have a point. The one person at the scene of every one of them fires is—Sadie."

It was as though my senses were now numb instead of my hip. Was Darby actually thinking Sadie started the fires? The numbness was quickly replaced with clarity. Miss Katty would have an even bigger squealing worm if she heard that people were thinking her Sadie was the presumed firebug.

As Darby and Grandma continued to sort through clues, I started to remember some of Sadie's questionable behavior and was gathering a few clues of my own. She'd become unusually excited while building the fire under the wash kettle that day. "*Let's get some big pieces of wood to make a big fire*," she had said while eagerly gathering wood.

"*I don't like school like you do,*" Sadie admitted, while sharing her and Katty's decision about quitting school with me.

"*Do you think school will still start on Monday?*" Had she

been wishing school would be delayed because of the bus barn fire, as she avoided her father's demands concerning Army?

*"Meryl, come go to the toilet with me. Come now."* I'd thought it was because of her urgency to use the toilet that she'd rushed me out of the house. Was she getting me to safety instead? Could Sadie actually be the firebug?

Reaching for a new sense of clarity, I probed Darby deeper, "Wasn't there other people who were also at all of the fires? I can't believe its Sadie either." Then, I recalled, as far as I knew, I was the only one in our house when it caught fire—that is until Sadie called for me to come outside.

"We don't want to go accusing anyone of anything that we don't have positive proof of. We're still looking for pieces to this puzzle. Now Meryl, you said you and Sadie were the only ones around when y'all's house caught fire, right? You were here with your grandma during the Green Fly's fire. And you and Sadie had just left the school yard and were on the road home during the bus barn incident. Is that correct?"

"Yes, all of that is the way it happened," I confirmed with a muddled brain.

"Your grandma said you lost sight of Sadie for a time while you were talking to the McCrady girl in the school yard?"

"Yes, but for only a few minutes."

"So, it's possible Sadie could have been at all three fire scenes, since she was unaccounted for, for a short time."

"It's possible but when I found her she was at the swings with Army Boone. They stopped talking when I approached so I don't know what they were talking about. I only saw her at the swings with Army and nowhere else," I debated.

"Well, maybe—just maybe; and I sure hope it's true, there's someone else involved but we just don't know it yet. The last thing I wanna' do is to confront Katty Simpson with unconfirmed suspicions about Sadie. We all know Katty and how she is about that little girl of hers." Darby was smart not to rumple Katty prematurely.

"Honestly, Darby, all us mother hens protect our little chicks. Katty's not acting out of reason." Grandma was probably remembering how she could get riled if she thought someone was coming against one of her own sons.

Darby was cautioning me again about discretion before being interrupted.

"Mrs. Strom, I picked us a big mess of purple hull peas. We can have some for supper and still have enough to can a few jars too. We'll get to 'em once we've wiped out the apples tomorrow. Meryl and Sadie can help us. They need to learn how it's done, and it'll also keep 'em in sight."

Had we not been so consumed with being shade-tree-detectives, Katty's arrival wouldn't have startled us so. Darby nervously bounced to his feet. I imagined for once, he'd been thankful for Katty's hearing problem and was confident she hadn't heard anything he wasn't ready to share with her.

"Mornin' Katty. Mrs. Strom, uh…I need to do a little more measurin' before the others show up," Darby's voice trailed as he darted toward our bedrooms. Grandma stood and bid me to follow and at the same time steered Katty toward home.

"Yes, we all need to get to work if we're going to get anything done today," Grandma said, still nudging Katty along.

A sleepy Sadie met us in the kitchen and dropped into the nearest chair. Grandma asked me to fix mine and Sadie's breakfast while she and Katty started peeling apples and boiling fruit jars.

Having been privy to Darby's and Grandma's conversation earlier, I viewed Sadie with a different pair of eyes. Surely this twelve year old, gobbling down her breakfast like a doe-eyed hound puppy at his feeding bowl couldn't be capable of causing all those fires—or could she?

## Chapter Fifteen

"I MISSED OLD Camp Meeting Time this morning. Simp thinks there's a fuse burned out in my radio. He's gonna look at it tonight after he gets home from the field," Katty said, while lifting the lid on her pot of beans to give them a stir.

That explained the morning minus a blaring radio. Grandma's early talk with Darby, Katty's quest to pick her garden before the heat of the day, and a blown radio fuse, equaled a longer sleep time for me. Once Simp fixed the radio, normal would resume. But for now, we had a reprieve from our early morning madness.

After finishing our breakfast, and after we had all the peas shelled Sadie and I were handed paring knives and cautioned many times over about their sharp edges.

"Now, y'all slice those apples real thin. If you peel 'em too thick, you'll be wastin' too much apple. People throw out about half as much apple as they get canned because they don't peel 'em right." Grandma referred to Proverbs 31, on the virtues of women and their role of caring for their households. Guess she thought if she warned us with scripture, we'd be under Katty's and her watchful eyes—and God's too.

The Simpson's were not regular churchgoers, actually hardly at all, but from hearing Grandma's frequent Bible references, they couldn't say they'd never heard what the Bible had to say about most everything. She attached scripture to nearly any situation.

"Y'all are peelin' too thick again. Waste not; want not." Sadie and I fixed our knives to peel as thinly as possible. If not, another Bible lesson could be in store for us.

By the time Simp got home that evening, we had the entire two bushels of apples and the bulging pan of purple hill peas canned for winter. I felt proud to be a part of it all.

Washed up from the field and awaiting supper, Simp resigned to the porch with Katty's radio to investigate its problem. Sadie set the table, and I was sent to throw the apple peelings, pea hulls, and a collection of other food scraps to the chickens.

Purple being my favorite color, I was drawn to the wild violets mingled among the weeds on my path back to the house. After parting the weeds to get a bouquet of violets for our supper table, I was met with an unsettling sight. A strewn collection of cigarette butts, one of which was still smoldering, was covered by the weeds. Of course, because they were rolled cigarettes, the first person to enter my mind was Army Boone.

An icy chill moved slowly down my back. A warm wave of sickness gripped my stomach. That warm wave rushed to my feet, filling them with fire and the need to run. Fear became panic. I held tightly to the violets as I sped toward the safety of Katty's kitchen and away from any peering eyes hidden in the dusk of night.

Without positive proof, I tried to dismiss my quick presumption. Army wasn't the only person around Muddy Ox who smoked rolled cigarettes. Of course, I'd never noticed any of them hanging around our chicken pen to smoke. But, for that matter, I'd never seen Army there either.

My lack of composure went unnoticed as I returned. Grandma smiled to see the flowers in my hand and found a small cut-glass jelly jar for my bouquet. The jar was small enough and the stems long enough for the blossoms to barely peak over the rim.

"I bet you couldn't resist these because they're purple."

"Grandma, you know me well," I answered, suppressing the desire to blurt out my discovery in the weeds. But I felt it wasn't the right time or place.

"Where'd the flowers come from," I was surprised Sadie noticed. She usually only went through the motions of being present around the table.

"Who but Meryl would stop to pick flowers on her way back from throwin' scraps to the chickens?" Grandma's tone reflected a compliment rather than a complaint.

"Katty, you're gonna be without a radio 'til we can

get to town Saturday. It's not likely The Big Store will have any of these gold-tipped radio fuses. This one's blown. See here?" Simp held up the darkened fuse to Katty as he reentered the kitchen.

Her countenance fell. I had mixed emotions. I knew how much she enjoyed her morning radio, but if Katty's radio was out of commission until at least Saturday, we could have two more somewhat quieter early mornings—if Darby's plan held true. I'd try not to let too much excitement enter my voice for our reprieve and Katty's dilemma as the evening wore on.

The chatter around the supper table was constant. Simp figured three more weeks of good cotton pulling remained before Asa let go of his field hands, except for possibly him and a couple more. This was welcome news to everyone, except for maybe Sadie. The Boone family could be moving on soon.

With most of their food put up for the winter, Katty and Grandma's conversation became about the quilts they could make during the long winter ahead. "Effie showed me the prettiest 'Dutch Girl' and 'Sunflower' quilts she'd been workin' on the other day. You shoulda' seen 'em. I'll cut us a pattern from hers. We can make us a couple of those," Grandma said.

"The Mexicans already left. Asa said the Boone's hadn't said nothin' about leavin' yet," Simp continued as though Grandma or Katty hadn't said anything in between. Obviously, he wasn't listening to them. Plus he must have been more bothered about the Boone's than he'd let on since they were high on his list of concerns.

"Good riddins' to 'em. I haven't seen that boy Army 'round here anymore, and I hope I never do." The mention of the Boone's name was a conversation changer for Katty.

Grandma and I continued to eat in silence, each harboring our own shared and individual secrets. She was probably brooding over Darby's and her suspicions about Sadie. I worried if I should confess finding that pile of cigarette butts in the weeds. Sadie wasn't talking at all. I wondered what thoughts were swirling around in that mind.

Simp retired to the porch with his pipe while we four ladies cleaned the kitchen. After joining Simp, I decided not to tell the already on edge group about finding the cigarette butts. Bringing it up would have presented a very anxious evening, not to mention a restless night for everyone. If a peacemaker really was blessed, then by the omission of one less thing to worry about in addition to my tranquil bouquet of violets to grace our supper table—I should be feeling very blessed.

The last thought I had alone on the couch before sleep overtook me was that one of Grandma's common sayings was right on target. *"Silence—especially in the case of a golden-tipped radio fuse this time, actually was—golden."*

## Chapter Sixteen

"I LIKE THE Dollar Store in Steele better," Sadie grumbled as we piled into the car.

"Well, Kennett's where we'll find your mother's radio fuse. I was told they'll have them there at Riggs Supply Store." Sadie was over-ruled.

"I haven't heard Old Camp Meetin' Time since Tuesday mornin'. I don't have any idea who died, or when and where their funerals will be without Mr. Rudy announcin' it after the mornin' news and weather report." Katty clearly needed her radio.

"Well, it won't take me but a jiffy to get it goin' after we get that fuse," Simp boasted. Katty was truly the love of his life. You never heard him voice it, but his actions shouted it almost daily.

I was glad they chose Kennett. There was a better selection of clothing there. The money donation amounted to a little over two hundred dollars. I insisted Grandma get a few church dresses, but she insisted louder that I buy what I needed first. In the end, I had no intention of letting her spend it all on me.

After Simp dropped us off in front of the Dollar Store, he left for the Farm Supply center in search of a special radio fuse. Katty trotted after Sadie as she darted in one direction, then another. Grandma and I made a beeline for the shoes.

It usually took ten pairs of those dollar a pair tennis shoes to get me through the winter. Ten pairs of tennis shoes might have seemed an extravagance to some, but the soles of those cheap tennis shoes pulled away from the canvas, and the toes would be full of holes in no time, because of my wide feet. That was probably why Daddy had insisted on those wider, more durable boy shoes when we lived in Illinois. But those ugly things only brought more unwanted attention and set an even greater stage for embarrassment and taunting. I'd been called Meryl the Barrel, fatso, and every other humiliating name imaginable in my previous schools. I couldn't chance that happening again. I didn't as much as glance toward the boy's shoes on my way to the ladies'.

Simp was sitting on a bench, puffing his pipe, as we arrived from the Dollar Store. His expression said he must have found Katty's fuse, which he soon confirmed. After tucking our packages into his trunk, we left for Graber's Department Store. Graber's clothes were less expensive than James Kahn's I couldn't even afford James Kahn's sale prices.

Grandma balked but finally consented to a few church dresses from the sale rack. After a second deposit into Simp's trunk, we returned to the Dollar Store in search of plastic, lavender curtains for my room. Grandma left me digging for curtains, while she went for some bar soap and a box of kitchen matches—she said.

We laughed after meeting in the middle aisle on our way to check-out. She had a pair of black leather, pointed toed shoes for me and I held a pair of brown, laced, every day, shoes for her. Making sure both pairs fit, we took shoes, matches, soap, and curtains to the register. Our shopping excursion was a success—with a little money left over.

Simp rosed from the bench as we returned. "I'm gonna go see if I can find Katty and Sadie. Anyways, I need some wire to fix a place in the chicken pen. We won't be long." Simp shook the ashes from his pipe and slid it into his shirt pocket.

"Okay, Meryl and me will be here when you get back…no hurry. Here Meryl, take these coins and get us an ice cream cone while we're waiting for 'em," Grandma said as soon as Simp was out of sight. My love for ice cream matched Grandma's. But I was happy to go into the ice cream parlor in hopes of seeing the teenagers that usually hung out there.

The smooth voice of Elvis Presley singing *Crying in the Chapel*, flowed from the jukebox, as I stepped inside. Two couples slow danced on a black and white, square-tiled floor. Groups of three and four sat at booths and tables scattered along the side of the room. Those that looked up as I entered, resumed their conversations once they didn't recognize me. The social limitations Grandma imposed on me narrowed my acquaintances to only the kids from school, cotton patch buddies, and a handful of friends from our church in Hayti.

Elvis's song ended as the parlor door closed behind me.

"Oh good, I forgot to tell you, but you got me strawberry anyway."

"It's your favorite, isn't it?" I grinned taking a lick of my chocolate cone.

The jukebox was the main reason Grandma sent me to the parlor alone. Like a lot of people her age, she saw the music of the day as the devil's music. To her, Elvis, Jerry Lee Lewis, and most other song artists of that era were a notch short of the antichrist.

I knew better. Elvis's voice was way too heavenly.

## Chapter Seventeen

"IT'S GOTTA BE a firebug," boomed a voice from behind our bench.

"There's been more fires in Muddy Ox here lately than I kin ever remember there a bein'," another man grumbled as they ambled toward Kennett Square.

"Word travels fast. We're not the only ones fearin' about a firebug," Grandma said once the men were past.

"I still don't want to think it's Sadie," I sighed.

"Well, she's bein' watched so close now, she'd have a hard time blowin' her nose without Katty or Simp wipin' it," Grandma joked.

"You're right about that, and Sadie isn't too happy about it."

"I don't want to think its Sadie, either. It has to be a fluke that she's been where all the fires were. Why, she's just a child. Someone else must be doin' this mischief," Grandma added between licks.

"Oh Grandma—I just had an awful thought. What if the firebug, whoever it is, burns our house again? I couldn't bear to have my clothes and shoes burned up twice—could you? People couldn't afford to give us any more money if it happened again."

"That's not likely. Whoever's startin' those fires would be silly to burn the same place twice. They'd risk gettin' caught for sure. People are watchin' too close." Grandma's conclusions made my heart a little lighter. I hoped they'd find the culprit soon to calm my fears and to take suspicions from Sadie.

Katty and Sadie finally appeared from the Hardware Store with Simp bringing up the rear. Of course, we heard Katty before we saw her. We smelled Sadie. She must have tried a dab from every bottle of cheap perfume the Dollar Store had. If I'd thought the Ben Hur perfume she usually bought was strong, it held no comparison to the smell of the mixture that now followed Sadie like a cloud. We'd for sure have the windows cracked on our way home, despite the brisk October wind. We'd get chilled and our hairdos would suffer. But at least we could breathe.

Simp opened his trunk one last time for their packages then perched on the fender with a small sack dangling from his hand. He beamed as he presented Katty with her fuse. She maneuvered into the front seat with a grin that covered her entire face.

"Looks like we're gonna make it home in time for me to work on your radio before bedtime. I'm pretty sure that come mornin', you'll be listenin' to Old Camp Meetin' Time and Mr. Rudy Pylant again."

"Well good. I sure have been missin' my radio and Mr. Rudy."

Grandma and I shared a look. We loved Mr. Rudy and Old Camp Meetin' Time too. Just not at Katty's volume level. I was thinking if Darby's predictions were true, we'd only have two more early mornings to experience Katty's radio dancing off its shelf. I imagined Grandma was thinking the same.

"Mrs. Strom, did y'all find some good bargains? I hope you found you a couple new church dresses. That money sure came at the right time for y'all. People mighta' come up with a dress or two for you, but I can't think of any girls Meryl's age that coulda' give her nothin'. For sure not sho… well, you know what I mean…uh…."

It was an awkward moment but knowing Katty, I realized she didn't intend to hurt me. Besides, it was true. I couldn't have worn any shared clothing or shoes.

"Grandma found three nice church dresses at Graber's, and we found her a pair of everyday shoes at the Dollar Store too." I interrupted, pulling Katty out of the hole she'd dug for herself, as though I hadn't heard her last remarks.

"Yes, but I made sure Meryl had her school things first. We even got her a pair of dress shoes for church." Grandma beamed.

"They don't have the stripe on the toe like the others had but they're the same style as the first pair I bought."

"Yes…pointed toed," Grandma's tone revealed her

distaste for the modern styles.

"Well, that's the style. It's okay, I won't be wearing them to school anyway—only to church mostly." Grandma understood my wanting to try to fit in, so she conceded. I was elated. I'd never gone on such a shopping spree. Getting all those things in a single trip to town was mind boggling—and so much fun.

While on the way home, it was a toss-up. Did we roll the windows up to keep the dust from flying through them? Or did we leave them cracked because of Sadie's perfume after we turned off 84 Highway onto the gravel road leading home. We left them down and dealt with the dust. There was a lot to be said for fresh air.

That gravel road just happened to go directly past the Boone's house. Sure enough, a few little ones played on the roof while Mrs. Boone sat on the porch puffing her corn cob pipe.

"Look at that," Katty grumbled, stretching her neck and straining to see firsthand what Simp had reportedly witnessed on his way to pay their electricity bill. Sadie perched to see as well. I figured she was looking for Army, but he was nowhere to be seen.

"I think it's disgraceful to see a woman smokin' a pipe like that." Grandma walked the straight and narrow. She didn't like to see women smoking at all, but a pipe was a special kind of offense.

"Looks like that kid Army, slouchin' down the road

toward us," Simp slowed the car a bit for confirmation. We all peered ahead in unison.

Army Boone was walking roadside as we passed. He locked eyes with Sadie and gave her a slight nod.

"Wonder where that boy's been and what's he been up to?" Katty huffed.

"Looks like he's probably just been to town," Sadie defended.

"Have you seen him walkin' past our house anymore, Katty?" Simp questioned.

"Not to my knowledge. Anyway, I'd a told you if I'd seen 'im," Katty grumped.

"Asa Bertram said he thinks they'll be headin' for the hills by the end of next week. The dad said the school officials were pushin' for 'em to start their kids to school if they stayed in Muddy Ox much longer. If they leave, the school's lucky and just don't know it."

"Good parents wouldn't let their kids run wild like they let those hooligans," Katty wedged in another insult toward the 'thorns in her flesh'.

"Besides, no one in town really took to 'em. They probably won't mind gettin' out of these parts," Simp continued.

Katty grunted. Grandma sighed. Sadie was quiet. I, as the others, was pleased to hear they were no longer going to be a concern for us and the community. Once home, Simp took the radio onto the porch to work on it while supper was being prepared.

"I got some new jacks. Wanna' play after we eat?" Sadie asked. Sadie was an expert at jacks. I rarely beat her, but it was fun trying. Simp soon placed the radio back on its shelf and plugged it in. A blast of static was proof of his success. He tuned to the Grand Ole Opry in time to hear Lester Flatt and Earl Scruggs sing about *Martha White's self-rising flour having hot rise.*

"Yep, it works." Simp promptly flipped the radio off and began washing his hands for supper. They might listen to the Grand Ole Opry on the evenings when it was too cold to sit on the porch, but the radio never played during a meal.

We sat down to a supper of fried commodity meat, cold slaw, and of course, white beans and cornbread. Grandma sliced a couple of large ripe tomatoes, as well. "We'd better enjoy these tomatoes while we can. They're almost gone for this year." Grandma pulled up to the table. After her Amen, we all dived in.

Sadie and I played jacks on the kitchen table after supper, while the others enjoyed the evening on the porch.

## Chapter Eighteen

SIMP TRIED NOT to do any *real* work on Sundays, but this time an entire section of the chicken pen needed to be replaced. He was hard at work when we arrived from church. Chickens aren't the smartest things on two legs, but they have an uncanny way of finding their way through a broken fence. The pen had to be fixed. Sunday or not.

Katty had purple hull peas seasoned with ham hocks, fried potatoes, and fried bean cakes, nearly ready by the time we changed from our church clothes. I wore my candy-striped dress and my new pointed toed shoes to church today. If my feet could have talked, they would have sighed with relief to be free of those crimping pointed toes as soon as I stepped inside the door. I could tolerate the discomfort for the sake of fashion for church and other special occasions—but that was all.

Grandma's navy blue dress was a welcome change from Katty's borrowed plaid housedresses. When Brother Castle asked for testimonies, Grandma was the first to stand and testify of how we'd been blessed with generous friends to help us recover from our loss. I thanked God quietly while sitting in the pew.

"Katty, what can we do to help with dinner?" Grandma offered.

"There's some onions and cucumbers by the sink, Mrs. Strom. You can slice 'em up while Sadie gets the plates and glasses if you want. Meryl, can you grab some silverware? The rest is under control. Okay now Sadie, go let your Daddy know dinner's about ready so he can get washed up." By its savory aroma, the cornbread was browning nicely.

Katty's remorse began once Sadie left to fetch Simp. "Mrs. Strom, I hated for Simp to have to fix that pen on the Sabbath, but he couldn't help it. He…had *an ox in the ditch*," Grandma and Katty said in unison as though they'd rehearsed it. We laughed.

"What's so funny?" Simp asked as he and Sadie stepped through the kitchen door. Katty started to tell him, but his expression stopped her cold.

"What's wrong? Did you hurt yourself? Why are you lookin' like that?" Katty questioned. Simp opened his hand to reveal a clump of rolled cigarettes butts.

"Where'd you get them?" Katty questioned.

"There's sure a lot of 'em," Grandma added.

I remained silent. I knew where he'd found them. Evidently, Simp found the butts before Sadie had called him to dinner. Her face proved she hadn't seen them before.

"There's several piles of these things out by the

chicken pen. I wouldn't a seen em' if I hadn't got mad and threw my hammer when I hit my thumb. I found the hammer when I cooled off—right in the middle of these nasty things."

"Wonder how they got there?" Katty asked redundantly.

"Lessen our chickens has took up smokin', somebody with the habit is lurkin' around the pen. From the number of 'em, they've been hangin' around a lot."

"That Boone boy rolls his own. He did the day I run 'im out of our yard, when he was here talkin' to Sadie."

Simp threw the butts in an empty coffee can he pulled from under the sink and set them at the far end of their porch, out of sight and smell. "Let it go for now. Dinner's gettin' cold. We'll talk about it later," he said disgustingly while washing his hands. I wondered exactly what later meant for us. The silence at the table was deafening.

## Chapter Nineteen

AFTER DINNER, WE joined Simp on the porch. We'd barely gotten seated before he began, "Sadie, do you know anythin' about them cigarette butts?"

"Y'all know I don't smoke." Sadie tried to sidestep her father's probing.

"Sadie, you know better than that. Has that Boone kid been 'round here and you didn't tell us? Have you seen him out by the pen?" By this time, it was hard for Sadie to avoid Simp's direct questioning. She sat wide-eyed for a second before coming clean.

"He wasn't doin' anythin' wrong. He never talked to me. He was just standin' there smokin'. I knew y'all would be mad, so I didn't tell you."

"We're madder that you kept this from us." Katty's face flushed with anger.

"Didn't I say I wanted to know if you ever saw him 'round here again? Weren't you supposed to tell us if that happened?" Simp was past hiding his rage.

"But I thought if he didn't talk to me, it'd be okay. He was only out by the pen for a little while; then he cut through Mrs. Strom's yard and went toward Muddy Ox."

"Sadie, you know better. We said if you saw him, not just if he talked to you. You shoulda told us. He coulda caught the grass on fire throwin' those butts down like that. Aint no doubt that peepin' tom hoodlum's been spyin' on us." Katty was boiling.

Suddenly, Katty did something I'd never seen her do before—she spanked Sadie. It wasn't the brutal beating like my dad usually gave me, but Katty was strong. Her big hand made a powerful impression. Sadie was stunned. It took her a few minutes to react. Eventually, tears streamed down her face, and she rushed inside the house. The screen door slammed loudly behind her.

"I'm mad but I'm more scared. I'm scared of that boy's intentions, his brassiness, and Sadie's lack of respect for what we told her." Katty slumped into her chair, holding her head in her hands.

"You did the right thing by spankin' her. I was about to do it myself."

That sounded good coming from Simp but not one of us believed him. He left the discipline to Katty. She wanted it that way.

"I've gotta lay down a while. This is gettin' the best of me," Katty moaned, her face fallen, her eyes brimmed with tears. "I can count on one hand the number of times I've spanked that child. It just scares me to death that she's bein' followed and watched by someone that we don't know what's goin' on in his stinkin' mind," Katty drooped. Her body looked deflated as she shuffled inside the house.

"Y'all know that thing about me spankin' Sadie was all talk. Katty might get to the point of spankin' that girl once in a long while. But she'd never tolerate anyone else to do it. Not even me," Simp said quietly once Katty had gone.

"We know how Katty is about Sadie. Simp y'all got your hands full there." Grandma rarely gave an opinion about how they catered to Sadie, but she let it slip.

"Mrs. Strom, Meryl, its clear Sadie ain't gonna tell us if that boy comes around. But I trust y'all would let us know if you see 'im." Simp seemed scared and disgusted as he appealed for our help. He appeared as though the calculated deceit of his child, and his wife's reaction to it had suddenly aged him considerably.

"Simp, you know we would. You can count on us. Meryl was quick to tell me about him bein' at the swings that day at the school. He may have an eye for Sadie, but he sure has a silly way of showin' it."

"I know I can always count on y'all. I'm gonna go check on Katty. It's a wonder she didn't have a stroke, she was so mad. Hopefully, she's settled down a notch." Simp dragged through the screen door as though he had anchors attached to his feet. He clearly wasn't ready to deal with suitors for Sadie, especially one like Army Boone.

I'd been sitting like a mouse in its hole, although I felt more like a rat. Maybe I should have told about finding those butts. But in my defense, I hoped to avoid the scene we'd just been a part of. After hearing Grandma assure Simp of our loyalty, I at least had to confess my secret to her. Loyal was nowhere near how I felt. Traitor was more like it.

"Umm…Grandma, I need to tell you something again. I thought I was being a peacemaker. Now I'm not sure."

"Peacemaker, what are you talking about, Meryl?"

"When I took the pea hulls and scraps to the chicken pen last night, I saw that pile of cigarette butts that Simp found today. They were in plain view after I pulled the weeds back to pick those violets. I suspected it was Army's doing but wasn't sure. A lot of people roll their own cigarettes. I didn't want to cause a worse ruckus than the one we just had. You heard how quickly Katty blames and gets upset with Army for everything."

"Meryl—yes. You shoulda spoke up."

"I realize now, that if I'd said something, maybe some of this today might have been avoided. But we were all so happy last night. We'd had our great shopping trip. We were getting to move back home. Simp found the fuse for Katty's radio. Things were going good. I didn't want to ruin our happy night. I thought I could be a peacemaker. When Simp asked for our help just now, and you assured him of our loyalty—I felt terrible." After my long confession, I took a deep breath and waited for Grandma's reaction.

"So you're sayin' you didn't see Army Boone—only the pile of cigarette butts?"

"I didn't see anyone."

"Well, then—in the future, if you see Army you should do as Simp has asked. After this, if you find any more piles of cigarette butts, or anything else that looks out of the ordinary, you should tell us about that too."

"I will. I promise."

"It could be mine and your problem as much as theirs. We'll be back in our house tomorrow night and be two women livin' alone again." Grandma was right. With our houses being so close, if Army or anyone else was spying around, our privacy could be invaded as much as the Simpson's. I again promised I'd share anything I saw or heard from that time on.

"Guess we can take our Sunday naps now too." Grandma stood to go inside.

I followed her, but instead of napping, I tried to read. My mind kept drifting to tomorrow and the first day of school and how glad I'd be to see Polly again. I'd try to get up a little earlier. Maybe her bus would arrive ahead of time. Then I remembered, I had no worries, Simp fixed Katty's radio. There wasn't a chance I or any of the neighbors wouldn't be awakened to Old Camp Meetin' Time a few minutes after Katty walked into her kitchen. As Grandma would say, "Bless her heart."

## Chapter Twenty

"THIS IS RUDY Pylant with your 'Old Camp Meeting Time here on KBOA, 830 on your dial this fine fall morning in Kennett, Missouri. Stay tuned for your Hometown News, right after we hear the Wilburn Brothers sing, *Don't Go Home Tonight Unsaved*."

I bounced off the couch. Yes, Katty's radio woke me. But this time I was glad. Saved—we had been saved by the town's generosity, a few devoted carpenters, and by sweet neighbors who gave us a home when we didn't have one. Home—we were going home this very night.

After breakfast, I jumped off the porch with Sadie in tow, and we were off. Sadie didn't share my enthusiasm concerning the first day of school. But she was consoled that after this year and one more, she could be free of school—forever. Her attitude got a bit better once we arrived at school. However, I couldn't label it excited. We parted at the entrance of her school.

I waited at the high school's east door entrance, but there was no sign of Polly. Had her dad moved them away in search of another harvest? The sound of my name eased my fears as Polly rounded the corner. "Jean, my bus was late." We hugged.

"Oh Polly, I feared your dad had made y'all follow the harvest again."

"I worried, too, but Emmet Tuttle offered him year round work on his farm for the next two years. Unless things change, I'll get to graduate at Muddy Ox."

We hugged again and hurried to the library for our schedules, books, and assigned lockers. After making a locker run, we parted again. Polly and I were in different homerooms this year but had Mrs. Tyree's second period English together. We could match the rest of our schedules once there.

Psychology was my first period class. Mr. Vondell, my homeroom teacher, was new to Muddy Ox. I chose a desk on the front row to his right. Discretely, I scanned the room to see who had the class with me. I kept my Psychology book, pencil, and notebook on the desk, then slid the rest onto a rack under my seat.

"Hi Jean, can I sit by you?" Darla Phelps asked, taking the desk beside me.

"Sure Darla. Hey, I don't know about you, but Mr. Vondell scares me. He sounds mean," I whispered.

"Maybe he sounds tougher than he really is," she whispered back.

"We hope," I moaned. Mr. Vondell's glance in our direction was enough to silence me. The students behind us sat at attention as well. I hoped he hadn't heard our whispers.

"Don't get too comfortable, Class. We have assembly right after roll call," he barked.

"I pray you're right about Mr. Vondell. But his voice is almost bigger than he is," I remarked as Darla, and I made our way to the gym for assembly. Darla usually paired with Pricilla Royal, 'Cilla' as she was called by everyone. I wondered why Darla had chosen to mesh with Polly and me instead. Guess she'd let us know eventually. "There's Polly," I said. "Come on, there's room next to her."

"Hi," Polly greeted Darla as we joined her on the bleachers. I figured she was curious why Darla chose to sit with us and not Cilla too, but also didn't ask.

"Hi, hope you don't mind if I join you and Jean?"

"Not at all," Polly replied warmly.

The squeal of the microphone shushed the assembly as principal Gaffin stepped forward. "As we begin, I want to welcome our new students along with you returning ones. We're glad to have each one of you here at Muddy Ox High School." He continued after a hearty applause. "With the cooperation of teachers and students, we hope for a successful and rewarding year. As some of you already know, we have rules that you will be expected to follow and respect. You were given a list at registration.

"Our school has a fine group of teachers whose goals are to help each student reach their potential and prepare them for the paths they choose. We expect you students to work when there's work to be done, and afterwards have fun when there's fun to be had. Umm…that is to have fun only once the work is completed. Do I make myself clear?

"We, the faculty promise to respect you as the self-motivated, mature, high school students that we know you all are. We expect cooperation and respect from you in return. Nothing less will be tolerated. Again, do I make myself perfectly clear?"

A silence swept over the assembly, I assumed Mr. Gaffin took that as agreement on everyone's behalf and continued. "I'd like to recognize our teachers at this time. Hold your applause please, until all names have been called. Thank you."

Each teacher stood upon hearing their name. Mr. Vondell, psychology and social studies; Mr. Wakefield, science and biology; and Mrs. Vickors, music and band were all new teachers. The others were long standing faculty at Muddy Ox. It was a small school in a small community where everyone knew everybody and who they had Sunday Dinner with. Teachers especially, were revered and respected. Following another hearty applause, the Pledge of Allegiance was said.

"Okay. Now Mrs. Vickors will lead us in our school song. Afterwards you'll go to your second period classes. Thank you again, and now I give you Mrs. Vickors."

*"Oh yes, we're true, we're true to Muddy Ox School. We'll ever sing her praises strong…"* After the song ended, the

entire assembly of students and teachers ended with a roaring "Rah, Rah, Rah," and everyone filed out in an orderly fashion.

## Chapter Twenty-One

THE THREE OF us went to Mrs. Tyree's class together. Again, I chose front row to the right of the teacher. Polly and Darla followed. Mrs. Tyree greeted us as we filed in. English was one of my favorite subjects. Mrs. Tyree was a passionate teacher who made each student feel as though they were the most important person on her roll. It was rare that anyone ever did poorly in her class. The English hour flew by for me. Darla had third period Band class alone, and Polly and I had Art. I enjoyed art and loved to play around with it, but Polly was gifted.

"Aren't you just a little curious as to why Darla has chosen to make us a threesome?" Polly pose that question once we were alone.

"More than a little but didn't want to bluntly ask. I figure she'll tell us in time."

We rejoined Darla for fourth period Economics with Mr. Anders. Mr. Anders didn't give an assignment for Tuesday—just because. He had a more casual, laid-back way of teaching compared to some teachers. This made him a very popular teacher—especially with the jocks. Dinner followed fourth period.

Darla's boyfriend was a senior and a basketball player. "I'll meet y'all after dinner. Coop's waiting for me, okay?" Having only eyes for Coop, Darla never noticed Polly and I didn't follow her to the cafeteria. I had fifty cents, so we headed for the Green Fly Diner for a coke and hamburger. One reason the Green Fly was so popular was a coke and hamburger were only a quarter. It was also where some of the 'cool crowd' hung out. Polly and I followed my preferred custom of entering through the front door of the Big Store to reach the back entrance of the Diner. I still vowed not to let anyone see me eat or even order food to avoid comments about the fat girl eating. So far, my plan was working.

The leathery smell of saddles, boots, gloves, and belts permeated the air as we walked through the doors of The Big Store. Those items were needed year round as opposed to the cotton sacks only needed for picking and pulling seasons. The fertilizers and sprays were replaced with coats, jackets, long handled underwear, and boggin' hats to ward off the sting of cold weather to come. The cold of winter that swept across the flat lands of the Bootheel was equally as brutal as the sultry heat of summer.

The wood floor creaked and cracked with each step until we reached the back door to the diner. The place was packed. I slipped Polly our money, and she did the ordering. We sat on the back porch as usual to be out of sight to enjoy our burgers and cokes.

"Are you going to do this the rest of your life?" Polly asked.

"Do what?" I replied.

"Sneak into an eating place, hide to eat, and cringe when the conversation leans toward weight or size or….."

"I don't know. Maybe—maybe not. Maybe someday it won't matter to me. Maybe someday it won't matter to others. I just know here and now while I am in school I can't let it get started. It's like a snowball rolling downhill. The ridicule gets heavier and heavier. The embarrassment gets larger and larger. Once someone hurls cruel words at me, others follow. There's never a stopping place or it never gets turned around. At least, it hasn't in the past. You ready to go on back?" I asked, changing the subject. By now, I was close to tears. I wasn't sure if they were tears of embarrassment or anger, but I fought to hold them back. Polly and I had waded through this sticky conversation before and as today, never got through it successfully.

As we rounded the Big Store building, I heard a banging and clanging. I looked in time to see a beat up old truck heading through town. The pots and pans tied to the wooden sideboards that wobbled with every movement of the truck were responsible for the disturbance. The heads of many children packed into the bed of the pickup confirmed it was the Boone

Family even before I saw Army Boone perched on a wooden keg near the tailgate. A trail of smoke swirled behind him as he puffed his cigarette. I could finally tell Katty, Simp, and Grandma that I saw them loaded up and headed out. I could hear Katty now, *"Good riddins to 'em."* To be honest, I couldn't think of anyone who wouldn't echo Katty—except for maybe Sadie.

Polly and I were met by Darla as we reached the east door. She joined us for fifth hour chorus class and again for typing and shorthand classes.

"Guess you're wondering why I'm hanging around with you all today?"

"Guess we thought it was because you liked us," I joked.

"I do. I do like you. But since Coop and I are going steady, I don't have time to do as much as I used to with the other girls. There was no falling out between us. I still love them as much as ever. But I noticed you all weren't as socially involved as the others. Running around with you two wouldn't be as much of a conflict if it's okay."

I guess it might have bothered someone else to have been referred to as *not as socially involved* but Polly and I didn't take offense. The truth was the truth.

"Of course it's okay," said Polly.

"Sure, we're glad you chose us," I agreed.

"All right, that's good then. If Coop doesn't have ball practice, I usually spend time with him after we eat and before the bell rings. We can eat together on his practice days though if you like?" Darla quickly added.

"Oh, we don't…," Polly began.

"Okay, that'll be good," I interrupted before Polly could tell Darla we never eat at the cafeteria. She'd find out eventually, but we didn't have time go into all of that now. Besides, my emotions remained tender from Polly's and my debate about my eating choices.

We claimed the first three front row chairs arranged in semi-circles, four rows, one behind the other, in the Chorus room. Before long the three of us were staring at each other from assigned sections across the room. Mrs. Vickors wasted no time in selecting me as first soprano, Darla second, and Polly alto. The boys, divided into baritone and bass, lined the back row.

Chorus was my all-time favorite class. I was impressed to hear the tones of Polly's and Darla's voices. I loved all music, but the sweet harmony that Mrs. Vickors soon had us singing soothed my soul. It was almost spiritual. I needed that right then.

Typing was where Darla shined. I related more to shorthand. Of course, the exceptionally bright Polly and Darla didn't have a problem with either. The bell rang and our first day as juniors was behind us. Polly and Darla boarded their separate busses. After a brief stop at my locker to sort books and papers, I started home. Sadie was waiting for me alone by the swings.

## Chapter Twenty-Two

"Hey Sadie. How was your first day in fifth grade?" It wasn't an empty question. I genuinely wanted to hear how her day went. I already knew her attitude toward school but was hoping possibly a classmate, a teacher, anything, might have sparked an ember in her somewhere to change it.

"I didn't like it. Rules. There's rules for everythin'. The only thing I liked was recess, but they even had rules for that." Rules came hard for Sadie. She knew how far to push Simp and Katty, but for the most part, did as she pleased.

"Did you make any friends?"

"There was one girl I kinda liked. We talked at recess. Her parents are gonna let her quit school after this year, too."

"Oh, then y'all have something in common." Naturally, she'd choose a friend who shared her distain for school. I decided not to challenge her. I might as well let it be.

"Anyway, I still hate school," Sadie grumbled.

"Don't you have any books to take home? Your teacher didn't give you any homework?" Sadie's hands were empty.

"Umm…I got it at school. No… she didn't give us no homework."

I wasn't sure which to believe. Did she get her homework in class or had the teacher not assigned her any? Because it wasn't my place to worry about her homework or the lack thereof, I let that go too.

"I'll miss our nights at your supper table, but it's going to be nice to move back home. It was kind of y'all to let us stay with you though." I reached for any topic of conversation other than school.

"I'll miss our jack playing. But can we still play sometimes, maybe?" Sadie asked.

"Yeah—sure," I agreed but figured our jack-playing sessions would be far and few between once we were back home. I suspected the demands of my junior year wouldn't leave me much time to spare.

The familiar sight of Grandma sitting on the porch swing like old times offered a welcomed sense of normalcy. The swing almost seemed to embrace me as I dropped next to her. Sadie gave Grandma a polite wave and kept walking toward home. We could hear her telling Katty about her non-eventful first day of fifth grade as soon as she walked through their door. Before long, we heard nothing. Maybe they were enjoying sugar cookies Katty probably baked for her.

I'd hardly sat down before I was up again. "I can't wait to see the rooms. How do they look? It will be great to sleep in my own bed again tonight."

"Well, let's go take a look." Grandma led the way, a big smile on her face.

"I put my things away, but I left yours, thinkin' you'd probably want to do 'em yourself. Your stuffs layin' across the spare bed in my room for you." The smell of clean, fresh paint, in contrast to the former stench of smoke, was wonderful as we passed through Grandma's beautiful new room to get to mine.

"I'll be in the kitchen. If you need any help, just yell," Grandma offered.

Standing in awe to see the transformation of my room brought a tear before I felt like jumping for joy. Blinking several times to confirm I wasn't dreaming, I began strategically hanging my clothes in color coordinated groups—dresses, skirts, blouses.

The shelves in the closet made up for not having a chest of drawers. I lined the remaining nine pairs of tennis shoes, less the pair I wore to school today, along with my dress shoes on the bottom shelf. Socks, sweaters, and undergarments went on the other two. Darby planned my closet and shelves just right for a space underneath precisely the right size for Mama's trunk. After seeing me almost risk my life to save it and my expression when we pulled it onto the porch, he had to know what it meant to me.

"I love it. Don't you just love it, Grandma?" I asked as she reappeared.

"Yes, I do. Want help with your curtains?" She asked, holding a pair of scissors.

After a careful trimming job for fitting the curtains to the short sliding window above the end of my bed, we stood back to survey out handiwork.

"It's hard to believe only about three weeks ago we almost lost our whole house," I said.

"We're sorta like Job. We came out of our tribulation even better than we went into it." Of course, Grandma would have a biblical comparison.

"Look, they put a light bulb in here." Most would not have been that excited about a closet with a light bulb—but I certainly was. I opened and closed my closet door and flicked the light a few times as absolute proof of its existence.

"Now, that's real pretty." Simp startled us. "I knocked, but y'all were so busy admirin' your handy work, I guess you didn't hear. Katty insists that y'all come and have supper with us one more night. She knows you've been over here workin' all day, Mrs. Strom. She's made chicken, dressin', and dumplins' as a celebration supper. Oh, and she made a cake too."

"Simp, y'all have done more…" Grandma began but he cut her off.

"Mrs. Strom, Katty insisted. We all know when Katty insists, you might as well give in. Come on. She was takin' the dressin' out of the oven when I left." We followed Simp without further objection. After all,

Katty did insist, and it was getting late in the day to start a supper of our own. It was also hard to pass up chicken, dumplings, and dressing—and a Katty cake.

"I have homework, so I won't be able to stay long," I warned on the way. Supper smelled heavenly, and we were hungry.

"If it's okay with you, I have a special blessin' to offer up before we eat tonight."

"You go right ahead, Mrs. Strom," Katty agreed.

*"God, we want to thank you for sparin' us and our home and thank you that it wasn't any worse than it was. Lord, please be gracious to all the people who helped us replace what we lost. Most of all, thank you for Simp, Katty, and Sadie Simpson. Give 'em a double blessin' for their kindness. Now, Lord, bless this wonderful meal and the hands that prepared it—In Jesus Name. Amen."*

## Chapter Twenty-Three

"YOU KNOW SIMP and Katty, God will surely reward you for helpin' us as you have. Just wait and see. You can't out give God. Look for it. It's a comin'." Grandma believed every word she declared. I think the Simpson's did too. I know I did.

"Well, God has already blessed us with one thing. That Boone bunch should be closer to Kentucky now than they are to the Bootheel of Missouri. Asa said they could be heard before they were seen, from all the clangin' of pots and pans they had tied to the sides of their truck." Simp beat me getting to tell it first, but it was good news anyway.

"Good riddins, I say again, good riddins to 'em," Katty added. I smiled remembering my prediction of her reaction.

"I sure hope they don't come back next year. I don't wish 'em any ill will, but I hope they find some place other than Muddy Ox to make their livin'," Simp added and dipped himself a generous portion of chicken and dumplings before passing it to Grandma.

Sadie was quiet. I wondered what she thought about Army's leaving, but I wasn't about to ask.

"Anybody Carl Chaffin found to work for 'im, as long as their younguns don't roll their own cigarettes and play on the roof top, or smell like a herd of goats, would be head and shoulders over that bunch," Katty spouted.

Grandma changed the subject. "Meryl has homework so she's goin' to the house as soon as she eats. I'll help you clean up, and then we'll let y'all get back to normal, maybe."

Now, Mrs. Strom, what did I tell you about that? We're gonna miss y'all 'round here." Katty didn't want to hear any more apologies.

"Thank you Katty. I'll surely miss our good suppers together and those yummy cakes—that's for sure," I said as I was leaving.

"We're only next door. The fire didn't move either one of us," Katty stated.

"That's right, Katty. Meryl, I won't be long."

"No rush Grandma. I'll be buried in Psychology, chapters one and two anyway. I sure don't want to start out on the bad side of Mr. Vondell, our new Psychology teacher."

"Psychology," Katty almost spit the word. "They need to focus on readin', writin', and rithmatic' and let that other stuff be," she continued as I was leaving. No mystery there, where Sadie got her attitude concerning school.

Grandma arrived with some of Katty's cake for us

to enjoy before bedtime just as I closed my Psychology book. "We won't be sittin' out here on the porch too many more nights. Feel that chill in the air?"

"Yes, I do," I said while pulling my sweater a little tighter. "Grandma, maybe if Sadie heard more encouragement about school, she might not feel the way she does."

"That's True," Grandma agreed.

"Her complaint today was about rules. She mostly fussed about the recess rules."

"Rules and Sadie don't mix. They all seem to agree this and one more year will be the end of schoolin' for Sadie. Course Simp don't say much on his own. Let's wash up and go to bed. You 'bout ready?"

"I'm ready. I was lucky to have had their couch, but it's sure good to be back home." I grabbed the baking soda and brushed my teeth, while Grandma rinsed off Katty's saucers.

Once I settled into bed, I heard Grandma saying her night prayers. "...*bless my boys and their families in Illinois and take care of Larson, Lord, where ever he is, amen.*"

The new mattress didn't keep her bed from creaking when Grandma crawled into it. But that was also a welcome sound. We were home. I began my prayers with, "*Thank you God for my new bed…closet…and..*," but never remembered getting to amen. I was so tired, and the bed was so comfortable. I barely got out that much of a prayer. Good thing God knew my heart.

# Chapter Twenty-Four

THE AROMA OF biscuits and bacon woke me and my senses this morning instead of a blasting radio. I don't know what she did to it, but Grandma could make bacon smell better than anyone. She turned a pan of steaming hot biscuits onto a plate as I sat down at the table.

"I slept wonderfully. Didn't you, Grandma? I don't think I turned over all night."

"Yes, it's good to be home for sure." Grandma was quieter than usual. I expected her to be as bubbly as I was this morning. But her bubbles seemed to have burst.

"Is anything wrong?"

"I went to bed with Larson on my mind. Maybe that's why I had a dream about him. He wasn't hurt or anythin,' but in my dream his voice sounded faint. He was like a tiny person in a huge room." A wrinkle creased Grandma's brow. I referred to it as her worry wrinkle. Daddy could put it on her brow faster than anyone.

"It's hard to imagine Daddy tiny. Are you sure it was Daddy in your dream?"

"It was Larson. I recognized his voice. Just couldn't make out what he said."

"Grandma, he's probably okay. If he was in trouble, he'd find a way to let us know."

"It just bothers me to have dreams like that—like there might be meanin' to 'em—or a warnin' of some kind. For now, though, I'll figure, no news is good news."

I was surprised she didn't dream of him every night, if having him on her mind was behind her dream. Her prayers usually started out about Daddy, and his name was consistently the last one she called.

Footsteps sounded on the porch. I assumed it was Sadie, but we were surprised to see Simp. Grandma waved him inside.

"Mornin' Simp." Grandma greeted him, but he addressed me instead.

"Meryl, Sadie ain't going to school this mornin'. So you don't have to wait for her."

"Is she sick?" I asked. Sadie missing the second day of school wasn't a good sign.

"No, she's not sick. It's the opposite. She's real fine. Katty and me have decided to let her quit school now instead of next year. She hates school and everything about it. We figured one more year wouldn't make that much difference. She can read and write and count money good enough that nobody cain't short change her. Katty don't want to make her go with Sadie hatin' it so bad. We'll be lettin' the school know today that she's quittin'." Simp's tone didn't match his message. We suspected that he had little to say about whether Sadie went to school or not.

Silence filled the room as if the three of us were searching for the right words. I figured at the same time, Sadie was next door sitting on her victory throne, probably basking in her triumph, while crossing school and everything it offered off her list.

"Simp, we're sorry to hear about this, but I suppose y'all know what you want," Grandma said, breaking the silence and trying to be supportive.

"It's probably best. We can teach her the rest of what she needs to know. I jest wanted to let you know, Meryl." He hesitated as though he had more to say—but didn't. Then he left, shutting the screen quietly behind him.

"I don't think for a second that he wants Sadie to quit school," Grandma said once Simp had gone.

"Me either. But if I'm going to meet Polly, guess I need to get going. Looks like Sadie won another battle with Katty and Simp," I said on my way out.

"It may look like she won, but I see a loss." Grandma's worry wrinkle was back. This time it had nothing to do with Daddy.

Throwing a kiss to Grandma, I scooted out the door. During my solo walk to school, I kept thinking about Sadie being allowed to quit school, just because she hated rules. One day poor Sadie would come against a hard rule and her mother wouldn't be around to help her. Sadie couldn't quit life. Oh well, I couldn't fix them. I had a day of my own waiting down the road.

Polly's bus was the last to arrive leaving little time before we had to part again. Darla was already in homeroom where she and I had sat the day before. I slid into my desk as Mr. Vondell checked roll. Voices buzzed throughout the room. However, for some reason, I was singled out by Mr. Vondell as I was about to ask Darla if she had studied the chapters.

"Jean Strom!" his voice boomed causing a hush to replace the buzzing. "Do I need to separate you and Miss Phelps?" I didn't move. Darla and I were only two whispers in a sea of voices. Why us? Why me? After a moment, he began the lesson. I was relieved.

"Okay then. Class turn to the first page of chapter one in your books." Pages rustled from front to back in the room. The reprieve I'd felt was short-lived.

"Question. Is a mother's love born or learned—Jean Strom?" He clearly intended to make an example of me this day. Singled out was the last thing I wanted. He caught me and the entire class completely off guard. As everyone's eyes, including his, were on me, he repeated the question.

"Born or learned. What do you think, Jean?"

Trying to decide if Mr. Vondell wanted my opinion or the book's, I cautiously chose the book's version.

Clearing my throat and finding my voice, I began. "Our book compares the bonding between a human mother and her baby to a mother monkey and its baby. Harlow's theory was that the need for affection between mother and child was stronger than the need for food. Food could come from another source. Although food was important for the baby monkey it also suffered from the lack of affection from its real mother. Harlow didn't say, but I imagine both kinds of mothers would also grieve."

Never taking his eyes off me, he gruffly cleared his throat. "It looks as though someone did their reading assignment. That's what the book says. What is your opinion about mother's who abandon their children?"

If I had been a child who hadn't normally been allowed to express their opinion at home, I might have been intimidated. But, if my dad did anything right, he valued my opinion. Grandma did as well. Now, Mr. Vondell wanted my opinion. So, I gave it to him.

"I think a mother's love is born. A mother who abandons a child or gives it away still loves it, even if she doesn't admit it. I believe the love she has for her child goes with her to the grave. In some cases, it's love that causes a mother to give up a child. She loves it enough to deny herself and give it what she thinks is best for its own good."

"Really, so giving up a child can be an act of love? How can you justify that? Does a mother, just because she loves a child, always make the best choice for it?"

By this time, I was thinking, *there are other students in this room. Why don't you pick on one of them?* But he didn't. He couldn't have known what I'd witnessed prior to coming to school that morning. I had first hand ammunition to fire back.

"I don't think all mothers love their children wisely. Wise or not, it is still love. Some mothers give children their way in everything, but it's not a right choice or decision to do that." I remembered how Grandma said Katty let Sadie quit school because she loved her unwisely.

"That's spoiling a child. What about giving a child up?" He pressed on. He was determined to pull an answer from me that he wanted to hear, but I didn't know what it was. I responded honestly and from lessons I had learned from Grandma.

"The Bible has examples of mothers showing love by giving up their children. Moses' mother gave him up to save his life. Another example is where two women went before a judge, both claiming to be a child's mother. The judge's solution was to cut the baby in two giving each of them a half. To save its life the real mother was willing to give the baby to the other woman. Mary, mother of Jesus, gave up her child to save souls—all of our souls."

That did it for him. He couldn't argue with that. Having my opinion valued and having learned Biblical examples after coming to live with Grandma proved to be an education beyond Mr. Vondell's text book.

He finally decided to quiz J.T. York in the back of the room. I felt sorry for J.T. It was evident he hadn't read the required chapters nor knew any Biblical examples to back him up. Mr. Vondell moved on to Chapter Two.

By the time he'd gotten a few responses about the effects of a full moon on one's personality, the bell rang, and a sigh of relief could be heard from all present. I think one of the sighs was that of Mr. Vondell. I figured he was relieved for that period to be over. Needless to say, so was I.

"I'm glad Mr. Vondell chose you instead of me today Jean. I wouldn't have known how to answer him," Darla said after we were safely in the hall.

"Gee thanks, I didn't know what to say either. It just came to me. I hope he doesn't ever do that to me again. I'll for sure be reading chapters three and four tonight."

"Me, too. I bet J.T. does, too," Darla agreed.

"Hey, what's this I hear about Mr. Vondell using you as an example in Psych class?" Polly asked as she caught up with us.

"Yes he did. How in the world did you hear about that so fast?" I questioned.

"I heard Tara tell Betty Ann and Mattie Lynn how glad they were he decided to ask you instead of them."

"That seems to be what everyone thought. Darla

just said the same thing."

"I don't think the rest of us could have come up with what you said, Jean."

"What did she say to him, Darla?" quizzed Polly.

"I can't remember all of it, but it ended with Jesus died to save our souls, his included."

"What?" Polly was shocked.

"Well, he finally moved on to poor J.T. Hey, Polly, do you know the moon has an effect on people when it is full?" I asked in an attempt to change the subject.

"Well, yes… that's in the Bible, too. Remember that if he quizzes you with that question." Polly came back quickly. I decided there must be very little about human nature that one couldn't find a Bible reference for. I knew Grandma never had a problem with finding one. Come noon time, Darla met with Coop. Neither Polly nor I had any money, so we circled the school yard a few times and then found a place to sit and wait for the bell.

"Can you believe our next door neighbors are letting their little girl quit school? She's only in the fifth grade."

"How old is she?" Polly's was a viable question. Sometimes grade levels didn't reflect age.

"Twelve, and she's their only child. She hates rules, especially the ones at school, so they agreed to let her quit."

"Wait until she's older and starts to deal with all that life brings her. She'll hate the rules then too but that won't make them go away," Polly echoed my feelings.

"That was my thoughts exactly on the way to school this morning. Her mom won't be around forever to fight her battles or bend the rules for her."

Hearing my own words made me realize that if my mother were still alive, she might have done the same for me also—sometimes loving me unwisely. Probably not when it came to school, but if there had been a way she could have sheltered me from almost anything else, she would have tried. Maybe I shouldn't be so judgmental of Katty. Nonetheless, to paraphrase Grandma's words this morning: Sadie might have won her battle today—but her victory was yet to be determined.

## Chapter Twenty-Five

THE MID-DECEMBER WIND was becoming less bearable every time I made the mile walk to and from school. Winter had hit hard. Our house was not far enough from school to qualify me a bus rider but was far enough to be a miserable trek in bad weather. Along with that misery, I hadn't added a coat to my shopping list.

Katty gave me one of Simp's old work jackets. It was easily large enough, but it also hung off my shoulders. And unfortunately, it looked like nothing less than one of Simp's old work jackets. But *"desperate times called for desperate measures,"* as Grandma would say. The jacket, however, didn't stand up very well to the bitter winds.

Polly and I didn't wait at the east door on really cold days. We met up in second period. This actually worked in my favor, allowing me to get Simp's jacket hidden in my locker before too many people noticed. The jacket was appreciated, but its size and condition could draw unwanted attention.

It was Friday. I'd have two more days before having to make that cold walk to school again. I stalled until the hall was nearly clear of students before pulling the jacket from the locker.

I'd just managed the last button when I noticed Mrs. Tyree beckoning me from the partially open door of her class room. She quickly shut the door once I was inside. I scanned my memory for anything I could have done to be in trouble.

"Jean, Mrs. Lonbreaker wanted you to have this." She pulled a beautiful, full-length coat from a bag and held it up to me. "It was her daughter's coat She graduated college a few years ago. Her husband is in the service, and they're stationed in Hawaii now. She sure doesn't need a wool coat there. Mrs. Lonbreaker said it was hanging in her daughter's closet and benefiting no one. It's a few years old but is still in good condition. Would you like to have it? It won't offend you, will it? I figured your coat must have burned in your house fire."

Would I love to have it? It was beautiful. I'd never had a coat like that before. It was dark maroon, with a fur-lined hood and silky smooth lining. Mrs. Lonbreaker was right. It fit perfectly. Unlike Simp's jacket, this beautiful coat came below my knees. It was double-breasted with silver clasps and could easily stand against the bite of winter. I'd be warm no matter how cold it got. I slipped my hands into its deep pockets and found a matching pair of fur lined gloves. Mrs. Tyree didn't wait for my answer. The glow on my face must have told her all she needed to know. "Oh, Jean, it looks so good on you. It's definitely your color."

"I love it. Please tell Mrs. Lonbreaker thank you. I'll take real good care of it and get it back to her, I promise."

"It's a gift, Jean. You don't have to give it back. Her daughter doesn't need it anymore. The coat and gloves are yours to keep if you want them."

"Yes—yes, I want them. Thank you, Thank you, Thank you, and tell Mrs. Lonbreaker thank you, too."

"You're perfectly welcome from both of us." She smiled.

I folded Simp's jacket into the bag that previously held my new coat. Giving her a big hug, I proudly stepped into the hall. This time, instead of empty, I wished it had been filled with school mates. But it was okay. Everyone would see my coat Monday and every winter day after that.

I walked home as fast as I could. Not because I was freezing, but because I couldn't wait to show my gift to Grandma. Mrs. Tyree had asked me if I'd feel offended. No way was I offended. Grandma often said there was pride and then there was false pride. When I asked her the difference, she explained. "Pride could be a bad thing if you were haughty about something, but a good thing if you were proud of what you had and took care of it. False pride was when you refused something in the name of pride like if you or a loved one really needed something and couldn't get it yourselves." She gave an example of a person whose family needed food, but they were too proud to accept it. I didn't have false pride. I needed a winter coat, was given one, and I was proud to have it.

"I've worried every time I seen you walkin' to school in this weather. It was sweet of Katty to give you that jacket, but there was nothin' to protect your legs from the wind. I don't think she'll care if you keep Simp's jacket for doin' your chores so you can save your pretty coat for school and church. She said the other day Simp got himself a new winter coat for this year. You can ask, but she probably won't want it back. Anyway, it's 'bout seen its best days."

I hung my coat on a hook in the front room near the stove as soon as I'd finished modeling it. Taking Simp's jacket out of the bag, I wore it for bringing in the night water and filling the oil bucket for the heating stove while Grandma put supper on the table. We didn't dawdle with supper or cleaning the kitchen. The heat from the oven in the kitchen didn't last long after it was turned off. We couldn't wait to feel the warmth of the stove in the front room. I curled up on the couch with my psychology book to be prepared in case Mr. Vondell decided to call on me again. Grandma worked on her quilt top.

"I don't know 'bout you, but I'm ready for bed," Grandma said after about an hour.

"I'm ready if you are." Reading made me sleepy. I'd

struggled to keep awake.

Grandma turned the stove off. She was afraid to let the stove burn while we slept for fear of fire. Her fears and conservative ways resulted in only needing to buy one barrel of oil for the entire winter. It also resulted in us sleeping in an unheated house, despite the cold temperatures.

To compensate, she borrowed four Army blankets from Katty. She hung one over the door between the front room and kitchen. The other barricaded the bedroom door to confine the heat to the front room. Every quilt and blanket she could find was draped on our beds along with Katty's two remaining Army blankets. A hot brick was wrapped and placed under the covers near our feet.

On some of the coldest nights, I wore a flannel night gown, a thick house coat, a head scarf, gloves, and bobby socks to bed. Even then, my nose still froze. I could barely turn over during the night because of the weight of the covers. However, I might have gone to bed freezing but my body heat along with my brick soon warmed my quilted cocoon. I slept warm and toasty except for my nose the rest of the night.

Grandma always had the front room warming in the mornings. She claimed that job. No one else was allowed to light the oil stove. Not even Grandpa lit the stove when he was alive. His chauvinistic mind probably saw it her duty anyway.

Come morning, Grandma would tap on the bedroom door to call me to breakfast. I worked my brick within reach with my foot, so I could take it with me. After slipping out of my cocoon, I'd leap to minimize my steps on the freezing linoleum to get to the heat as quickly as possible. Always hanging my clothes and coat near the stove before bed assured they'd be warm in the mornings when I put them on.

The water bucket sometimes had a thin sheet of ice on top. The house had no plumbing, so we never worried about pipes bursting. The kitchen might have been freezing but my walk to school would be more bearable now because of my new coat and gloves. I hadn't ever seen a coat like it before, not even in the Sears or Montgomery Ward catalogs.

Mrs. Lonbreaker's daughter must have also had a weight problem for me to fit into her coat so well. If so, she was an example of how someone who was not a perfect size ended up okay after all. Mrs. Tyree said she lived with her military husband in Hawaii. Was it possible that could be me one day? My mind was working overtime and wandering in so many directions. Anyway, I'd be warm, as well as fashionable now during my walks to and from school.

## Chapter Twenty-Six

I WAITED THIS morning for Polly by the east door, despite the temperatures, to show her my coat and gloves. "Wow, nice coat, Jean." Polly was one of the few who'd seen Simp's jacket, so she recognized the difference right away. "Did you get it over the weekend? I love it, and it looks so good on you."

"Isn't it beautiful? Mrs. Tyree gave it to me last Friday after you'd left for your bus. It belonged to Mrs. Lonbreaker's daughter who is married and lives in Hawaii now. I just love it. It's so warm. Feel the inside." Together, we admired every inch of my coat.

"Yes, it's beautiful. I love it," Polly agreed.

"Guess you can make a silk purse out of a sow's ear," I said.

Polly came to a dead stop, stood back and looked at me. "What?" Polly's expression equaled shock and anger.

"Katty is always using that term to describe how hard it is to make something out of nothing."

"Jean, how does that apply here? I don't get it?"

"When I'm wearing this coat I don't feel unattractive or like someone who got dumped on her

Grandmother's porch," I said as I hung the coat in my locker.

Polly remained motionless. We were eye to eye when I turned. "You surprise me. Yes, that is a beautiful coat, but it's just a coat. It doesn't change who you are or always have been. It wasn't your fault your dad left you with your Grandma. It for sure wasn't your fault your mother died. And let's get this straight. You are not unattractive, nor have you ever been. It's not your size, clothes, or circumstances that make you attractive. It's who and how you are. After you shut that coat away in your locker, you're still my sweet, smart, beautiful, friend, Jean. Don't you ever forget that. And don't ever compare yourself to something like a sow's ear again. That's just silly. You're a silk purse if I've ever seen one."

I wasn't prepared for Polly's reaction. If I'd ever doubted it before, I then realized I had a true friend in Polly. I was ashamed I'd turned such a glowing act of kindness into a demeaning view of how I saw myself.

"Jean, if you only see a sow's ear in yourself, the prettiest coat in the world can't change what others will see in you too."

"All right, I hear you. I wasn't thinking. I'd heard Katty say it so many times it just came to my mind. You're right. I don't really feel that way about myself, and I'd be mad if anyone else did."

I'd never felt like anything connected to a sow.

What was I thinking? A sow is a pig, and a pig is fat. Fat, in any description, is a word I desperately tried to evade. I vowed to never use Katty's saying again in any way attached to me. "Thank you my friend, for setting me straight—love you too," I gave Polly a hug.

The remainder of the day I felt better about myself. Not because of the coat, but because of Polly's characterization of me.

Winters in the Missouri Bootheel were typically unpredictable. Temperatures might be what Simp referred to as tolerable then drop to brutal without warning. Nights were uncomfortably cold for sleeping in unheated bedrooms, even if the days were tolerable. Grandma and I had our brick regimen down to a science. We'd place them on top of the heating stove after supper and by bedtime they'd be hot enough to take to our beds.

December was almost gone. Christmas was five days away. It was the Friday before Christmas break. I welcomed and also dreaded Christmas break. School was my outlet. I still felt if Sadie had given school a chance, it might have become more pleasurable for her, as well. Then again, maybe not. Katty and Simp loved her so much they were constantly trying to lower the hurdles to make her path easier. Grandma loved me so much she constantly raised the bar for my hurdles, so I'd work harder and jump higher.

I'm not sure how cold the thermometer had dropped during the night, but ice chunks were floating in the water bucket where Grandma had broken it to fix breakfast. I'd be especially thankful for my coat and gloves during my frigid walk to school today. Bracing for the inevitable, I bundled up tightly. My normal gait soon became a trot. The wind stung my cheeks. My nose was so cold it felt as though it could easily break off.

Things would worsen once I reached the main road. With only bare, flat, fields and no trees or buildings to filter them, I'd be hit full force by the winds. I gave thought to asking Mrs. McCrady for a ride. Maybe they wouldn't mind being crowded in their car on a cold morning such as this. I also knew that if Mrs. McCrady saw me, she would probably insist that I ride. This was one time if I refused, my pride could definitely be labeled false.

I heard the whirring of a motor from behind after I reached the main road and moved closer to the road ditch to give the approaching vehicle plenty of room. After the car stopped, I looked up expecting to see Mrs. McCrady. Instead—I saw Daddy.

"Get in, Baby, I'll take you to school. I almost didn't

recognize you with the hood of that pretty coat pulled up so tight around your face," Daddy smiled.

I was never happier to jump in and feel the warmth of a car. "Daddy, I sure am glad to see you. It's freezing this morning," I stuttered through chattering teeth.

"I'm just gettin' into town, Baby. I'll be goin' back in a week or so. I wanted to come see you and Mom. It's almost Christmas, ain't it?" Daddy smiled. He loved to tease me like I was still six years old.

"Did you hear that our house caught fire, Daddy?" I responded solemnly. His expression changed to serious.

"I just heard about it a few days ago. That's another reason I came home. Baby, you know I would have been here sooner, if I'd known."

"I was sure you hadn't heard. We didn't have a way to reach you. Daddy, we need a way to reach you in cases like this. We didn't get hurt, but all our clothes burned. I worked so hard picking cotton all fall, and everything I worked for was destroyed."

"That's awful, Baby. I'm sorry."

"But Daddy, you would have been proud of Darby and Obe and the others for how they helped us. Obe and Darby actually kept me from running into the house when it was on fire. I wanted to save my clothes. I couldn't though. They were already burned."

"Baby, it scares me that you'd try somethin' like that. I'm glad they was there to stop you. They're good men. I'll be thankin' them when I see 'em. We'll try to get you some more clothes while I am here, okay?"

"That's another thing you'll be proud of. People from the cotton gin, the lumber yard, and some other people in town all chipped in money for us. And guess what? Carl Chaffin matched the amount that everyone gave. They ended up giving us two hundred dollars. We had a big shopping trip the weekend before school started. It was such fun."

"I sure want to shake those guys' and Carl Chaffin's hands before I go back to Florida. That there's a fine bunch of fellas."

"And this coat came from Mrs. Lonbreaker. She used to be a teacher at Muddy Ox. Her daughter didn't need it any more. People have been so good to us, Daddy."

"That's a pretty coat and a pretty little girl wearin' it for sure. We'll still be goin' to town though. I want to get you and Mom somethin' for Christmas."

"Well, if you want to I could use another outfit or maybe another pair of sho…uh…another outfit. And Grandma needs another church dress. I don't know how much money you have. Have you had steady work?" The last thing I wanted was the kind of shoes Daddy would buy for me. I was glad I caught myself.

"Well, we'll see what we can do." Daddy skirted my question about how much money he had or his work.

"After today, school is out until January 2$^{nd}$ for Christmas break."

"That's good. Tomorrow's Saturday. Maybe we can go to town tomorrow."

"Okay, but we still need a way to get in touch with you. What if Grandma or I got bad sick? Neither of us have any real problems, but you never know."

"I know, Baby—I know. But I haven't stayed put long enough to give y'all a way to do that. I've been workin' just here and there. When I go back, though, I have a lead on a good job that should last at least until the spring. Then, maybe I can come back here and work for Asa again. I'm gonna try and talk to him while I'm in town."

I didn't want to tell Daddy I feared Mr. Bertram might not have work for him when he came back in the spring because he bought a new tractor. I figured he could find that out from Mr. Bertram himself. Besides, I could be wrong. Even if he didn't need Daddy to work on his tractor or do other work for him, maybe he'd know someone else who might need him.

"So where have you been working?" I pressed again.

"Oh, I hauled sugar cane for a while, worked at a few garages; even repaired some air-boat motors in the Everglades for a guy."

"The Everglades—did you see any alligators?"

"Oh yeah, there's gators everywhere in the Everglades. You can see 'em in the road ditches as you drive by. I was workin' on an air-boat motor for this guy one day, and I almost put my hand on one stretched across my tool box, right there on the boat."

"What did you do?"

"I had a pretty good size wrench in my other hand, so I hit the thing right 'tween the eyes. Then I kicked it, and it wiggled back into the swamp."

"Leave it to you Daddy. I knew you would tackle most anything, but I never thought it would be an alligator."

"Well, Baby, it's like this, when you come up against a gator, you either fight or get eaten. I figured I was a little too tough to chew. That alligator just THOUGHT he wanted to bite into me. Now, what about this fire? How'd it start?"

"They don't know for sure. They're thinking there's a firebug around town."

"A firebug, huh?"

"Yes, our house, the porch of the Green Fly, and the school's bus barn were all set fire. The Green Fly and the bus barn were the week before school started. But there haven't been any more fires since October. Maybe the firebug is afraid he'd get caught so he stopped."

Daddy didn't respond, which said he didn't agree. His vagueness about his job history told me little had changed with him. He was probably drinking pretty heavily again, or he'd have a steady job. However, I didn't smell any liquor on him today. That was a good sign—I hoped.

"Can you drop me off on the west side of the school, so I won't have so far to walk to get inside?" I leaned over and pecked him on the cheek when the car came to a stop. I was so thankful again that Daddy showed up when he did.

"I'll be here to pick you up when school lets out today, okay?' Daddy said as he slipped two quarters in my hand.

"Thank you Daddy. Be here right at 3:30. I'll be at this door, okay?"

"I'll be here Baby. You can count on me." I closed the car door. Daddy gave me a wave as he drove off. Grandma was going to be so surprised and happy to have him home, even if it would be for only a week or so.

## Chapter Twenty-Seven

ICE DANGLED FROM the school bell that sat near the west door entrance. If Daddy hadn't showed up when he had, ice would have probably been dangling from my face, too like that on the bell. My guardian angel must have still been alive and well.

There was a wave of excitement in the halls in anticipation of Christmas break. Choir members were excused fifth hour to warm up for the performance. I wished I'd told Daddy to come to the program and bring Grandma. They would have loved my solo part. Maybe he'd be back for spring concert and could bring Grandma then.

Once the program was over, Christmas break officially began. I was excited and thankful that Daddy was picking me up after school. The afternoon was not as cold as the morning but would have still been a cold walk home. After saying good-bye to Polly and Darla and wishing them Merry Christmas before they ran to their buses, I stashed my books inside my locker, grabbed my coat, and rushed to meet Daddy.

A sick feeling swept over me as I stepped through the door where Daddy was supposed to have been waiting. Surely he hadn't forgotten me. I was minutes from stepping back inside to leave by my usual way when his car pulled into the circle.

"Hello Baby. I know—I'm late," Daddy slurred. The car smelled of alcohol.

"I…was afraid you weren't coming…but I'm glad…you're here." My voice was weak with disappointment.

"Hey Baby, you want to drive?" Daddy slurred again.

I didn't have a license or even a permit but right or wrong, I justified my driving, considering Daddy's drunken state. I knew how to drive. Daddy had let me drive on his lap and on back roads since I was ten years old. He slid to the passenger side, and I took my place behind the wheel. The parking lot was empty of buses and car riders, and the road between the school and Grandma's house was mostly clear. Ice crunched beneath the tires that was refreezing after the noon day thaw as I pulled into the yard. As usual, Grandma had supper on the table.

"I was wonderin' if you'd remember to pick up Meryl. Where have you been, son? You've been gone since noon?" Grandma's face fell once she smelled the liquor.

"What do you mean I'd forget Meryl? Didn't I tell you I was goin' to go pick her up? Meryl didn't I tell you I'd be there, and wasn't I there? And here we are."

Daddy's alcohol was talking so we knew it was best to let it be.

"Grandma, I wish I would have thought to tell Daddy this morning about the Christmas program today. Parents were welcome. I had a solo." I was reaching for anything to change Daddy's mood. He never reacted while bent on one elbow over the wash pan. At least he remembered the hand washing rule despite his drunken state.

"I hope he'll go to bed and sleep it off after he eats. Before it gets dark, can you go out by the shed and get another brick? Your daddy will need one for tonight," Grandma whispered while Daddy's back was turned.

I went to find a brick to warm Daddy's bed. My suspicions about his drinking heavily again were confirmed. I was amazed at the things in our world that we couldn't fix. Daddy was the biggest one of them. That morning, I had been excited about his coming home. Now, I was anticipating him heading back to Florida—or wherever.

I wiped the brick clean and placed it alongside of Grandma's and mine on top of the oil stove. If Daddy went to bed early as we wished, it needed to start warming.

"You're the best cook I know, Mom. Ain't she a good cook Meryl? Mom, you need to teach Meryl how to cook like you do." Daddy rambled on when he was drunk. We let him eat and talk while we ate in silence, only answering when necessary.

"You know what, Mom? I been thinkin'. How'd you like to go see the brothers for Christmas? We haven't been back to Illinois since me and Meryl moved away."

Grandma was noticeably surprised, as was I, at Daddy's suggestion. Under other circumstances, we would have welcomed a visit to her sons, to my uncles and their families, to the place where Mama was buried. However, making the trip with Daddy if he was drinking was not enticing to either of us. She couldn't avoid answering him now.

"Well…I don't know. Do you think Christmas is a good time to go? They'll be havin' their own family things going on. And the roads; do you think the roads will be safe to travel that far north? I worry about the roads that close to St. Louis, this time of year." I knew she was stalling and hoping against hope, that either of her objections might change his notion to go. Brooksville, Illinois was only a little more than two hundred miles north of Muddy Ox. However, the distance was daunting to Grandma who had only been there a handful of times.

"Daddy, she's right. Remember how it always seems to snow more up there than it does here?" I added.

"Aw…snow don't bother me none. I can drive on anythin', in any kind of weather. They'll be glad to see us," Daddy argued.

"But…" Grandma was searching for another excuse

when Daddy cut her off.

"If I didn't know better, Mom, I'd think you didn't want to go see your boys."

"I'd love to see the boys and their families up there, it's just…"

"…just what? Daddy interrupted again. "We can leave Tuesday mornin'. Ain't Tuesday Christmas Eve, Meryl? This is Friday, ain't it? We could go sooner but I got some business to take care of tomorrow. And the car needs tunin' before we go. Then it's settled." Daddy closed the conversation as if the three of us were in total agreement. We might as well have been. It was evident we'd be going to Illinois Tuesday morning.

"Right now, I gotta' get me some sleep. I'm beat." Daddy's words were becoming more slurred. Fatigue mixed with alcohol was pushing him to an early bedtime.

"Meryl, find a towel for your Daddy's brick. I'll grab some blankets for his bed."

By the time I had Daddy's brick wrapped, she had his bed ready. We led him into the bedroom. She turned down the covers, and I positioned the brick. Daddy fell into bed, clothes and all. His snoring began while she was pulling the covers over him and tucking him in as she would a small child.

We returned to the kitchen to finish our now cold suppers. I figured we both were too consumed with thoughts of our impending trip for it to matter—I know

I was. It would be great to get to see our Illinois family again. But I worried how they'd feel about us crashing their Christmas. Also, I knew Grandma was as concerned as I was about our safety if Daddy insisted on drinking while driving.

I added another scarf tied around my head to my sleep attire, not only for warmth, but to help block the snorting and rumbling of the snoring 'bulldozer' in the next room. Having Daddy home had its ups and downs for sure. Poor Grandma, her bed was in the same room. Daddy's snoring could practically rattle window panes.

Sleep finally came but was mingled with visions of wrecks, twisted metal, and bolted doors from which I worked most of the night trying to escape. I felt anything but rested come morning.

After waking, I stayed huddled in my warm blanket cocoon momentarily to gather and sort my thoughts. I so hoped to find the Daddy that was full of funny stories and laughter sitting at the table when I walked into the kitchen. If only he wouldn't drink himself into the Daddy we feared and mistrusted, he'd be a pleasure—not a dread.

In three days, we were actually going to Illinois for Christmas. Despite the worries of us intruding on our unsuspecting relatives, and our lives being at risk by an alcohol impaired driver, I still couldn't help but be a little excited about going. I so missed our Illinois family. I also knew Grandma would be happy to see her sons and other grandchildren.

Unable to delay the shock of my warm feet on the cold floor any longer, I took a deep breath, threw back the covers, grabbed my brick, and vaulted to the front room. After shutting the door behind me, and tucking the army blanket back around the facing, I returned my brick to its corner home behind the stove. Once past the next blanket barrier to the kitchen, I found Daddy and Grandma having breakfast. Two large crates of Florida oranges sat on the far end of the kitchen table.

Daddy sounded hung over, but sober. Grandma did her usual thing of asking if I was ready for breakfast. I automatically agreed. Had I said I wasn't hungry, she would have given me at least five reasons to discount my choice. That is, if she heard me at all. Grandma assumed—sun's up—you're in the kitchen—you eat breakfast—in that order.

## Chapter Twenty-Eight

"MORNIN' BABY, DID you sleep warm? I sure did after somebody put that hot brick to my feet. You take good care of your old Daddy don't you, Baby? Your Grandma told me what you did."

Evidently she hadn't told him it was her idea. After washing up, I took a seat and flashed him a weak smile as an answer.

"Hey, Mom, I need to run to Kennett for a few things to give the car a tune up before our trip. I want you and Meryl to go, too.

"If we're goin' to Illinois I..." Grandma began, but Daddy broke in.

"We can do a little Christmas shoppin' while we're in town." Daddy gave me a wink. Of course, my face lit up at the mention of Christmas shopping.

"Son, I don't have money for shoppin'—Christmas or otherwise. My check won't be here 'til January 1st. I've spent my limit this month. After I paid the light bill, I've got a few dollars put back for emergencies and to pay burial insurance for all of us and that's it." One of Grandma's greatest fears was that one of us would die with no money to bury us. Our burial insurance was paid like clockwork.

"Now, Mom, I got a little money. I planned to give y'all some to spend in town. First though, I gotta' go to the blacksmith shop and deliver these oranges and sugar cane to the guys. They said they'd pay me for 'em. Y'all can get ready while I'm gone." Daddy pushed his plate back and stood to leave. Grandma's expression was one of forced consent. We were interrupted by a knock on the door. Daddy answered since he was already standing.

"Hello Larson. I figured that car with Florida plates was yours. You comin' or goin' right now? It's another cold one today, ain't it. I reckon the farmers got their crops over with and their fields plowed just in time." A nervous Simp rambled as he scooted inside.

"I'm goin'. I gotta' take some things to the blacksmith shop," Daddy answered bluntly. "I won't be long, Mom. Y'all be ready when I get back—all right?" Grabbing one of the crates of oranges, and a bundle of sugar cane, Daddy grunted as he brushed past Simp and was out the door before Grandma could answer. Instead she addressed Simp.

"What you up to this mornin', Simp?"

"Nothin' really, Katty saw Larson over here yesterday. Said his steps didn't look none too steady walkin' from the car to the porch. She wanted me to check on y'all."

"Yes…well…he was drinkin' a little yesterday but

other than bein' a little grumpy, he seems to be his self and sober this mornin'. Don't know how long he'll stay that way though."

"Daddy's taking us Christmas shopping in Kennett when he gets back." It was hard to hide my excitement of going from a nondescript Christmas to one with presents.

"Simp, will y'all keep an eye on my place? Larson's insistin' on us goin' to Illinois over Christmas. He wants to leave early Tuesday mornin'. I'd love to see my boys and their families, but I fear goin'. If I knew Larson wouldn't drink and drive, I'd feel better. Also, I hate just showin' up. They all probably already have their Christmas doins' lined out."

"You know Katty and me will look after your place. I understand why you worry about getting there and back in one piece. But as far as just droppin' in on your sons, why I don't think there's a one of them that won't be tickled to death to see you—and Meryl Jean, too. They'd probably be glad to see Larson—if he'd leave that bottle alone."

"I hope you're right. But even if the boys will be glad to see us, I wonder how their wives will like three people bargin' in on 'em. Anyway, we gotta' hurry now and get ready. Larson will be poppin' back through the door any minute for us to go to town. Here, let me give y'all some oranges. The one I ate this mornin' was as sweet as the peaches we used to pick in Anna, Illinois when Omar and me followed the harvest. Here's a stalk of sugar cane, too, for Sadie." Grandma handed Simp three oranges and the sugar cane and wished them Merry Christmas.

"Thank you Mrs. Strom. And tell Larson thanks, too. Y'all be safe, ya' hear? Go on and have a good visit with them boys and their families. It's been a while since you've seen the grandbabies up there ain't it?" Simp asked as he reached for the door.

"The last time I laid eyes on any of them was at Edna's funeral 'bout four years ago. Bless them boy's hearts. Their jobs and big family responsibilities makes it hard for 'em to break away and come down here all the time. Duncan's got nine children, Brayden's got seven, and Paulie's got three. Each of 'em has baby girls I'll be seein' for the first time."

"That alone's worth makin' the trip. Katty and me will be lookin' for your safe return. No need a wishin'. I know you'll have a Merry Christmas with all them grandbabies in your arms and all over your lap."

As soon as Simp left, Grandma said for us to run and get ready for town.

"I hope we can get the dishes done and the kitchen cleaned up before we go." It went against Grandma's grain to leave things undone. I warned her after we came to live with her that she might as well get used to it. Daddy never gave Mama any notice when he decided we were going somewhere either. Planning ahead wasn't

Daddy's way of doing anything.

The frigid bedrooms helped to speed up our getting ready time. As soon as possible, we ran back into the kitchen and started slinging dishes and pot vessels. Grandma washed, I dried, and put away. Almost as if it were planned, Grandma met Daddy at the door with a pan of dirty dish water. He emptied it across the road while she finished wiping the table. We did it. At least Grandma could go to town a little less stressed on one level anyway.

Back from pitching the dish water, Daddy emptied all the money from his coat, pants, and shirt pockets onto the kitchen table. After giving us fifteen dollars each, he raked what was left back into his pockets and barked, "Let's go."

I didn't smell liquor on Daddy. That was the makings of a good trip to town.

## Chapter Twenty-Nine

INSTEAD OF DROPPING us off at the Five and Dime, as I suspected he'd do, Daddy tagged along. He said he'd get his car stuff on the way back home.

"I'm gonna go look over here," Daddy said as he sauntered out of sight.

"Okay, let's meet at the door when we're done?" Grandma said and left for the opposite side of the store.

When I knew they were gone, I darted to the cosmetic and jewelry counter. Grandma never wore cosmetics other than maybe a pat of face powder, but she loved pretty combs for her hair and wore breast pins occasionally. I had just found a pair of cameo hair pins when I heard familiar voices.

"Hey Jean," Tara and Melly chimed from across the counter. "Are you shopping for stocking stuffers?" Tara asked.

"Stocking stuffers? Oh, yeah, we're doing some last minute shopping before we leave for Illinois, Tuesday. Daddy's home and is taking us there for Christmas." I tried to sound casual, which wasn't easy. Stocking stuffers. We didn't hang stockings. We didn't even have a tree. Our shopping really was last minute. That part was legitimate. "Is that what you're doing, looking for stocking stuffers?" I asked?

"We thought we might find a few, but we're really here to get scotch tape, bows, and wrapping paper. So you're going to Illinois for Christmas?" Melly asked.

"Don't you think this praying hands pin is pretty? I think Grandma will love it. She prays more than anyone I've ever seen," I said, trying to avoid questions about Daddy or our sudden trip.

"Yes, it is. I bet she'll love that. Is there another one like it? Melly, let's see if we can find one for Grandma Bertram. She prays a lot too," Tara said.

They evidently knew their grandma better than I did. But when I thought of Mrs. Bertram, I pictured the whip-cracker of the cotton field. While they rummaged in the display of pins, I was drawn to the men's wallets. Daddy could use a wallet. He surely didn't have one, remembering him emptying his pockets onto the table before we came.

"Guess you got the last praying hands pin they had. We've decided to get Grandma Bertram this gardenia scented hand and body lotion instead. See ya after the holidays," they said as they left in search of wrapping paper and such.

Trying to think of what else I could get for Daddy, I wandered into the tool department. He was always saying a man could never have too many tools. I didn't know what tools he had but decided a man surely couldn't have too many screwdrivers or flashlights. I got him one of each. Heading back to the front of the store, I passed the sock department. I grabbed a pair of black socks for Daddy and a pair of white fuzzy ones for Grandma to wear to bed. Those socks and her brick would keep her feet warm, even if her nose did freeze off. If they made nose socks, I'd have gotten us both one of those.

Lost in the thought of how if Grandma and I put our heads together, we might invent a nose sock, and turning quickly, I banged my face into the chest of none other than—Mr. Vondell.

"Hello, Jean. You Christmas shopping?" It was strange seeing Mr. Vondell outside of the classroom. In my mind, teachers were like superior beings on high pedestals. After seeing him in the Five and Dime store and on common ground, I realized they lived, breathed, and yes, even shopped like the rest of us common folks. Pulling my nose from his chest, I apologized for banging into him.

"I'm so sorry Mr. Vondell, I didn't see you. I was picking out socks for my Grandma and wasn't watching where I was going."

"That's okay. I'm looking for socks, too, to use as stocking stuffers."

"Hmm...yes, stocking stuffers; these socks will make good ones. Did you see Tara and Melly here? They were looking for stocking stuffers, too." Stocking stuffers, again. I hadn't realized they were such a vital part of Christmas shopping. Just getting something to go under a Christmas tree, if we'd had one was hard enough.

"No, they must have already found what they were looking for and left. You have a Merry Christmas and see you January 2$^{nd}$," he said as he started to leave. This Mr. Vondell was different than the one behind the school desk. He smiled and was personable—unlike in the classroom with his gruff voice and stiff jaw. My palms got sweaty remembering how he singled me out on the first day of class. The Mr. Vondell I nearly knocked down in the Five and Dime didn't seem like the kind of person that would stress anyone that way.

"You doing anything special over Christmas?" He stopped and turned to me again. I couldn't believe Mr. Vondell was interested in my holiday plans.

"Yes, my dad's home from Florida. We're leaving for Illinois Tuesday morning to see family there." I made it sound like something we did every Christmas.

"Illinois, huh? Well, have a safe trip and again, Merry Christmas." As he was walking away for the second time, daddy suddenly appeared behind me.

"Who was that? Do you know that man? You were talking to him for a long time." Daddy asked. Had he been watching me, and did he see me pick out his gifts?

"That's one of my teachers, Mr. Vondell. He's nice. He was wishing me a Merry Christmas. How long have you been standing there?" I asked, trying to hide his wallet under Grandma's socks.

"Not long. I wasn't spying on you. I looked up and saw a strange man talking to you, and it worried me—that's all."

"Daddy, we need to get wrapping paper and tape to wrap our gifts." I was glad Tara had mentioned that. I wouldn't have given it a thought.

"Okay, we'll get some before we go. What do you think your grandma would like to have for Christmas?" Daddy questioned.

"Maybe some house slippers or some hand and body lotion. I saw the McCrady girls earlier, and that is what they got Mrs. Bertram." I guessed my first suggestion of a new church dress for Grandma probably wasn't within Daddy's budget.

"All right, you show me where the lotion is, and we'll get her some."

As I led Daddy to the lotion counter, I noticed he had a bag of something he'd already purchased. After making his choice, he handed me the lotion and more money to pay for it and the wrapping materials. Seeing me trying so hard to hide what I had in my hands, was probably why he offered to go round up Grandma. Before long, I headed to the register with my purchases, lotion, wrapping paper, tape and a roll of thin curling ribbon—just because.

"This is fun," I said as I rejoined them.

"Yes, it is," Grandma agreed.

"I ran into Tara and Melly earlier getting a few more last minute things for Christmas. And, Grandma, you will never guess who else I ran into. I literally ran into him because I didn't see him behind me. It was Mr. Vondell, my Psychology teacher. I had to look twice to realize it was really him. I would have never thought I'd run into one of my teachers shopping in the Dime store," I exclaimed as we were leaving the store.

"Well, don't you think maybe teachers shop for Christmas too?" Grandma chuckled.

"I know, it was just strange seeing him anywhere other than behind his desk or in the halls at school," I said, as we climbed into the car, each clutching our own little bag of secrets.

## Chapter Thirty

"I WON'T BE long," Daddy said before going into the auto parts store. We were certain that nothing in that automotive store would have interested either of us. Grandma told him we'd just wait for him.

"I wish I could buy the boys and their families a nice gift. At least, I wish I could get somethin' for the grandchildren," Grandma sighed once we were alone.

"They'll all understand, Grandma. Anyway, just giving them yourself will be a gift since they never get to see you."

"We only got what we did today because Larson gave us the money to do it. Fifteen dollars wouldn't begin to get things for all of them. Besides, anythin' I could get 'em wouldn't hold a candle to the kind of things they're used to getting."

"Wow Daddy, you needed a lot of stuff to get the car ready." He was carrying a huge bag when he emerged from the parts store.

"It's not all car stuff. They had a barrel of giant, paper shell pecans straight from Black Island, gathered fresh today. I bought a bunch of 'em."

Black Island, named for its rich, black, soil was an

area near the west bank of the Mississippi River by Caruthersville. Maybe the richness of the soil was why the large pecan groves at Black Island produced an abundance of what the locals called paper shell pecans. The shells being so thin, gave easy access to the sweet pecan meat within. Pecans could be found or bought many other places, but Black Island pecans were extra tasty.

"I figured the brothers, and their families would like these. They can't get pecans like these up north. We'll take 'em these pecans, the rest of the oranges, and the sugar cane I brought up from Florida. That way we won't show up empty-handed."

Daddy surprised me. For him to say, 'showing up empty-handed', let me know he'd also had a reservation or two about our unannounced visit. I was sure he hadn't worried about it as much as Grandma and I had. But I now realized it had crossed his mind.

"I was worried about that, too, son. Maybe we should go another time," Grandma seized the opportunity to suggest he change his mind about the trip.

"Mom, don't you worry. There's not a one of 'em that won't be glad to see us," shooting down any chance of his plans changing.

"Will y'all be goin' to church in the mornin'?" Daddy asked as we pulled into the yard. I held my breath. Was Daddy offering to take us to church—or maybe even go with us?

"Yes, Meryl has a special Christmas song to sing in the program," I felt Grandma holding her breath, too.

"Well, get me up in the mornin' when y'all do, and I'll get to workin' on the car so we can get a early start Tuesday. It won't take more than five hours to get there if we don't have any car trouble to slow us down."

"Daddy, why don't you go to church with us? You can hear my song." I should have known it was too good to be true. Daddy had no intentions of going to church. It was silly of me to even think he did—but I asked anyway.

"Now baby, you don't want the ceilin' to fall in at that church, do you? You can sing your song to me in the car all the way to Illinois."

"Yes, I can sing it for you in the car, but it won't be the same as hearing me sing it at Church. Other people will be singing in the morning too," I argued.

"Now, Meryl, I never was a churchgoer. You know that. Besides, I want to get started on the car to have it ready to roll."

"I…can't wait to wrap our presents," I said curbing the subject of church. I knew to ask him anymore was pointless. I could have argued that he had Monday to work on the car. He would have had some other excuse if I had—or got angry.

"Those presents sure won't be wrapped long. We'll have to open 'em Monday, since we're leavin' out early Tuesday," Grandma said.

"It'll be fun anyway, even if they are only wrapped for two days," I said, still trying to hold on to our new found holiday joy. Knowing her so well, I knew Grandma would have rather he not tune up his car on the Sabbath. One good thing, if he was in her yard and under the hood of his car, we'd know where he was and what he was doing. As soon as we got home, Grandma rushed to light the oil stove in the front room. The house was freezing since it had been off most of the day.

"Y'all don't come in the front room 'til I say. I'll get my presents wrapped while you're fixin' supper. Now Meryl, don't you be peekin' around that blanket," Daddy teased as he went to wrap our gifts.

He couldn't have paid me to peek around the blanket and ruin the surprise. This was our first Christmas with presents since Mama died. I might have been sixteen, but I felt almost like a four year old, looking for Santa Claus again. I was an overly inquisitive child of five—too bright for my own good—when I figured out about Santa. I wished I would have lived in the fantasy a little longer. The reality of life came soon enough without me rushing my childhood along.

"Okay, you can come in now," Daddy said about the time supper was finished.

One entire couch cushion was covered with tiny presents. Some were wrapped into round balls, others into cylinders, squares and triangles. It was impossible to figure out what they were by their shapes and sizes. He didn't have names on them but said he would tell us who they belonged to when the time came. That only added to the mystery. Grandma disappeared into the bedroom for a moment and reappeared with a piece of bright red cloth which she smoothed across an end table. Daddy scooped up his presents and laid them on the cloth.

"I need to run up to the blacksmith shop for a little while. I won't be long. I'll be out of your way while you do your wrappin'," Daddy said as soon as supper was over.

Grandma's countenance fell. I figured she'd love to beg him not to go. I knew I wanted to, but it would have only made him mad and spoiled our happy moment.

"Son, you won't be long will you?" Grandma asked sheepishly.

"Now Mom, I told you I wouldn't be," Daddy said sounding as dependable as anyone would ever want to sound.

"Hurry back Daddy, so you can see how many presents you have," I said in the most cheerful voice I could find.

"I will. Y'all can snoop all you want with 'em presents there. But I don't think you can figure 'em out," he said, chuckling as he left.

"I wish he wouldn't have gone to the shop tonight.

It turned out to be such a nice trip to town. This could ruin it all," Grandma said when we were alone.

"Me, too. Maybe if he doesn't stay too long, he won't get real, real drunk. Remember how he brags he can hold his liquor better since he drinks a lot? You know, better than those who drink only a little?" I knew I was insulting mine and Grandma's intelligence, but hey, if we were going to try to pretend about the magic of Christmas, then I could try to believe in the nonsense of his claim of tolerance.

After the table was cleared, I volunteered to wrap my gifts in the kitchen while Grandma wrapped hers in the front room. In addition to the combs and breast pin, I got her some milk chocolate and peppermint candy. She loved candy. I always thought she probably didn't get much of it when she was a child, so now she was making up for it. Before long, she signaled she was finished. We arranged our presents alongside Daddy's on the festive covered end table.

"We'll have time to pack Monday. There's no need to try to do it now. It'll be warmer during the daytime on Monday anyway. I hope Larson won't come home drunk," Grandma's fears surfaced again.

"If he does, he'll have time to sober up before Tuesday morning." I tried to remain hopeful but knew he could get drunk and sober, and drunk and sober, and drunk again before Tuesday. This was only Saturday.

"There's one thing for sure, if he does come home

drunk, I won't be wakin' him up at the same time we leave for church. He can sleep 'til we get home and maybe sleep it off."

"If he's going to do it, I'd rather he drink now, instead of on the way or during our Illinois visit," I reasoned.

"Well, of course. Oh Larson, why are you plagued with such a habit? Oh Lord, help us." Poor Grandma. Daddy worried her more than she ever needed or deserved.

## Chapter Thirty-One

I PRACTICED MY song several times and read a chapter ahead in Psychology. Grandma stayed busy cutting quilt pieces and putting them in piles of like colors and shapes. It was after ten o'clock and still no sign of Daddy. We'd already gotten dressed for bed. I considered asking her about inventing a nose-sock but decided to wait. The subject of socks could lead to her guessing what I'd gotten her.

"We might as well go to bed. Waiting up won't make him come any sooner. It'll only cost us a night's sleep. I'm gonna leave the kitchen door unlocked so we won't have to brave the cold to get up and let him in. Besides, only a crazy person would pick a night like tonight to break in on someone." She placed Daddy's brick under his covers.

"To think of it Grandma, if there is a mean or crazy person running around out there somewhere tonight, aren't those the ones who usually do break-ins anyway?"

"You're right I guess." She laughed. After my comment about vandals, Grandma dropped to her knees by her chair to say her night prayers. I imagined she added a stronger request for protection from any burglars who could be on the prowl.

"I'm going to trust God to hear my prayer from my warm bed," I justified.

"God always hears His name, but kneeling is my way to pray. I'd just as soon keep doing it that way." Well, so much for me feeling justified.

I think I was between sleep and consciousness when I heard a thud in the kitchen. It was Daddy. Good—he'd made it home before his brick had gotten cold and hopefully before he'd put too much liquor under his belt. Several more thuds indicated he probably wasn't as sober as I'd wished.

A flick of light pierced the darkness in my room as Daddy turned the ceiling light on for a second. I hated for Grandma to have the light flashed in her eyes, but I figured she'd rather have the light than a repeat of what happened a few years back.

Daddy had arrived home staggering drunk in the wee hours of morning. Trying to avoid waking Grandma and getting a scolding, he felt his way into the darkness, hoping to crawl into bed without circumstance. Little did he know earlier that day, an old tom cat had sneaked inside the house unbeknownst to us and soiled the floor behind the dresser. Grandma's compulsion to clean and sanitize the spot overshadowed her forethought. She'd pulled out the dresser and moved a dressing table from their regular places to let the saturated floor dry completely and innocently left both pieces of furniture out of place.

Daddy usually laid his pants on the dressing table that Grandma had left disarranged. When they fell to the floor, he bent over to pick them up and hit his head on the dressers' edge that was also not in its usual place. Then he stumped his toe on the metal roller of the dresser leg and staggered into the cold wet spot on the floor. The final straw broke along with the light string when he reached to turn it on. That—was when the cursing began.

This episode caused the entire dog population of Silver Leaf to begin barking. Before long, lights popped on in every home within ear shot. Simp and Katty ran out on their porch in their night clothes to see what the ruckus was about. Yes, Grandma would have much rather had a little light pierce her eyes for a few seconds, to avoid a repeat of that fiasco. I could barely keep from giggling, just remembering the tom cat episode and the big, bruised, lump daddy had on his head the next morning. To our surprise, he didn't flare mad but from then on, had a new tale to spin with his drinking buddies or any other time he had an audience.

His moan and grunt, then a snort and a snore, as disturbing as they were, gave me reason to sigh for relief before I settled back to sleep. I had no doubt it did the same for Grandma. When he was miles from home, there was nothing she could do but ask God to take care of him. Having him home made her feel like she could *fix* him, even though Grandma knew—that only God could fix Daddy. Or for that matter anyone else.

Grandma had a dilemma the next morning. Should she let Daddy sleep or wake him before we left for church, as he'd requested? "Meryl, you sneak into the bedroom and softly ask your Daddy if he wants to get up. If he does, that's fine. If he doesn't, then we can say we tried." I did as she asked.

I touched his arm from a safe distance. Anyone who knew him very well, knew how to keep a safe distance when trying to awaken Daddy. It had something to do with when he was in the Army but if he was startled awake, he was prone to come up, fist first. "Daddy, we're leaving for church now," I whispered softly trying to arouse him—and not.

He snorted a couple of times then responded. "Okay baby, I'll get up here in a minute."

"Well…just letting you know we're leaving now," I repeated, then quietly returned to the kitchen.

"Is he gettin' up?" Grandma questioned.

"I told him twice. He said he'd get up in a minute," I reported.

"Well, I'm gonna cover this bowl of gravy and this plate of biscuits and leave 'em here on the table. If he gets up or not, he can't say we didn't try to wake him."

The crunching of gravel announced the Walby's arrival. We grabbed our coats and rushed out the door.

"Mornin' Mrs. Strom. Y'all lookin' forward to the

Christmas program this mornin'? You got your song ready Jean? Is that Larson's car in your driveway?" Effie managed to get everything including an inquiry about Daddy all said in one breath.

"Yes, my song's ready. I practiced it last night while we were wait…"

"Huh mmm," Grandma cleared her throat.

"…waiting to go to bed," I finished.

"I worked on my quilt pieces a long while last night, too, Effie. I've about got 'em all cut and sorted." I figured Grandma hoped to get Effie talking about quilts, so she'd forget about Daddy and his car in the driveway. That proved to be only wishful thinking. Effie skipped right over the quilting part and went straight back to Daddy.

"So…I guess Larson's home? The plates say Florida. Has he been in Florida all this time?" Effie asked. Her gold tooth glistened as it caught the morning sun when she turned to us in the back seat. Effie Walby and Mrs. Bertram were sisters, and they each had a gold tooth. Until I came to live with Grandma, I had never seen one person with a gold tooth, must less two. I was fascinated by her gold tooth. However, I didn't think I ever wanted to have one.

"Yes, he's been working in the sugar cane fields and orange groves down there." Grandma didn't elaborate.

"Has he moved back for good? What's he gonna work at if he has? Lord knows there ain't much to do around here in the dead of winter," Jake chimed in.

"No, he's going back to Florida after Christmas," Grandma said short and sweet.

"He's taking us to Illinois for Christmas," I chimed. I think if she'd had a piece of tape, Grandma would have promptly put it over my mouth, maybe even tied a bow on it from the look she gave me. I got the point. The less we talked about Daddy—the better. Beyond him saying he was going back to Florida after Christmas; we didn't actually know much to tell. Besides, most inquiries about Daddy usually became prying and personal.

"I'm going to sing The First Noel. Also, I've worked up a skit for the young people to do." Now, I was the one trying to divert the two of them.

"Didn't Larson want to come and hear Meryl Jean sing her special this morning? Looks like he would have wanted…"

"Oh, I'll sing it while we're in the car going to…" Grandma shot me another look. "…later tonight…or…or some other time."

"Well…looks like a father would want…"

"Mr. Walby, what do you think about them wanting to get new carpeting and pews for the church?" The last thing I usually wanted to do was get Jake Walby in a fury about church goings on—but it worked in our favor this time. No one got another word in edge or otherwise the rest of the way to Hayti. Jake's opinion of how the people were so quick to spend money and of how primitive things used to be in his day, compared to how fancy everyone wanted to make them now, filled the remainder of our trip. We, Effie included, couldn't pile out of the car fast enough when he reached the entrance of the church.

## Chapter Thirty-Two

ONCE WITHIN THE sanctity of the church, Jake would be fine. No one but us ever knew how he really felt about church issues. Of course, Grandma and I never shared anything about our conversations to and from church with the other members. That would have cut poor little Effie to the quick. Besides, we loved them. Jake wasn't a bad person. "It's just his personality," Grandma would say.

Jake had a big heart and was among the first to help a person in need. However, he was a self-made man and had worked hard for everything he had. He didn't take to change easily. His rants made for a long half hour or longer ride to church and back, especially since he always drove below the speed limit.

As for Effie, if she were not so inquisitive, she wouldn't know so much about people and their business—neither would everyone else. Effie had a knack for asking what others were only thinking. "Why, if it wasn't for Effie, we wouldn't know near as much about goin's on in Silver Leaf—or for that matter, Muddy Ox neither," Grandma would say.

Our ride home was all about the Christmas program. One would have thought that I had been the entire program instead just a small part, to hear Effie talk. "If them people didn't already have a Christmas spirit, they sure got one now, Jean. You did so good."

"Thank you, Mrs. Walby." We were almost home and so far hadn't heard one critical word or prying question.

"So, how long y'all stayin' in Illinois?" Well—we were *almost* home."

"We're not for sure. I suspect we'll be headed back a day or two after Christmas, though," Grandma answered honestly.

Daddy's car hood was raised with him under it when we arrived home. "Look, Larson's out in this cold and not even wearin' a coat. He's liable to freeze to death," Jake commented.

"I know. Seems the cold don't bother Larson like it does the rest of us. I'm always remindin' him to grab his coat. Grandma quickly scooted out of the car to avoid more questions or comments. I wanted to say the cold probably didn't bother Daddy because he was so hot blooded and quick tempered, but Grandma would have found some tape for my mouth for sure if I'd said that.

"Mrs. Strom, y'all be safe now. Tell Larson to get plenty of sleep for your long drive."

"Okay, we will, Jake. Thank you again for takin' us to church. Have a good Christmas. Gotta go now—thanks again—bye."

After changing our clothes, I was sent to pump a fresh bucket of water. Daddy raised his head long enough to say he wouldn't be much longer. I let him know dinner was already cooking.

Grandma automatically filled the wash pan when I returned and placed it on the back burner to start heating. "Larson'll need some hot water to get that grease off before he eats. He always could get more grease on him than anyone I ever seen when he works on cars."

I mashed the potatoes as Grandma took the chicken from the skillet. "Want me to see how much longer Daddy will be?"

"Car's ready to go. I need to wa…" Daddy said as he suddenly appeared.

"Here son, I already got you some hot water to wash with," Grandma said as she set the pan of water over into the dry sink—next to a bar of lye soap.

"Good. I got a lot of the grease off already with a little gasoline. Maybe it won't be so hard to get the rest." Daddy now smelled like oil and gasoline. I hoped the hot water and lye soap could take care of the gasoline smell as well as the oil and grease stains.

In the time it took for him to scrub, we had the food on the table. Despite his efforts, some grease remained on his rough hands, especially within the creases in his thumb and around his finger nails. No wonder Daddy's hands were so cracked and rough.

They'd weathered cold, dirt, grease, oil, gasoline, and lye soap on a regular basis.

Had Grandma not seen his efforts, she might have balked at him coming to the table with his hands looking as they did. But, she saw him try his best. They were stained and scarred—not dirty. At least the gasoline smell was gone—mostly.

"How long are we stayin' in Illinois?" Grandma asked once we were seated and had offered grace.

"I figure 'bout four or five days—depends," Daddy said between bites. *Depends* meant, we'd find out later, I guessed. So, we were actually none the wiser.

"Mom, ain't no one can make fried chicken, biscuits, and gravy like you can."

"Meryl made the mashed potatoes."

"They're good, too, Baby. I figure one day you'll be a good cook like your Grandma."

"I'm trying, but I'm not sure if my biscuits will ever be as good as hers." Grandma beamed as Daddy and I sang her praises. She was a modest person but loved it when people bragged about her sons, her flower and vegetable gardens, or her cooking—especially her biscuits. Since coming to live with her, I'd also got added to her bragging list.

## Chapter Thirty-Three

I WONDERED WHAT we'd use for packing since our suitcases were lost in the fire. Not to worry. Grandma had a solution. Three large tow sacks lay over the back of the couch. Those burlap tow sacks once held the corn mash we fed our chickens. Because of her obsession for saving everything, Grandma had washed and saved every one of them.

"I was about to think you two were never gonna get done packin'," Daddy said as we carefully placed the last items into our sacks.

"Packing's harder when you're usin' sacks and not suitcases. We couldn't just cram our stuff down in the bag or it'd be a mess once we got there," Grandma muttered.

"Then don't look at my packin', Mom. You wouldn't like it." Daddy stood to leave.

"Where you goin'?"

"To get somethin' from the car. I'll be right back, Mom."

"I hope he's not gone after more of his clothes. It's too late to clean 'em up now." Grandma fretted. It was Monday afternoon. We were leaving early the next morning.

I hoped he wasn't going for a swig from the bottle he usually kept under the front seat. We were both wrong. Daddy came in with more presents.

"What you got there?" Grandma was grinning.

"Oh, I ran into San-dee Claus again. Y'all ready to have Christmas?"

"I've been ready," I exclaimed.

Grandma took to her chair, and Daddy and I sat on opposite ends of the couch. I was nearly out of patience to discover what was in those tiny, unmarked presents of Daddy's.

"Okay, but I want us to save the mystery gifts for last." Guess I had to find a little more patience. Daddy's little mysteries were pushed aside as we passed the other presents to one another. I had given those little odd-shaped bundles a squeeze and a shake every time I passed by them. Grandma did the same when she thought no one was looking. I bet she had to dig up a little more patience, too.

After all the other gifts were passed out, I got to say "when" and we tore into our packages all at once. Of course, Grandma loved her cameo combs and praying hands breast pin from me, and the lotion and slippers from Daddy.

Practical Grandma got Daddy a couple pairs of socks and a flannel shirt. Her impractical side got him a small harmonica. Daddy held the harmonica in his hand with a look on his face that I couldn't decipher as one of pleasure or confusion.

"I wanted to give you something else to do besides take cars apart and put 'em back together. I'm pretty sure I remember you blowing on one of 'em things when you was growin' up and findin' a couple tunes on it."

"Thanks mom, I'll try," he said casually slipping it into his shirt pocket. "Baby, I really needed that billfold. And you know I'm always sayin' a man cain't never have too many tools. This one fancy little screwdriver. Come give your old Daddy a kiss."

"I needed more pencils for school, thanks. Umm…I don't think I've ever tried to wear Ben Hur perfume before but…it smells…nice," I said as I moved over to peck him on the cheek. I didn't want to tell him how Sadie nearly suffocated us in the car on our way back from Kennett with her bottle of Ben Hur on our first Saturday shopping trip with the Simpsons. He would have thought I didn't like his gift. Maybe Sadie put too much on at once. I'd try dabbing only a drop or two. If it was more than I could handle, I'd only wear it during our Illinois trip and whenever I was with Daddy.

"Open what I got you Meryl. I hope you like it," Grandma said.

Laying aside the purple lace bow I was sure she purposely chose for my package; I was shocked to see a small diary. I would have never expected Grandma to buy me something you couldn't either eat or wear.

"A diary."

"I thought you'd have a lot of things you'd want to make note of 'tween now and the time you graduate."

"Grandma, thank you. Yes, I know I will. This is a perfect gift." After hugging her as I started to move back to my side of the couch, Daddy slipped another crudely wrapped package into my hand. The wrappings easily fell off to reveal a small Brownie camera and a package of film.

"It's not new but, one of the guys at the blacksmith shop swapped it to me for some oranges and sugar cane. It still works good though. I thought you'd like to take a few pictures while we're on our trip."

"I'd like to take some while we're there, but I want to take some right now, too. I love it Daddy," I said, popping a roll of film into the camera to snap a few candid shots of our surprisingly happy Christmas.

"Hey…we're not done yet." This was the Daddy I loved. Not because he was showering us with gifts, but because he was happy and fun—and sober.

"Oh yes, we still have our mystery gifts," I said.

"Meryl and me have tried to guess what they could be, but you stumped us, son."

"I figured y'all would be shakin' and squeezin' them every time you passed 'em." Grandma gave him a 'cat that ate the mouse look'.

"There are no names on them. How do we know

who gets what?"

"It don't matter, Baby." Daddy pitched them to us until we each had an equal pile on our laps. "This time though, open one at a time so you don't spoil things."

Grandma and I had way too much fun opening those oddly shaped little packages. Daddy tricked us—they were all the same thing. That small collection of ten cent lady's handkerchiefs wrapped into various sizes and shapes, gave us a priceless Christmas memory we never forgot.

## Chapter Thirty-Four

"Hey, it's still early. Can't we play a game or something?" I asked trying to savor our moment.

"The only game I have is dominos. I haven't played that game since Omar died. The Walbys use to come and play with us almost every Friday night. I'm not sure I even remember how to play dominos anymore."

"I sorta' wanted to go see the guys at the blacksmith shop before…"

"But I don't mind trying to remember," Grandma flipped-flopped.

"Oh Daddy, you can wait to see the guys when we get back, can't you? Please, we haven't had a more fun time…in years. I don't want it to end."

"Well…okay Baby. But two against one ain't fair. I don't think I remember how to play dominos neither," he confessed. Daddy probably would have rather played a card game, as would I. But to Grandma, cards were the devil. No one could have paid her to have a deck of cards in her house. Cards meant gambling, gambling meant sin, and sin was of the devil. Grandma labeled a lot of things of the devil.

She would have been appalled to know I could play a mean hand of Black Jack or Poker. We played with matches not money, but I'd been allowed to sit in many times when my parents played cards with friends. Sometimes Mama and I would play Rummy or Spades while Daddy was coon hunting. Both Daddy and I knew better than to even suggest cards with Grandma—unless it was a game of Old Maids. She approved of those. They weren't gambling cards. I sure didn't see Daddy playing Old Maids. Truthfully, even I would have rather suffered through learning to play Dominos.

"Larson, put our bricks on the stove, so they can be warming. Meryl, you set up the game. I'll put on some coffee," Grandma instructed.

Playing Dominos was more fun than we'd expected. An hour flew by before we realized. The game must have come back to Grandma better than she'd thought. She easily won the first game.

"We had such a big dinner. Are y'all okay with gleaning for supper?" Grandma asked.

I had never heard the term gleaning before coming to live with Grandma but had now grown quite familiar with it. Gleaned left over fried chicken was as good cold as it is hot as far as we were concerned. Of course, Daddy raked cold grease off a bowl of beans and ate some of those too—with some *gleaned* biscuits.

"Okay, our gleaning is done. Let's play some more. I think I'm catching on now." Not only did I want to redeem myself at dominos; I didn't want to give Daddy a chance to escape.

After a slight hesitation and in response to our nudging, Daddy once more surrendered. He won the second game, but I slaughtered them in the last. By that time I'd caught on and mastered that simple game of numbers.

"My goodness, it's after ten o'clock. We should go to bed if we're goin' to get up early in the mornin'," Grandma exclaimed. Before Daddy could say anything, I asked him what time he planned for us to leave. I so hoped he wouldn't insist on going to the blacksmith shop this late. If he did, there was no telling what time he'd get home or what shape he'd be in when he returned.

"I figured 'bout nine. That'll get us there 'tween two or three, dependin' on how many times we have to stop. But I wanted to…"

"Then we'll need to get up around six thirty," Grandma interrupted. Daddy gave her a look of protest, but she continued before he could put it into words. "We gotta get breakfast, clean the kitchen, load the car, and check the house over before we go. Second thought, maybe I can get up at six thirty and get y'all up a little after seven." If Daddy got going too early he might decide on an early morning run to town. Staying with us meant he'd be less likely to grab a drink for the road. Smart, Grandma.

"I guess it's to bed then. Our bricks should be good and warm. They've been on the stove a long time now," I said summing it up quickly.

"Larson, if you and Meryl want to go on, I'll lock up and make sure the stove's off and say my prayers. I've been praying here by the chair on these cold nights. You'll have plenty of time to get settled before we come through," Grandma took my cue.

Daddy had been out maneuvered. He scowled before grabbing his brick and wrapped it in a towel on the way to bed. Grandma and I looked at one another and released mutual sighs of relief. After giving him ample time, I followed. No doubt Grandma's prayers would be more fervent tonight for our trip. So were mine.

I didn't sleep well, being nervous about our traveling. I kept picturing a bewildered Uncle Bray's face when we appeared unannounced. Daddy said we should go there first. If his calculations were correct, we'd be storming in on them right before supper, which Daddy saw as completely acceptable.

The last thing I remembered was the squeak of Grandma's bed spring as she climbed in, and Daddy's '*put-put-put*' before he coasted into slumber. The '*puts*' usually came before he brought his snoring motor to a full '*roar*'. When morning came, I opened my eyes and ears to '*put—roar—growl—put*'. Daddy was still sleeping. I giant stepped to the warm front room and dressed for the day. Even the thick blanket blocking off the kitchen, couldn't hold back the beckoning aroma of breakfast for me.

"You're up. That's good. Set the table so we can get your Daddy up." Grandma's body language screamed tension. I washed my hands and got to work.

"I admit I'm excited we're going to Illinois for Christmas," I said searching Grandma's face for a positive reaction.

"I can't lie. It'll be good to see 'em all. They're bound to know we would have wanted to tell 'em we were comin'. Nothing we can do 'bout it now. Go get your Daddy up so we can eat."

The only positive factor in Grandma's response was that she and I *positively* shared the same dreads which made us equally apprehensive about our trip. I cracked Daddy's bedroom door enough to call him to breakfast. After two invitations, he finally grunted awake.

Grandma and I cleaned the kitchen after we ate while Daddy loaded the car, checked the oil and water, and kicked the tires. Once she was satisfied the windows were locked and barred, and after rechecking the stoves in the front room and kitchen several times, Grandma tried the door one last time. It was locked solid. As we were pulling out of the yard, Simp waved on his way back from feeding and watering the chickens.

The lights of Hayti, Missouri soon dimmed in our rearview mirror, as we headed north onto highway 61. Grandma settled into the front seat, and I had the entire back seat to myself. The first entry into my diary was dated December 24, 1963. *"Dear Diary, I hope our family in Illinois will forgive us and be glad to see us. I hope we get there and back safely. I hope I can put a flower on Mama's grave—and I hope Daddy stays sober."* It wasn't long until my restless night and early morning wore on me. The hum of the car engine and the thudding of tires lulled me to sleep.

"I COULD USE a cup of coffee. Y'all want anything? This would be a good time to go to the bathroom if you need one." Daddy's voice along with a blast of cold air as he opened the car door startled me awake.

"I'd like a Pepsi. You want one Meryl?" Grandma asked. I never turned down a soft drink.

When she and I returned to the car after our bathroom break, Daddy had us each a bottle of Pepsi Cola waiting. As we drove off, he pitched a pack of peanuts and a Baby Ruth candy bar to me in the back seat and gave Grandma two Hershey chocolate bars.

"Here Mom, I got you one for now and one for later. I know how much you love your milk chocolate." Daddy could do some of the sweetest things at times.

## Chapter Thirty-Five

After pouring the peanuts into my Pepsi, I took one bite of the candy bar and decided to save the rest for later. This tranquil moment brought on a song. *"The First Noel, the angels did say, was to certain poor shepherds in fields where they lay."* I couldn't believe it when Daddy and Grandma joined in on the chorus.

"See, Mom, I told you. Edna and I never needed a radio. Not with our little song bird in the back seat."

"That was the song she sang yesterday morning at church. You shoulda heard her. She did so good. Everyone was talking about her song and skit," Grandma boasted.

"Skit?"

"Yes, Meryl writes skits for the church now. She's young people's leader, too. You can be proud of that girl. Everyone at the church loves her. She…"

I continued to sing softly as their conversation faded into the background. Daddy smiled at me in the rearview mirror. Still singing on autopilot, my mind wandered to a very sad and different kind of trip. The one Daddy and I made when we stole away like thieves, in the middle of a rainy night in 1959. Our destination was—Muddy Ox and Grandma's house. I remembered peering through the window, my face turned from him, trying to hide my tears.

A few months after Mama passed away, Daddy decided we needed to move to Missouri. I cried for my past and feared for my future while watching the haphazard swirls of rain trickle down the window and thought how they mirrored my life. Like the rain drops, I couldn't control which direction I was going either. It was sad to leave our home even though it felt empty without Mama. Also, leaving our family and everything familiar to me was scary.

Our family—thinking of the unsuspecting family at the end of this journey, brought my song to a halt. I numbly reached for my candy—for comfort.

After only two more hours, Daddy needed another cup of coffee, a bathroom, and some gasoline. Grandma and I also took advantage of the stop. It was on our way back to the car from the ladies room that I realized I had been at this truck stop before. These very gas pumps were where my dad sped away leaving a stranger in utter confusion during another trip to Grandma's, a few years prior to Mama's death.

At the time, we had many animals including a huge, long-horned billy goat we called Red, a nanny goat, and her two babies, Snowy and Billy. Daddy also had two prize blue-tick coon dogs, Queenie and Old Blue, plus several other hunting dogs. Queenie had a litter of puppies eight weeks old. To add to our zoo, he had a mean old boar raccoon that he used to train his hunting dogs.

We couldn't go to Missouri for any length of time and leave our zoo unattended. We had to take them with us. After seeing the need to do a little down-sizing, Daddy sold all of the hunting dogs but Blue and Queenie and either sold or gave all the pups away but four. We took the rest with us.

Most would have seen this task nearly impossible, but Daddy had a plan. Red and Old Blue were tied to opposite sides inside the trunk. The boar raccoon was secured between them, under the spare tire and out of the reach of Blue. The back seat was removed altogether to make room for Nanny, her babies, Queenie, four hound puppies—and me. Mama cushioned a can for me to sit on. Problem solved.

I knew the last thing Mama wanted was for me to make the trip to Missouri under such conditions. But she couldn't argue with a man who'd consumed a half pint of whiskey and thought his way was the only way.

While Daddy was pumping gas, one of the baby goats stepped on Queenie's foot, and she bit Nanny's ear. Nanny blared and started slinging blood all over everything, including me. The baby goats were bleating. The puppies began barking. Blue was howling in the trunk. I was crying, and Mama was yelling to try and quiet all of us down.

A man at the pump next to us, after seeing first a goat, then a puppy, then me, bob our heads in the window, asked my dad what he had in the car, goats, kids, or dogs? Daddy who had finished filling his tank looked at the man and replied, "Yes." We drove off, leaving the bewildered man to figure it out on his own.

Smiling to remember the look on that man's face and cringing to recall the vision of my reflection in the window during our last trip, reminded me that our present trip was so far a welcome change from at least two of the worse trips I had ever taken with Daddy.

## Chapter Thirty-Six

As Daddy predicted, we arrived in Brooksville, Illinois a little after three in the afternoon. Brooksville was unique for having a water tower built in the shape of an enormous catsup bottle. My eyes locked onto the bottle and followed it as we drove by. *Look Meryl, we're home, there's the catsup bottle,* I remembered Mama saying every time we returned from our visits to Grandma's as soon as the catsup bottle came into view.

*Look Mama*, I thought. *We're back.* Oh how I wished we could have made a right turn and followed Lebanon Road to our house and found Mama there waiting for us.

Instead we turned left, past my school of horrible memories of taunting and ridicule and continued to Uncle Bray and Aunt Gwen's house on Seminary Street.

A brightly lit Christmas tree covered their entire front window. Shadows of raucous, children with their heads bobbing beyond the sheer curtain, created a new sense of excitement in me. I hoped the welcome mat on their front porch meant what it said. Daddy boldly approached their wreathed door. Grandma and I stayed in the car with the window cracked to hear their response.

"It's Uncle Larson," Bray Jr. announced. I was glad he was the one who answered the door. Had it been one of the younger ones, they may not have remembered an uncle they hadn't seen in over four years. Uncle Bray towered over my dad by at least seven inches. His broad shoulders filled the doorway as he greeted his brother. After a few minutes they shared manly pats on the back, and Daddy motioned for us to come.

Grandma wept as her grandchildren took turns greeting her. She especially became teary-eyed to see their three year old baby girl, Chrissy, for the first time. That was when I positively knew this trip was a good thing, if only for Grandma to get to meet Chrissy and reconnect with the others. Uncle Duncan and Uncle Paul each had baby girls within months apart that she had yet to meet for the first time as well.

"Meryl, Meryl," the cousins squealed as we hugged and danced with joy.

"Gwen, set three more plates," Uncle Bray said, releasing Grandma from a near rib-breaking hug. Throwing his arm around my shoulders, he led me with the others to their dining room.

"We were about to sit down to an early meal since it's Christmas Eve. You all are just in time." I always loved Uncle Bray, but this warm welcome made me love and respect him now, even more.

"We get to open one of our presents after dinner.

We have to wait for morning for Santa Claus to bring the rest," Betsy, their oldest daughter whispered in my ear.

I was a few months older than Betsy. Bray Jr. was born ten months after Betsy. The next four—Lily, Mona, Artie, and Phoebe—were only a year or so apart. There was a seven year gap between Phoebe and their last child Chrissy.

"Artie, help Bray Jr. get more chairs. Betsy, you fill three more glasses with ice." Aunt Gwen directed.

Possibly wondering if she'd cooked a meal large enough to feed three extra mouths could have made Aunt Gwen a little less warm toward us. She also might have resented having a visit from her mother-in-law sprung on her—and rightly so.

"When Larson decides to do something, you can't change his mind. I'm glad to get to see y'all and the others for Christmas, but I hate that we surprised you like this," Grandma whispered apologies later while helping Aunt Gwen with the dinner dishes.

"Well, we would have liked to have known you all were coming. But I don't blame you or Meryl. We know Larson well." Aunt Gwen whispered back. After hearing that she understood our part in the visit, I was sure Grandma felt better. I knew I did as I followed the cousins into the living room.

I loved the way the older children related to little Chrissy. Of course, those big blue eyes and bouncy blond curls would have captured anyone's heart. My cousins were the closest things I had to siblings. I never knew the joys or pains of having a baby sister or brother.

"I love your tree," I marveled while surveying the plethora of beautifully wrapped presents under it. Of course, what could one expect with seven children? I couldn't imagine where 'Santa Claus' planned to put the other gifts he was expected to bring.

Uncle Bray helped Daddy carry in our tow sacks, along with our goodies from the car. Daddy happily passed out the sugar cane, oranges, and nuts to the crowd, which in his eyes was penance for our intrusion.

"Do we get to open our Christmas Eve present now?" Artie asked as he sat by the tree.

"We can't wait." Mona beamed as she joined him.

"Let's open our presents now," echoed Phoebe as she plopped down beside them.

Lily, Betsy, and Bray Jr. lined behind the younger ones. I sat on the chair arm next to Grandma. Daddy pulled up a kitchen chair beside us, and Chrissy climbed onto his lap. Children loved Daddy. In this setting, wearing his 'happy side', what was there not to love? Aunt Gwen and Uncle Bray handed each child their Christmas Eve gift.

Paper and ribbons flew as they tore into them. A tinge of envy and yes, a little jealousy ripped inside me—which had nothing to do with me not being handed a gift. Why did they get to have both their parents, and I was robbed of one—sometimes both of mine since Daddy was gone so much? Also, I was fairly sure they never had to dance around Uncle Bray to see which side of him would surface.

Nine year old Artie opened a collection of Wild West figures and began assembling his version of the gunfight at the O.K. Corral. Bray Jr. got a football. Phoebe combed and styled the long blonde hair of her Barbie doll. Lily dug into a paper doll kit and systematically arranged the outfits into casual, dressy, and playtime. Mona, the quietest of the seven, got an art pad, some charcoals, and drawing pencils. She found a corner and began what was sure to be a choice work of art.

To practice throwing and aiming his new football, Bray Jr. appeared with an emptied clothes basket and placed it in the opposite corner of the living room, all the while promising his mother he'd pick up the dirty clothes he'd dumped from the basket—later. After pictures turned sideways from the jolts and the broom pounded the floor in the kitchen a few times, Uncle Bray strongly suggested he find another place to practice. Before long, not wanting to be isolated from the group, Bray Jr. returned to the living room and though it was below his age level, he joined Artie in arranging his reenactment.

Betsy got a cute pair of saddle oxfords and some

bobby socks. I watched as each cousin enjoyed their Christmas Eve gifts. However, I was mostly drawn to Betsy bopping about in her stylish shoes.

"Meryl, aren't you going to open your present?" Daddy asked.

"Present, where?" I smiled.

It wasn't hard to spot, once Daddy pointed under their tree, his wrapping techniques were hard to miss. A present was the last thing I'd expected. Every eye in the room was plastered on me as I untied the twine knot and removed the lid from the box. The dam at Niagara Falls couldn't have held back the tears that flooded my eyes as I pulled out a pair of black, suede, boy shoes from the box.

"Put 'em on. I thought you needed a good pair of shoes instead of those old, rundown, flimsy tennis shoes you been wearin'."

"But Daddy."

"Go ahead, put 'em on."

"But Daddy, I…"

"Meryl—put 'em on. They'll last you all winter."

Then I noticed his red eyes and got a whiff of his breath. Evidently he had been drinking. Daddy probably either had a bottle hidden under his car seat before we left Missouri or had gotten one during one of our many bathroom stops on the way. It didn't matter, he was drunk enough now that if I gave an argument, it would have not gone well.

"Those are boy's shoes," yelled Artie. "You gonna wear boy's shoes?"

Aunt Gwen shooed him into the other room to help his brother pick up the dirty clothes, but it was too late. It was out there. I couldn't blame Artie. He didn't know better. He was only being a kid—a little boy who instantly recognized his kind of shoes.

"They're not so bad, Meryl," Grandma said trying to soften the blow.

"Put the da…uh…put the things on." By now it was a power of wills. Daddy was not going to be outdone. I wiped my cheeks with the back of my hand, only to have a new stream of tears fall in their place. Removing my weathered, but beloved tennis shoes, I sat them aside and replaced them with the big, bulky, black, disgraces. My plan to cross off my 'nevers' had now been set back four years.

1. Never to be belt-whipped by an alcoholic father.
2. Never be tormented because of my weight.
3. Never—wear boy's shoes again.

If I wasn't careful, not only were my efforts to avoid number (3) being over-ruled and nullified by an inebriated, over-bearing father but 'never' number (1) could be in jeopardy, too. The last thing a sixteen year old girl wants on Christmas Eve is to be belt-whipped in front of her cousins and their parents. The only never remaining on my list was number (2).

"Mommy, why does Uncle Larson make her wear boy's shoes? Is it because she's fat and her feet are fat, too?" whispered Phoebe.

Even though she whispered, I heard and so did everyone else. In less than a blink of a Christmas tree light, my entire list of 'nevers' was erased as though it never existed.

"Let's take a picture. Gwen, get our camera." Little did Uncle Bray know that a picture-perfect moment would only add to my embarrassment.

Daddy inched closer and everyone said cheese. Of course, there had to be two pictures, as if one wasn't humiliating enough. One posed with Uncle Bray and one with Aunt Gwen since they took turns being photographers. Due to the wonders of Polaroid we didn't have to wait to see the finished product. I was so hoping they'd cut my shoes out of the picture. Not a chance. To me, the picture was one of my big, hideous shoes and the rest of us were only by-products. My facial expression in the picture said it all. No caption necessary. To add to my humiliation, Daddy asked, "Meryl, where's the camera I got you for Christmas? We need to get a picture on it, too."

Aunt Gwen saw it on Grandma's lap and told Betsy to take a picture of all of us with it. Betsy saw my dismay but did as her mother asked.

Afterward, Uncle Bray and Daddy went to the kitchen for a cup of coffee. Aunt Gwen left to figure out sleeping arrangements, and the cousins were sent to get dressed for bed.

"Meryl, I'm sure your Daddy meant well. He didn't set out to embarrass you. He wanted you to have sturdy shoes for school," Grandma consoled when we were alone.

"I won't ever tell Daddy, but I'll never wear these ugly things to school," I muttered through clenched teeth.

"I understand—really I do. He'll leave for Florida as soon as we get back home. What you do about wearin' the shoes will be your decision. He's drinkin' now though, and you know you'll have to wear 'em while we're here."

Grandma was right. When we visited the other two families, I'd have to wear Daddy's shoes. I called them Daddy's shoes because I had no intentions of claiming them. They were one more confirmation of how disconnected he was to me and my feelings. Sadly enough, I couldn't trust his reaction to tell him how much emotional pain his *meaning well* caused me.

The younger ones were sent upstairs to get nestled in their beds so Santa Claus could come. Betsy and I followed, if not to sleep, to fill in the gaps created by so many years apart. We heard a few muffled curse words from downstairs, as Uncle Bray fought with directions trying to assemble some of Santa's final treasures. The front door creaked open and shut a few more times. I figured Daddy was finishing his bottle.

Grandma was given Mona's bed, and she bunked with Phoebe. Lily curled next to Chrissy. The boys paired off, and I slept with Betsy. Daddy was given the couch. By this time, he was tired and tipsy. He probably could have slept hanging from a hook in a corner.

Before long, all was quiet upstairs and downstairs. Betsy's slow breathing let me know she'd also given into sleep. I was reminded of the Christmas poem, *The Night Before Christmas*. Not a creature was stirring in their big house, not even the big, drunk daddy rat on their couch—for now.

All their children went to sleep with great expectations of what the next day would bring. I wondered the same. However, it had nothing to do with presents.

## Chapter Thirty-Seven

CHRISTMAS MORNING AT Uncle Bray's and Aunt Gwen's was a loud, frantic, fun-time example of controlled chaos. I loved it. It didn't matter that 'Santa' didn't leave anything under the tree for me. Actually, I was thankful nothing else black, wide width, with laces, and had my name on it was there.

Seeing all the cousins open their gifts was joyous. Their living room looked like a toy store had been dumped into it. Paper, ribbons, and boxes were everywhere. The walls seemed to expand with laugher and squeals of joy. So, this was what Christmas morning was like for a big—real—family? I felt privileged to get to witness it. Christmas morning with their family was a first for Grandma, too, considering the miles between Brooksville and the Bootheel. Daddy might have had his own reasons for us to make this holiday visit to his brother's homes, but getting to share Christmas morning with this family, was one of the best gifts Grandma could have ever had.

Uncle Bray and Aunt Gwen had Christmas dinner and gift exchange plans with Aunt Gwen's family that afternoon and evening. We were invited to Uncle Paul's and Aunt Jackie's. Getting to see and visit with Aunt Jackie was a gift in its self for me. To me, she was beautiful, funny, sweet, and kind. I met her for the first time when I was seven years old, and it was love at first sight. She was eighteen when she and Uncle Paul married and moved to Brooksville from Easley, South Carolina. Now that I was sixteen and Aunt Jackie was so young at heart, she seemed like just another teenager at times.

Queen Victoria McGehee, her mother's actual name, and Aunt Jackie were not blood-kin, but I couldn't have loved them more had they been. Christmas evening would be memorable, if for only getting to be with them. All they had to do was to be themselves.

Grandmother Queen, as she was called by most, came to live with Aunt Jackie and Uncle Paul not long after they married. It was a great arrangement. They soon realized what an asset Queen was to their family. After the children came, if they needed a baby-sitter, she was there. If Aunt Jackie needed motherly advice, Queen was on hand to give it. Should Uncle Paul need an extra hand or hammer, his mother-in-law worked alongside him as diligently as a hired hand.

Queen always joked that Daddy named his prize coon dog Queenie after her, because the dog was so smart and good at what she did. Daddy would remind her that his dog was already named when he got her. But if not, he would have considered naming her Queen for that very reason.

Grandmother Queen was definitely one of a kind. She was never without an opinion on anything and didn't mind giving it. People said she was like Listerine; her advice was sometimes strong, but they needed her every day.

Aunt Jackie and Uncle Paul were my idea of the perfect couple. Their love story could have been scripted for a Doris Day and Gordon McCrae movie. She was a sweet, saucy southern belle. He was a handsome Paratrooper, in town on furlough. They met, fell in love, and got married. I wished to have a love story like theirs one day.

Aunt Jackie adored my mother and was happy to share memories of her with me. She was also a great listener. No subject was ever off limits with Aunt Jackie. We talked about girl things Grandma avoided completely or topics that made her uncomfortable.

Uncle Paul and Aunt Jackie's children were another Christmas treat for Grandma. Walter, age seven and Monty, age six, were drawn like magnets to Grandma's love. If she was on the couch, the boys were on each side of her and three year old Nettie was in her lap. As she stroked Nettie's dark brown hair and gazed into those snappy brown eyes that were a replica of her own, we could practically see Grandma's heart melting. Cute little Nettie would fake a cough so Grandma would give her a cherry cough drop from her purse. Of course

Walter and Monty had coughs, too. If there was a Grandma Heaven on earth—Grandma surely found it during our Christmas visit to Brooksville that year.

We gathered around Aunt Jackie's piano and had a sing-along after dinner. But with the close harmony we shared, we could make music with or without an instrument. Daddy even got into the act by playing a few songs on his harmonica. He made train whistles and animal sounds for the kids causing them to be drawn to him, too, after that.

Nine o'clock was the children's bedtime and time for us to go. Uncle Bray and Aunt Gwen should be home. I hadn't realized how I'd missed family until this visit. Uncle Duncan's was next on our list. Maybe we had at least a couple more days left before Daddy planned to leave for home. Here I was wishing for a longer stay for a trip I had been reluctant to take at all.

I managed to slip into Betsy's bed without waking her when we returned.

## Chapter Thirty-Eight

WE LEFT FOR Uncle Duncan's the next morning after breakfast. Nine cousins awaited me there. As an only child, to be a part of Uncle Bray's and Uncle Duncan's large families, if only for a short time, was such a treat.

When we reached the end of Uncle Bray's street, I was surprised when Daddy turned in the direction opposite from where Uncle Duncan lived. "Thought you might like to see our old house again," Daddy said. I'd wished for as much but didn't know how he'd feel about it.

Daddy briefly glanced toward the factory he had quit without notice, as we passed by. His expression was unreadable. Our house was just beyond the factory, on the very next corner. Christmas lights blinked around the front door window. Mama used to hang lights around that same window pane. The new owners must have had a child or children, judging by the big Santa Claus figure on the front porch. Wonder what they did with all our furniture and stuff since we could only cram so much into Daddy's car that night we stole away like thieves. A thief pretty well described us. Daddy left his debts, along with his job, the house and our Illinois family—with no intention of ever paying them.

I remembered how I had tried to think about what Mama would have thought most important after being given her job of packing. When loading the car, I insisted we give priority to her trunk. Then we stuffed our clothes and other assumed necessities in around it. All else was left where it stood. I was haunted for some time after our move, about possibly leaving some irreplaceable treasure behind. But now, after all this time, and after Grandma and I losing so many things in our house fire, I realize *things* hold little significance. I'd kept Mama's trunk, and it almost got destroyed. I managed to take my Saucy Walker doll, and she got burned to a crisp. Things were and are—just things.

If we'd knocked on their door and they'd let us in, what would we have said? "*We used to live here. Sorry for the mess we left.*" I might have asked to see my old bedroom or glanced at where Mama's sick bed had been and visualized her lying there. However, I knew a knock on their door wasn't possible. Daddy hadn't left any trails to be followed back then. I was sure he didn't want to blaze any new ones now. Although it seemed to be the theme of our trip, an impromptu visit with the new residents of our old house was not an option. Willing myself to let go of the past was necessary and—realistic.

Daddy made a U-turn. As we passed back by, the parents and two smiling children were walking to their car. Once again, the house of my childhood was left behind. Hopefully, that place would hold happier memories for them.

"We'll be going by the cemetery on the way to Uncle Duncan's. Want to stop?"

"Yes," I said. I'd wish for that, too.

"I think we'll have time. Duncan and them don't know we're comin'."

Of course they wouldn't. I became anxious again to be barging in on yet another unsuspecting family. Daddy turned off St. Clair Avenue into the cemetery. We parked as close to Mom's grave site as the path would allow. Grandma stayed in the car. A dusting of overnight snow made the downhill slope to Mama's grave too great a challenge for a seventy-four year old.

"I wish I had a flower, Daddy," I said as we struggled to keep footing.

"Your mother wouldn't worry 'bout flowers. She'd just be glad you came, Baby."

I brushed the snow from her marker with my glove. Mary Edna Strom, born August 11, 1909—died July 16, 1959. Only forty-nine years of life. I felt cheated that I couldn't have had more years with her. I had so many questions for her. *Mama, why did you say you were ashamed of me in my dream?* She couldn't answer but if it was true, she'd tell me one day.

"Here, Baby." Daddy startled me and interrupted my one-way conversation with Mama. He was holding a small bouquet of plastic flowers. "I found these against a bush over there. We don't know whose grave they blew off of, but I'm sure whoever it was won't mind sharin' with your mama. What do you think?"

"Probably not," I agreed. Daddy helped me push them into the frozen ground by Mama's stone. As we struggled up hill to the car, I wondered if my angel let those flowers show up where Daddy could find them, so I didn't have to visit Mama flowerless.

The closer we got to Uncle Duncan's the more nervous I became. Yes, we were family, but even family needed a little advance notice of visitors, especially during a holiday.

Again, Grandma and I sat in the car while Daddy approached their door. We were parked too far away from their house to hear what was said. However, what we saw caused us to gasp. Their front door opened—then abruptly slammed shut.

"Oh my," Grandma exclaimed. "They slammed the door in Larson's face."

My heart sank.

Almost immediately, the door reopened, and Uncle Duncan stepped onto the porch. As with Uncle Bray, there was a short exchange of words before a manly embrace. Daddy motioned for us to come. They said their youngest, Lola, had answered the door. Not recognizing Daddy, she slammed it and ran to her parents. It was an honest reaction from Lola, but a scary one for Grandma and me.

Controlled excitement was a good description of their family setting. Their children were quiet, disciplined, and well mannered. They worked together and moved about like a well-oiled machine. I supposed that was necessary with a large family.

The two oldest girls, Joan and Veronica, only nineteen and eighteen seemed much older since they were expected to help so much with the younger ones. It was as though four adults were running their household and the girl's birth order had robbed them of their youth in a way. Ethan, their oldest son was seventeen. Daniel and I were sixteen. The other five children were stair-steps with baby Lola being a month or two younger than her cousins, Chrissy and Nettie.

Lola and the two other baby girls had contrasting, but adorable features. Chrissy, with her big, blue eyes, and waist-length, blond hair was a show stopper. In addition to having Grandma's beautiful brown eyes, Nettie's thick dark brown hair hung in soft curls and waves to framed her face perfectly. She could also turn heads in any crowd. Lola's hair was a mass of curly, blond ringlets outlining her cherub like face. Her tiny lips looked like rosebuds when she went into a pout. Either child would have presented a beauty contest official with a judging dilemma. I imagined Grandma's heart swelled with pride.

Chrissy and Nettie had taken to us right away. Lola

was more aloof. We discussed later, that had Aunt Nadine encouraged her a bit more, maybe she would have been warmer. It might have also helped if Aunt Nadine, herself, had been a tad warmer. But she, like Aunt Gwen, probably didn't appreciate an unannounced visit from her mother-in-law. I also suspected she and Uncle Duncan might have had a little tiff going on before we arrived, judging from her icy tone and the daggers in her eyes toward him.

Things got a little less tense after Daddy and Uncle Duncan went outside to talk cars. Lola finally warmed up to Grandma and climbed onto her lap. I tried to make friends with her, but it seemed she only had so much generosity to share at one time.

"I like you," I told her.

"I don't like you." She pouted.

"Well, I like you, and I love your cute little curls," I insisted.

"I don't like you," she persisted.

"Why don't you like me? I'm your cousin, and I still like you even if you don't like me," I argued playfully.

"Okay, I'll like you, but I don't like your boy."

The room roared with laughter. I gathered she meant she didn't like Daddy. Had he stayed inside with her longer, he might have won her over, but he and Uncle Duncan must have had a lot to talk about. They were outside more than inside during our visit.

Aunt Nadine excused herself and disappeared into

another room. Joan offered us something to drink and Veronica placed a plate of spiced cookies on the table. Daniel pulled out the Monopoly Game. It was the first time I had ever played Monopoly. Mom and I never played board games. Monopoly probably wouldn't have been much fun for only the two of us. Daddy would have never been interested in a child's board game.

I loved the chatter and friendly rivalry between the siblings around the table. However, the game of Monopoly, didn't appeal to me. Maybe I was overly serious, but it was too much like life—get money, have hardships, and worry about paying debts. If the dice rolled in your favor, opportunity presented itself. But all too soon, you could find yourself in a mess. I preferred games of skill as opposed to those of chance.

Aunt Nadine finally came from her room and served up some sandwiches and chips. Daddy and Uncle Duncan moved their car conversation to the living room. I lost all my monopoly money and went bankrupt—game was over for me. Before long, Aunt Nadine said she had another headache and excused herself again to lie down. Joan and Veronica resumed the hostess duties. I think they, along with the other children, were truly glad to get to see us, especially Grandma.

After a while, Daddy said it was time we get back to Uncle Bray's. He added we had to start making plans to head back home the next day since he had to get back to his job in Florida in a few days. That was the first time those bits of information had been shared with us. But I was okay with going home. I'd be glad to get back to Missouri and see Daddy off to Florida so I could ditch those ugly shoes. Grandma was a homebody and often said home was her favorite place to be—not to discredit one minute of our holiday visit.

Daddy and Uncle Duncan had their time together, and Grandma and I had a great time with the rest of the family. Grandma literally had to coax Lola off her lap for us to leave, rendering that first time introduction a success. Aunt Nadine's headache never got better. We didn't get to say goodbye to her before leaving.

After a few minutes in the car with Daddy, we suspected his staying outside with Uncle Duncan wasn't all about car talk. His speech was slightly slurred. The smell of liquor was evident.

Grandma and I looked at one another. I could see her fuming, but she remained silent. We sure didn't want to make him mad while he was driving. No wonder Aunt Nadine was anxious during our visit with them. I imagined Uncle Duncan had shared more than a few drinks with his brother, and she probably had expected as much of them.

## Chapter Thirty-Nine

WHEN WE ARRIVED at Uncle Bray's, Daddy let us out at their doorsteps and said he'd be right back before he sped away. Of course, I didn't doubt where he was going. I assumed he and Uncle Duncan finished off his stash of liquor, and he wanted more Southern Comfort for our trip back down South.

"Where's Larson?" Aunt Gwen asked when Grandma and I came in alone.

"He…said he'd be right back," Grandma said and gave Uncle Bray a look.

"Well, dinner will be ready soon. He'd better hurry back if he doesn't want to miss it. I made a big pot roast since you all are leaving tomorrow," Aunt Gwen said.

Daddy must have shared his plans with Uncle Bray, too, for her to also know we were leaving. Uncle Bray went into the living room with Grandma trailing behind. I was sure she planned to warn him of Daddy's condition. I joined them in time to hear Grandma end with, "He smells like a brewery."

"I'll take care of it Mom," Uncle Bray promised.

"Him and Duncan stayed outside for most of our visit. I hardly saw Duncan at all. I figure they were drinking the whole time." Grandma sounded disappointed, disgusted, and embarrassed.

"It's okay Mom. Maybe, he'll sleep it off after dinner," Uncle Bray consoled.

"Well, I hope so," Grandma sighed.

"He's probably gone for liquor now," I added.

"Don't worry Meryl. I'll talk with him." I loved that about him. He had a way of stepping in and calming situations. If anyone could impact Daddy, it was Uncle Bray. Guess we'd wait and see.

Dinner came and passed with still no sign of Daddy. The adults stayed talking around the table. The younger children went into the living room and played. Betsy and I went upstairs to her room.

"Does Uncle Larson get drunk all the time?" Betsy asked.

"If he wants to he does."

"I'm sorry about those shoes." It was the first time Betsy had mentioned them. It was also the first time I thought of how no one at Uncle Duncan's mentioned them at all.

"He's clueless about how cruel kids can be. Would you want to wear those things?

"NO!" Betsy's reaction was even a notch stronger than I'd expected.

"I'll stuff them into the darkest corner of my closet when we get back to Missouri where I won't even have to look at them."

"Won't Uncle Larson be mad?" Betsy's eyes grew large.

"He would be if he was there. But he'll leave for Florida as soon as he can after we get back to Grandma's."

"Doesn't it bother you that he'll be leaving you again?"

"The first time he left, I felt deserted. I didn't have either parent around anymore. Had it not been for Grandma, I would have felt like the left over dinner scraps your mother threw in the trash a few minutes ago. You know Grandma didn't have to let me live with her—but she did. Betsy. I don't wish my circumstances on anyone, but I wish you and all the other cousins could know our Grandma like I do. I also wish we didn't live so far away from one another."

"Me, too. I miss you. I can't imagine how it would feel to have a parent die."

"It's a helpless feeling—and scary."

Betsy and I were still talking about death, me living with Grandma and having to work in the cotton fields after the others had gone to bed. I figured Grandma was lying in bed awake. Probably Aunt Gwen, as well.

When Daddy stumbled through their door downstairs, Uncle Bray was waiting up for him. Their conversation over coffee and the leftovers put aside for Daddy must have been short and to the point. Uncle Bray directed Daddy to the couch, turned off the lights, and joined Aunt Gwen in their bedroom.

Only minutes passed before Daddy's snoring rumbled the living room walls.

"Does he always snore that loud?" Betsy laughed.

"Sometimes—louder." I giggled.

We talked a while longer about her school activities and the boy she liked before we fell asleep. She was allowed to date at sixteen. So far, there'd only been one special guy for her. She glowed when she talked about her Jimmy. I couldn't imagine how it would be to sport a cute pair of saddle oxfords and bobby socks and have a steady boyfriend, too. I couldn't deny my envy of Betsy.

Daddy was still snoring on the couch the next morning. He was oblivious to the children playing around him. The constant snap of Bray Jr's new baseball hitting his glove had everyone else in the room on edge, but Daddy slept through it all. Even the smell of bacon didn't arouse him.

I had mixed feelings about him sleeping in. The longer he slept, the more sober he'd be. However, we hoped to get home before dark since drinking and driving in the dark was an even greater risk. It was nearly noon. Our margin for leaving at a safe time of the day had narrowed.

Uncle Bray had an idea. Daddy had told him he wasn't expected back at his job until January 2nd. He and Aunt Gwen would suggest we stay one more night and go see Christmas lights, since they would remain on display until after New Years. There were a couple of neighborhoods around that practically made a competition of their light displays. I remembered Mama and Daddy taking me to see them on occasion when we lived in Brooksville. Betsy declared the displays had gotten bigger and better.

"It will be dark enough to catch the lights after dinner," Aunt Gwen began.

"Yeah, Larson, I think we can all fit into my station wagon to go see them together. Mom has never seen lights like these," Uncle Bray added.

"Pleeez…stay one more night, Uncle Larson, so Meryl and Grandma can see the lights with us. Pleeez…," Betsy begged. The others followed her lead, begging in unison.

"We'll even see if Paul and Jackie want to follow us in their car. They can come over afterwards so we can all get together again before you go home. Duncan and his family might can come too." Uncle Bray proposed after Daddy had finally gotten awake, had his coffee, food and been worn down by begging children.

Daddy balked at first but saw how mean he'd look if he cheated Grandma and me out of a chance to see the lights or deny Grandma another evening with the families. His battle was lost almost before it began.

Uncle Duncan and his family declined. Aunt Nadine said they already had plans with her family if another one of her headaches got better. They were out on two counts.

"You all can leave out early in the morning Larson, after you've had a better night's rest. And you'll get home before dark." Uncle Bray finally wouldn't take no for an answer.

After all it was his mother, too, who would be on the road with someone nursing a hangover or likely drinking and driving in the dark.

What fun we had. Every house shone with brilliant Christmas lights. The displays were so popular that one neighborhood had police directing people in and out of its entrance because of the traffic. All the windows were filled with automated Santas, elves, revolving Christmas trees, or teddy-bears. Toy-filled sleighs, snowmen, and nativity scenes adorned nearly every yard. Grandma kept saying how she'd never seen such a fuss made over Christmas decorations. There wasn't a child in the car that strained their neck any farther to see out the windows or whose eyes were any brighter that night than Grandma's. What a great plan Uncle Bray and Aunt Gwen had.

Aunt Jackie and Grandmother Queen brought cookies to add to the coffee and hot chocolate Aunt Gwen had waiting for us back at their house. What a beautiful memory we'd have, despite Daddy's drinking and my present of those ugly shoes.

After singing Christmas Carols, Uncle Bray sang his

favorite ditty, *You're Some Ugly Child*. He was so animated as he sang that song—in the most loving way.

Daddy joined him on the harmonica for a few other songs and made his train whistle and animal sounds again for all the children. The evening ended with a request for me to sing Oh Holy Night.

"I remember your mother's smile every time you sang, Meryl. She was always so very proud of you," Aunt Jackie said.

"Was she ever ashamed of me?" Aunt Jackie would know that if anyone did.

"NEVER—she never was ashamed of you about anything I ever knew of. Why would you ask?" Aunt Jackie questioned.

"Oh—no reason. I was just wondering." I didn't want discussing my dream to put a damper on our beautiful gathering.

"I know one thing," Aunt Gwen said. "The light in those pretty green eyes and that beautiful voice will steal the heart of a special young man one day. He'll fall in love before he knows what happened."

I blushed. I didn't know how Daddy would take the mentioning of a boy or a man falling in love with me. That subject was never brought up in Daddy's, Grandma's and my circle before. Still, Aunt Gwen's prediction warmed me from head to toe.

It was way past their children's bedtime when Uncle Paul and Aunt Jackie carried their sleeping two younger children to the car with Grandmother Queen and Walt in tow. Daddy and Uncle Bray talked around the table while Grandma and Aunt Gwen cleaned the kitchen. The younger kids were sent to bed. Betsy and I stayed behind trying to stretch our remaining time together as long as possible.

"You sing beautifully, Meryl," Betsy said. "I wish I could sing. I envy you."

Betsy envied me? I envied her—her life with both parents, her siblings, her cute shoes, and her boyfriend. I couldn't believe she envied me. That last night of our visit was so special. The lights, the singing, and just being a part of it all made it a most beautiful way to end our wonderful holiday visit.

## Chapter Forty

WITH A MIND full of sweet memories and a heart warmed by family, I locked my eyes onto the catsup bottle water tower again, as we left Brooksville. A tearful memory shot like an arrow and landed by a lonely tombstone in the cemetery on the bluff. I felt sadness and solace to have revisited Mama's grave.

*"There's the catsup bottle, Mama. I'm leaving you again—but I'll be back."* I decided to believe my guardian angel had helped to provide those flowers for Mama.

Uncle Bray had made an early morning trip to the bakery. A quick breakfast of donuts and coffee put us on the road by nine.

"We'll be home by early afternoon." Daddy sounded sober and alert. Strangely enough, Muddy Ox was home now—Brooksville was a place to visit.

"This trip was good, son," Grandma said.

"Yes, it was. I loved seeing everybody again," I added from the back seat.

"I sure do have some sweet grandchildren. I think I managed to get a hug from everyone of them several times over. Those three little ones were something else. Each of 'em has their own special dose of beautiful."

"Bray and Paul said they're gonna work on visitin' more often, Mom. Duncan said he will too when he can."

"I hope so. Children grow up fast. I want 'em all to know and love me. That's hard to do when you only see 'em every three or four years."

They continued to talk about one, then another of the grandchildren. Daddy assured her love was the only reaction they could have toward her. Yes, he was sober.

"Who doesn't love you, Mom? Just name somebody."

"Nadine had me wonderin'. I didn't know what I'd done, except for us to show up and them not expectin' us."

"Mom, Nadine and Duncan had a little fuss going on. You know how married people do sometimes."

"I'm glad it wasn't about me, but I hate to hear how her and Duncan was at odds. Young people don't realize how short and precious life is to waste it on not gettin' along."

"That is, until one or the other is planted in a grave on a bluff." Daddy added.

I was sixteen. Daddy, his brothers nor their wives seemed young to me—except Aunt Jackie. Grandma's seventy-four years gave the word young a different definition.

"They'll get over it. Don't worry, Mom," Daddy reassured.

A silence fell. I figured we were all reliving our visit. Betsy's and my late night bonding had robbed me of sleep. About an hour down the road, I drifted off.

"I need a bathroom stop," Daddy's voice jolted me awake.

"Me too," said Grandma, and I agreed.

We returned to the car before Daddy. "You must have been tired. We wasn't much out of Brooksville 'til you was asleep," Grandma said.

"Betsy and I talked for a long…"

I cracked the window after hearing loud voices and deep growls. A circle of terrified men had gathered around a large, angry dog.

"Better watch 'im. He's a mean'un. He broke loose from that chain he's draggin' behind 'im," said a bystander.

"Be careful," another cautioned.

"Grab somethin' to protect yourself if he lunges for ya," another warned.

A break in the circle revealed Daddy slowly approaching the growling beast. Daddy's eyes never broke contact with those of the angry dog.

"My dog's mean. I'm tellin' ya, man. He's ripped open the arm of more than one who's tried to corral 'im." The dog's owner held a large iron pipe.

"Stay back and lower that pipe, man." Daddy directed. The drooling dog growled louder, revealing his teeth. "He's scared," Daddy said, never breaking eye contact with the dog.

"Don't sound scared to me—sounds mad," spouted a man from the crowd.

With his palms upward, Daddy slowly reached toward the dog allowing him to sniff his fingers. "Everybody stand still and keep quiet. And lower that pipe I said," Daddy ordered.

Eventually, the dog dropped to the ground in submission and Daddy stroked his head and back. Grasping the broken chain attached to his collar, he led him to his owner and returned to our car.

"How did you do that, Daddy?" I asked, watching the white faced crowd through the car's back window as we drove away.

"What on earth kind of dog was that Larson? It looked like a baby horse."

"It was a Mastiff. They're big dogs, but they aint born mean. Mom, you could tell that owner had mistreated him to make him that way. The owner needed that chain around his neck instead," Daddy grumbled.

"How did you know you could back 'im down? Larson, you take some mighty big chances sometimes."

"When the dog saw I wasn't afraid and wasn't going to hurt him, he calmed down. Dogs can smell fear. His owner was scared and ready to hit him. Naturally, the dog was going to fight back. Poor thing probably had been mistreated more times than we'd ever want to know about," Daddy said as though taming angry animals was an everyday occurrence.

"You coulda got hurt bad, Larson," Grandma said, her voice shaking.

"Well, I didn't. I'd a handled him if he'd attacked. My boot was too thick for him to bite through. But I was pretty sure that wasn't goin' to happen." After that encounter, I wondered if there was anything at all my dad feared.

"Hey, I remember the coffee and hamburgers at this truck stop a little before Chester as being some of the best. Y'all want to stop and get a burger and some coffee when we get to it? We'll be there in about an hour? My donuts have about wore off. I'm hungry." Daddy had driven from Brooksville to Muddy Ox so many times, he knew every crook and turn along the way.

"All right now, those burgers and fries should hold us till supper. We have about two and a half hours of drivin' to go," Daddy said as we crossed the Illinois/Missouri State Line.

"Son, we'll be tired from the trip when we get home, and it'll take us a while to get the car unloaded. Wanna' stop in Hayti and get some bread and lunch meat to have sandwiches for supper? I don't think I'll feel like cookin' after travelin' all day."

"Sounds good, Mom. By the way, I'm leavin' for Florida in the mornin'." Daddy finally shared his plans with us.

## Chapter Forty-One

"HEY...GET OFF MY bumper you son of a..." Daddy shouted at the driver behind us. Our car suddenly accelerated as Daddy floored the gas pedal.

"Son, please be careful. There could be a patch of ice on the road. If you're goin' too fast, you won't see it 'til you're right up on it," Grandma begged.

"Crazy drivers. They musta got their driver's license out of a gumball machine. Get off my bumper, you idiot." Suddenly, Daddy jerked the stirring wheel, lunged over on the shoulder of the road and slammed on the brakes. I was thrown against the back of Grandma's seat, and she was thrown into the dash and the windshield.

The car behind us went into a skid to keep from ramming us and barely missed a guard-rail. Fortunately, the driver regained control and sped off. For a split second, I feared he was going to stop and confront Daddy. I breathed a sigh of relief when he was gone and out of sight.

"Grandma, are you all right?" I screamed when I saw she was holding her hand. She must have hurt it trying to brace herself against the dash. Then I saw she had an angry bump and a trickle of blood on her forehead.

"Daddy, what were you thinking? You've hurt Grandma. She's got a bump on her forehead, and she's bleeding. I hope her hand isn't broken." Daddy's eyes glared; his face reddened. For a moment, I thought he was going to slap me for yelling at him. Instead, he got out of the car and paced angrily behind it.

"Do you think your hand is broken, Grandma? Can you move it? Let me see your head."

She was crying. "I'm ok, I think. I hope it's not broken. I couldn't stop myself from hittin' the windshield. He didn't give us any warnin' before he pulled over to stop like that."

"I know, Grandma. He's walking around behind the car now. I don't think he's drinking. This time it's just his crazy temper. We can never predict him."

"You okay, Mom?" Daddy solemnly asked as he got back behind the wheel.

"I…think so," Grandma managed.

"Meryl, are you hurt?" I hadn't noticed until then that I had a gash on my knee. The muscles in my arms were twitching from trying to brace myself. I wasn't about to complain though. I'd gotten by with sassing him already about Grandma. Daddy was calmer now. I didn't want to set him off again.

"I'm okay," I said quietly.

He cautiously pulled back onto the road. We made

the remainder of the trip in silence and without any more stops or mishaps. I think seeing Grandma hurting scared Daddy more than he would have wanted to admit.

When we arrived home, Daddy got the house keys and opened the back door. Together, we got Grandma into the house. As proof of how badly she felt, Grandma didn't object to Daddy's lighting the oil stove. I draped a quilt over her on the couch then rushed to pump a bucket of water. I put cold cloths on her hand and the bump on her head while Daddy unloaded the car.

"Do you need to go to the hospital, Mom?" Daddy asked meekly.

"Let's give it a little while. We'll see if these cold cloths make the swellin' and the bump go down. Time will tell if my hand is broken or just sprung."

"Mom, I'm sorry. I was mad and wasn't thinkin'. I didn't mean to hurt you."

"I know you didn't, Son. Let this be a lesson though. You gotta control your temper better than that. You coulda hurt us and the people in that other car, too."

"I know… I know, Mom…I'll try."

I could count on one hand the times in my life I'd heard Daddy say he was sorry. I knew he meant it.

"My goodness. We didn't stop in Hayti to get stuff for supper. I don't have anything to scrape together for us to eat after while." That was a sign Grandma was feeling a little better. She remembered supper. Daddy diverted her when she tried to stand.

"I'll run to the Big Store and get something. Mom, you don't worry about it. Meryl, can you put on a pot of coffee? I'll be right back."

When he returned, Daddy had lunch meat, a loaf of bread, Pepsi Cola's, Grandma and me a candy bar—and a guilt-ridden face.

"Mom, haven't I heard you say that you didn't have an ailment that a good cold bottle of Pepsi and a candy bar couldn't fix?"

"Yes, I've said that," Grandma agreed allowing a half smile.

"Well, you should be feeling a lot better after supper then." Daddy told her to stay on the couch while I fixed the sandwiches. Again, she didn't put up a fuss—more proof of how badly she felt.

"We need to eat here in the front room where it's warmer anyway," Daddy decided.

The swelling on Grandma's head got better. However, the bruises had darkened. She looked pitiful but still refused to go to the doctor. Being tired from the trip and stressed from the incident, we took our hot bricks and went to bed a little before nine. For the first time that I can remember, she said her night prayers while sitting in her chair, instead of kneeling. That was yet another clue of how much she was hurting.

I had a lot to thank God for once I snuggled into bed. I was most thankful for Him protecting us when Daddy lunged off the road and that Grandma didn't get hurt any worse than she did. Also, that those people in the other car escaped injury from the guard rail and had the good sense not to confront Daddy. I prayed for Daddy's safety during his trip back to Florida. Finally, I thanked God for our wonderful visit to Illinois.

The next morning, Grandma had two black eyes and her hand and forehead were an even deeper shade of purple. I had bruises and a cut on my knee. My neck, shoulders, and arms felt like I had been beaten with the iron pipe that man with the dog had earlier.

Grandma's injuries didn't stop her from rising early to light the oil stove and having breakfast ready. Daddy didn't waste time in pointing his car south. After seeing him turn onto the blacktop from our lane, I made a mad dash with the ugliest pair of black oxford shoes you could imagine and stuck them as far back into my closet as I could get them, out of sight—and out of mind. I didn't know what I would do when Daddy returned and asked me about them, but I figured I'd deal with that problem when the time came.

## Chapter Forty-Two

"OH, MRS. STROM. What in the world happened to you?" Katty paled at the sight of Grandma's black eyes and bruises. I was surprised to see her brush the back of her man-sized hand across her tearing eyes—an out-of-character reaction from Katty.

"Did Larson do this? Mrs. Strom, did Larson lay hands on you?" Simp asked. His face flushed with anger.

"No, Larson didn't hurt me. At least it wasn't intentional. He stopped too fast on the shoulder of the road, and I couldn't brace myself fast enough." Grandma downplayed the accident for their benefit—and Daddy's.

Katty sprang into action as soon as she noticed Grandma's swollen hand. "Let me look at that, Mrs. Strom." After a closer look, Katty turned to Simp.

"Simp, get the car. We gotta take her to Kennett. I think her hand is broke."

"Honestly, Katty, I think it is, too."

"But Grandma, you told Daddy it was okay. You even lit the oil stove and made breakfast this morning."

"Well, I didn't want anything to delay Larson's leaving. I didn't want him driving on New Years Eve, especially if he might be drinking with all the others on the road doing the same." I understood. I feared after he filled his car with oil, water, and gas he'd fill his belly with liquor."

"I'll go get the car while y'all help her with her coat." Simp flew out the door.

"I can't believe Larson left you like this, Mrs. Strom."

"He wanted to take me to the doctor or hospital either one last night, but truth be known Katty, I didn't want us to get back into that car with him. His temper this time got the best of him. Besides, I was hoping I'd be better this morning."

"Daddy did ask her if he could take her to get it seen about," I confirmed. I didn't want Katty and Simp to think he was heartless.

"Can we go to the Dollar Store while we're in Kennett?"

"No Sadie," Katty snapped. "We're going to Kennett for Mrs. Strom. This ain't no pleasure trip."

A few hours later, Grandma reappeared with her hand in a cast, her arm in a sling, and a bandage on her forehead. The doctor scolded her for not getting to him sooner. It was only a small fracture. There was no need for stitches on her forehead, and her shoulder was only sprained. But the doctor cautioned that seventy-four year old bones and muscles didn't heal as quickly as a younger person's might. She went home with pain pills, an appointment to see him again in six weeks, and restrictions. He quickly scanned my injuries and dismissed any problems.

"I'm glad our cannin's over with. But how am I gonna quilt with this cast and my arm in a sling?"

"Mrs. Strom, you can quilt when the cast comes off," Katty assured.

"It'd be easier if it wasn't my right hand, but I'm thankful it wasn't my left. I didn't need it broke again. Omar wouldn't agree that my hand was broke years ago and doctored it himself. The bone never healed straight. That's why it's so weak."

"You said I should learn how to quilt, Grandma. Maybe now's the time."

"Honey, you'll need to start makin' your stitches smaller, or we'll hang our toenails in 'em when we put your quilts on the beds." Yes—Grandma was feeling better. What she tried to make as a joke was really a dig about my sewing. The previous winter I'd started a quilt for my hope chest but never finished it. Anyway, mine could have been called a hopeless chest. It was as hopeless as my non-social life. I couldn't believe Betsy had a steady boyfriend, and I hadn't had as much as a date.

Six weeks later, when we took Grandma back to have her cast removed, the doctor was amazed at how well she'd healed. He credited it to her strong bones and healthy living. Of course, she credited it to the Lord.

FINALLY, WINTER WAS over, and spring had arrived. April that year not only brought showers but also my seventeenth birthday. I'd added another never to my list. After graduating, I hoped to never set foot in another cotton patch again.

The May flowers were beautiful. Grandma's bush alongside the house was heavy with fragrant roses. Her constant care, along with the warm spring showers had paid off.

"Umm…smell those roses. They make our evenings on the porch all that more pleasant. You have the prettiest and fullest rose bushes in all of Silver Leaf, Grandma."

"It's 'cause I give 'em plenty of water and tender lovin' care. I tell 'em every day how pretty they are and how glad I am they live and bloom in our yard."

"Well—it's working, whatever you're doing."

"Almost anythin' will give you its best if it knows you love and appreciate it."

"Grandma, can you believe in three more days I'll be a senior?"

"Time flies like the wind. It doesn't seem very long

ago that you came to live with me. You done better workin' in the fields than I ever thought you would, though."

"I had a good teacher. Emmy Bertram is a lot like you. She doesn't settle for anything less than one hundred and ten percent."

"I know Emmy pushed you hard, but you took to work easier than some children. Your daddy never took to field work like that. And remember how Army Boone's father said he could never get him to work?"

"I think your letting me keep all of the money I made for school clothes was an incentive. I haven't worn boy's shoes in four years—except in Illinois last Christmas."

"Your Daddy probably forgot about those shoes by now."

"If not, I hope he thinks I've outgrown them."

"With choppin' season here, Larson could show up any time."

"I hope Mr. Bertram has work for Daddy since he had to buy that new tractor."

"New tractor or not, he'll still need help with his crops."

"That's true, and there are things Daddy can fix other than tractors, I'm sure."

"Are you about ready for bed?" Grandma stood, not waiting for my answer. I knew to follow. She wanted us to go inside together so she could check and recheck that the door was secure.

Grandma changed into her nightgown while I brushed my teeth. She was kneeling for her prayers when I tipped-toed through her room. I imagined the mention of Daddy's name had prompted a little longer prayer.

I opened my window wide to allow the fragrance of the roses to drift through. The night noises, minus the thump of a hard-shelled bug or two against the screen, sounded like a symphony of sorts. I closed my eyes and said my prayers.

*"Lord, I don't know what your plan in my life may be, but if you plan to put someone special in it, can you send him soon? I hate being seventeen and have never had a date. But thank you for everything else. Bless Grandma, and please keep your hand on Daddy—wherever he is…Amen."*

## Chapter Forty-Three

"HERE CHICK, CHICK, chick," Katty's voice screeched as she threw handfuls of corn mash to the chickens. Her shrieking and the pounding of Simp's hammer as he repaired yet another spot of fence in the chicken pen, told me it was time to get up. After joining Grandma at the table, I saw that her worry wrinkle had found its place across her forehead again.

"I had another dream about Larson last night. I guess he was on my mind when we went to bed. I can't remember many details—just him whistlin'. You know what his whistle sounds like. Well, it echoed like he was in a tunnel or a chamber." Grandma spoke as though she was in a trance.

"Well, if he was whistling, he probably wasn't in any trouble. Doesn't he usually whistle when he's happy or plotting something?" Daddy's whistling didn't sound like a distress call to me.

However, the mention of the echo in the tunnel reminded me of my dream when Mama told me she was ashamed of me. I hadn't thought about that dream in a while. Surely if she could know I was about to be a senior, she would be proud. Aunt Jackie promised her being ashamed of me wasn't ever so or possible.

We ate in silence. I mulled over my past dream, and I imagined Grandma was fretting about her recent one. Before long, I was out the door and headed toward school, leaving my mulling behind. Grandma would probably busy herself with the garden or her flowers or maybe check in on Simp's repair job and put her dream to rest as well.

I was especially anxious to get to school this morning. Polly was supposed to have had a date with a boy from her church. I couldn't wait to hear about it.

"All right, Polly. I want to hear every detail," I asked when we were alone.

"He was nice. We went to midweek service at church. Afterwards, we went with another couple for burgers at McGee's then he took me home. It was fun. He was nice."

"You said that already. Did he hold your hand or kiss you goodnight?" I needed to hear more than only how nice he was. The dog I petted on the way to school was nice.

"No he didn't kiss me. It was only our first date." Polly wasn't nearly as excited as I expected. She was so low-key that at times it was hard to tell when she was excited or not.

"Did he ask you out again?"

"Did who ask her out again?" Darla quizzed as she caught up with us.

"Polly had a date. So far, all she can say about him was that he was nice. Polly, do you even like him?" I was more excited than Polly, and it was her date.

"I liked him. He's really ni…"

"I know, I know, he's nice," I mocked.

"This conversation is to be continued," Darla said as we reached our class.

Polly smiled on the way to her homeroom, leaving us hanging and disappointed.

"If I'd been on a date, I'd have been more gushy—actually a lot more gushy."

"Oh Jean, you're funny. I'm sure she'll tell us more during noon hour. Oh…wait a minute. I promised Cilla I'd have lunch with them today. Do you mind?"

"Darla, no I don't mind. I'll let you know what I can pull out of Polly later. It's okay." Darla had more time to spend with Cilla and the girls since Coop graduated the year before. Polly and I understood.

"Where's Darla?" Polly's tone hadn't changed.

"She's having lunch with Cilla and the other girls, but she wants to know all about your date too. So go ahead. We'll fill her in later." Polly never responded.

"Hey, is something wrong?"

"Maybe." Polly's brow was knitted like Grandma's.

"Okay, what is it?"

"I overheard my dad and Mom talking this morning about a job in Michigan. He never said he was going to take it. He was only talking about it."

"Oh, Polly, surely he wouldn't give up his sharecropping job and ruin your senior year?"

"I hope not. Changing schools would be hard enough, especially during my senior year. He wouldn't be purposely ruining it. He'd only leave if it would better our family. But I so wanted to graduate with you and my other friends here at Muddy Ox."

I understood that if Polly's dad took another job, he wouldn't do it to be mean. He had a large family to provide for. My brow was now knitted. We avoided the topic of Polly possibly moving the rest of the day. I knew she was silently praying—and so was I.

## Chapter Forty-Four

WORRYING ABOUT MY senior year without Polly took a little bounce out of my step as I walked home. I mindlessly passed the McCrady's house and robotically turned down the gravel lane to home. About mid-ways, I saw Grandma had company.

"Meryl, this is Mrs. Conner and her son Hutcheson." Grandma said as I arrived.

"Hutch—people call me Hutch." The tall, ruggedly handsome, boy up-nodded instead of shaking my hand. I felt a little offended.

"Hi, I'm Meryl," not offering my hand either.

"Mrs. Conner, her husband, and uh…Hutch have moved here from Arkansas. They're rentin' Sid Carson's house next door."

I sat and leaned against the post opposite Hutch.

"We're glad to have a few more pairs of eyes close by," Grandma added.

As I'd suspected, Grandma was still uneasy about us living alone again, even if she felt more confident with me around. She'd discovered that I was afraid of very little, other than conversations about dress and shoe sizes and possibly stinging worms in the cotton patch.

Actually, conversations about shoe and dress sizes could creep up on you the same way as the worms. I'd learned maneuvers to avoid both uncomfortable stings.

"Well, we need to go home. I gotta start supper. It was good to meet you, Meryl. I'm glad to have nice neighbors too, Mrs. Strom," Mrs. Conner said as she stood to leave.

Hutch waved before helping his mother across the road ditch between our houses.

"Meryl and me most always sit a spell here on the porch in the evenings before bedtime. Y'all are welcome to come sit with us after while if you like."

"Sounds nice. We'll do that." Mrs. Conner accepted Grandma's invitation. Hutch gave me another nod before they disappeared inside their house.

"Now, that's a nice young man. Did you see how he helped his mama across the road ditch? A man who's good to his mama will be good to a wife one day."

I shot Grandma a look.

"Well...at least that's what I've always heard. Do you have homework to do while I fix supper?" Grandma asked.

"My last final test was today in English class, but Mrs. Tyree asked us to write a poem for tomorrow anyway. I started one, but it still needs work," I replied.

"Well, it looks like we're havin' company this evenin' I'd get it done, if I was you."

"I thought he was arrogant to just nod instead of

shaking my hand. Didn't you?"

"Well maybe he's shy. Give him the benefit of a doubt," Grandma urged.

Was Grandma trying to matchmake me? Was she also embarrassed that I was seventeen and had never had a date or a boyfriend? Ralph Fredrick's kissed me a couple of times when we played truth or dare. But if that was how a kiss was supposed to feel, I guess I hadn't missed much. Anyway, I never told Grandma about Ralph. It was that insignificant. I never truly had a date or a *real* kiss.

Going over my poem, I wondered again why Mrs. Tyree wanted them. It wasn't for a grade since finals were over. However, it was as much of a challenge as an assignment for me. Since I hadn't met a challenge I could ignore, I was eager to do it.

Grandma was in the swing humming, as soon as supper dishes were done. She began to sing as I came out the screen door. I joined in while dropping next to her on the swing. *"Farther along, we'll know all about it. Farther along, we'll understand why."* Our harmony rode the breeze while the scratchy voice of a cicada tried to sing along but never found its place.

*"We'll understand it all be and by...,"* a rich baritone joined in.

"You sing good son," Grandma complimented Hutch.

"Oh, he sings all the time," Mrs. Conner commented as she appeared behind him.

"Meryl's like a little song bird herself. She sings all time, too." Hutch and I sat in silence while the two discussed us as though we were ghosts.

"Sing us a song Hutch," Grandma didn't hide her fondness of him.

I thought he was going to be shy but after a pause, he sang *Running Bear*, a song about forbidden love between a squaw and a love struck brave. It was like an American Indian version of Romeo and Juliet.

I didn't think Grandma was familiar with the song, but I was. Hutch did well. We applauded, and he blushed. "Okay, Meryl, it's your turn." Grandma had taken over Mama's job of thrusting me into the spotlight. Not being shy at all, I chose *The Wayward Wind*, a song I knew well.

"Child you sing like an angel," Mrs. Conner said when I finished.

"Thank you." For a second, it felt as though Hutch and I were auditioning.

"Meryl's been singin' as long as she could talk. She got it honest. Her mama could sing and play anything she picked up; God rest her soul. Her Daddy sings too."

"Where is Meryl's daddy? I haven't seen anyone around here but you two," Mrs. Conner asked.

"Larson…is working in Florida right now. He sort of comes and goes since his wife passed away, and he brought Meryl here to live with me."

"He sounds a little like my husband. He comes and goes a lot, too," Mrs. Conner added.

## Chapter Forty-Five

GRANDMA AND MRS. Conner continued to chat. Hutch hadn't broken his stare with me, even as I met his gaze. "Ugh…would anyone like some iced tea?" My face was flushed as I stood to make my offer good. When I returned with the tea, Hutch was lying in the grass, looking at the stars. He motioned for me to join him.

"That song was nice," I said. He sat up to take a swig of tea. Lying back down, he again patted the grass for me to join him. If Grandma or his mother thought it inappropriate or unusual that we were lying on the grass together, they never protested or missed a word.

"You know, probably Running Bear and Little White Dove did this very thing under the night sky."

"Did what very thing?"

"Laid in the grass and looked at the stars like we are now."

"You think so?" I teased.

"Yeah, but they didn't have an audience." He grinned.

I giggled. He was lucky Grandma had taken a liking to him, or she would have ordered me back on the porch and insisted I act like a proper lady.

"You sing very well you know?" I said, trying to break another long stare.

"I do okay for an old country boy. You're the one with the voice. Singing is a thing we have in common. Hey, there's the big dipper. Can you find the little one?"

"There it is. It's to the right, above the big one. I can always find the big dipper by finding the three stars in a row," I boasted, having met another challenge.

"Yep—you found it. The three stars in a row are actually the bear's tail. See the bear? Bet we have another thing in common, too."

"And that would be…?" I questioned.

"Bet you can't wait for the day you'll never drag another sack in a cotton field."

"You're right about that. I recently added that to my never list."

"Your never list? What's that?" he asked.

"Oh, it's a list of goals I made for myself. I seem to be adding to it a lot lately."

"Well, I can't wait to hang my cotton sack up for the last time," Hutch said, downing the last of his tea. I offered him more, but he declined.

"I sure don't plan to pick cotton my entire life. After graduation, I'll move away, get a good job, or maybe go to college, or…"

"Or get married and have some kids?" He was staring again.

"Marriage and—for sure, kids, are far into my future. Yes, I'd like to get married and have a family—someday. But I can't even think of that until after high school."

"Why, there's girls all over this place who are married at your age and already have a house full of kids. They seem to be happy and doing all right," he argued.

"And I'm happy for them—if they're happy. But I want more. What do you want? Did you graduate high school?"

"No I got dragged around so much I dropped out of school. But I'm going to get my GED someday."

"So, if you don't want to work in the cotton fields forever. What's your plan?"

"Well, I…I…" Hutch began but Grandma interrupted.

"Meryl, you'd better be careful to not get grass stains on that skirt."

I figured Grandma would eventually find a problem with me lying in the grass, but it took her longer than I expected to come up with one.

"Okay, I'll be careful," I answered vaguely since she didn't actually tell me to get up.

"You sure can get fired up quick." The bewildered look on Hutch's face said I might have been a little too pointed with my comments.

"I'm sorry. I didn't mean to…"

"Guess we just had our first argument."

"Maybe, but I'd call it simply a difference of opinions," I answered a little softer.

"Call it what you want, but it felt a lot like an argument." He scratched his head, obviously feeling he'd struck a nerve in me.

"Although you're right about me not wanting to pick cotton forever, on the other hand, I've actually welcomed the opportunity to get to do it for now," I added.

"I've heard working in a cotton field called a lot of things, but an opportunity has never been one of them." Hutch smiled.

"Grandma lets me keep all the money I make in the field to buy my school clothes and books. It's an opportunity because I can be independent. I can chose my own clothes and—things."

"I see. So your dad doesn't do that for you? You know, help with school clothes?"

"Daddy's gone most of the time. He has his way of living, and Grandma and I have ours."

"So you don't get along with your Daddy?" Hutch asked.

"Oh, we get along fine. I love Daddy, and he's crazy about me."

"Then why is he gone all the time?"

"He has a different way of coping with my mom's death than I have. I'm ok with him being away if he needs to be. Grandma and I do fine—just the two of us."

"How old were you when your mother died?"

"I was thirteen and Daddy was thirty-nine."

"Well, there's another thing we have in common. I was thirteen when my real dad died." He was delighted to find we had more in common.

"Do you like your stepdad?" I asked.

"We do okay. He's not around a lot either. What kind of work does your dad do that he's not around…and works?" Hutch eluded my question.

"Right now, he's working in the sugar cane in Florida. Sometimes he does factory work. He's a really good mechanic, so he can always get jobs doing that."

"There's another thing we have in common. Your dad's a mechanic. I love to do mechanic work. I'm not great at it yet, but I plan to be one day." Hutch grinned.

"So, that's your goal, to be a mechanic?"

"My goal—was to join the Army and get a GED and do something when I got out. But now, maybe I'll put that off a little while."

"Why put it off?"

"Maybe there are a few things I need to tend to before I take that step." Hutch sounded conflicted.

"Oh…like what…?"

"Okay, Hutch, we need to get on home. Meryl's got school in the mornin' and weren't you goin' early to see about that job in Doodlum Switch?"

He almost seemed relieved when his mother interrupted us. Guess I was asking too many questions. He was starting to squirm. But he asked a lot of questions, too.

"That's my cue. Got to go," He turned to help me, but I was already standing.

Hutch and his mother disappeared across the lane as quickly as they had appeared. Grandma gathered the glasses, put them in a pan till morning, and we were soon settled into bed. I lay quietly remembering how Hutch kept looking for things we had in common. "*Looks like we just had our first argument,*" Was he saying he saw more arguments for us in the future? He was nice and—older than the guys in my class. If he's going to put off going into the Army, when does he plan to get his GED?

Oh well, I had my own issues to think about. Wonder what Polly and Darla wrote their poems about? Thoughts of Hutch and my poem dwindled, as my mind and body slipped into slumber.

## Chapter Forty-Six

I WAS NEARLY to the end of the lane on my way to school the next morning before I thought of looking back to see if Hutch's car was in their drive. It wasn't. His mother had mentioned he was going to Doodlum Switch. He must have gotten a very early start.

I was anxious to give my poem to Mrs. Tyree. I knew some kids saw writing poetry as a punishment, but I found it rewarding. Still, I wondered why Mrs. Tyree would give us such an assignment with only one day left of school before chopping season.

Polly and Darla appeared at the east door together. They were laughing so hard they hadn't noticed me waiting for them.

"Hey, you two. What's so funny?"

"Polly was telling me about J.T. York's poem." She could barely talk for giggling.

"Everyone will be rolling if Mrs. Tyree has him read it in class," Polly added.

"Knowing J.T., I can only imagine any poem he'd write would have to be funny. I've never seen a serious bone in his body. What'd he write about?"

"Not what—who—did he write about?" Darla

squealed.

"Who?" I questioned.

"He doesn't use his name, but we'll all know it's about Mr. Vondell," Darla said.

"Oh no. Do you think Mr. Vondell will be offended?" I was sensitive to such.

"I don't know, but the title is *The Bear Who Taught Our Class.*" Polly grinned.

"Yes, it starts, His voice is a growl. His face has a scowl. It was hard not to stare. Was he a teacher or a bear? Then he ended it like, the bear went into hibernation while us kids leave for vacation. Guess J.T. is getting even for being singled out all year."

"Only J.T. could get by with something like that," I added.

"He hasn't gotten by with it, yet. We'll see if Mr. Vondell recognizes himself in the poem and how he reacts if he ever sees a copy of it," Darla said giggling.

"What did you write about Darla?" Polly asked.

"I wrote about learning the piano. What's yours about?"

"Growing up with so many brothers and sisters," Polly said.

"What's your poem about Jean?" They asked in unison.

"My Grandmother. The title is *That Grandmother of Mine.*"

First hour seemed to drag by because we were anxious to get to English class. Finally, we slid into our desks a few minutes before Mrs. Tyree arrived.

"Well, are you ready for school to be out?" Mrs. Tyree questioned.

Laughter, sighs, and moans could be heard across the room. The moans could have been from those who feared they had not done well in their classes, or maybe because the surety of a sharpened hoe and a cotton row awaited most of us.

"You'll be pleased to know that everyone passed this class. Some barely made it. Some did very well. But no one failed. Mrs. Tyree wasn't one to give a grade when it wasn't earned. But she was also known to spend extra time with those who struggled.

The moans and sighs turned to relief and joy. "Just think, depending on how well you did in your other classes you'll be seniors next term. Congratulations," She continued over the murmurs in the room. "I hope you brought your poems. I guess you're wondering why I asked you to write them. No, they won't be graded. Yes, I intend to read every one, but will do it while school breaks for chopping season. I've always felt like poetry is a marriage of one's heart and mind. Your poems will say a lot about you."

"I—I want you to know my poem is not serious," J.T. spoke up.

"That's okay, J.T. I can learn about you, even through humor. Humor is good. Now, will every one please pass their poems forward? Since you've worked so hard all year, you can have the remainder of the hour to talk quietly—quietly," she emphasized.

Those of us who knew about J.T.'s poem were disappointed. He was especially disappointed. The class clown always welcomes the spotlight.

The remainder of the day went quickly. Not needing to stop by my locker, I could walk with Polly and Darla to their buses. I think I might have been disappointed even more than J.T. that Mrs. Tyree didn't read or talk about our poems. As it was, only she and I would know what my poem said. I hadn't shared it with anyone, not even Grandma. I'd have to wait now until the middle of July to get her feedback. Chopping season usually lasted about six weeks. One good thing, Mr. Vondell would probably never know about J.T.'s poem if Mrs. Tyree saw what the others saw.

It was a hot and sticky mid-May. The cotton field would be worse. Still, I was anxious to start making money again. I smiled remembering Hutch's reaction when I said I saw working in the fields as an opportunity. Well, it was for me anyway.

The sputtering of a motor, clearly in need of maintenance, and the squeals of children's voices amid a much louder sound of metal clanging and banging, brought me back to the present. They were back.

It had to be the Boones. That was the same sound show I'd heard last fall when I saw them leaving town. I moved as far off the blacktop as possible, without actually stepping in the road ditch. When they passed by, the mysterious eyes of Army Boone locked with mine. It was as though he had never moved from his place in the bed of that truck the entire time they'd been gone. I dreaded telling Simp, Katty, and Grandma about their return. I imagined Sadie would be pleased.

Had Mr. Chaffin actually allowed them to return to his farm? It sure looked like they were heading back to the same shotgun house they'd lived in before. If that was the case, Mr. Chaffin needn't run for any popularity contests in Muddy Ox in the near future. Knowing Mr. Chaffin's attitude toward trying to please people, I figured he didn't care. His primary concern was getting his crops harvested the least expensive way possible. One couldn't blame him for that. There were many pairs of hands in that Boone family, even if one pair—Army's—didn't produce much work, the others made up for it in the long run. Plus, they wouldn't care about the condition of their living quarters as long as the roof held up to the children climbing on it, and Mrs. Boone's rocking chair didn't fall through the front porch. *Lord, help us.* I could already hear Katty's voice in my head.

I didn't have to be the bearer of bad news. The Simpsons were sitting on the porch with Grandma when I arrived. Before I could say a word, Katty announced, "That Boone bunch is back."

"How did you know?" I was relieved and a little

disappointed not get to share the news.

"Effie Walby just left. She saw 'em earlier at the Big Store stockin' up on supplies. Effie overheard 'em talkin' with Carl Chaffin about that shot gun house they lived in last fall," Katty said disgustedly.

"I can't believe Chaffin let them people come back to work for him," Simp growled.

"Well, who else would live in that run-down-shotgun-shack?" Katty spouted.

Sadie hadn't said a word, but it was obvious she didn't like their comments by the faces she made behind her parents' backs.

"Maybe they won't be as bad this time. The kids are all a year older. Could be they've settled down a bit." Grandma looked for a positive side if there was one.

"Kids that have had the right kind of raisin' might get better, but it's the same two parents raisin' the same litter of hooligans," Katty grumbled.

"One good thing, it's not easy to run down a field row with a hoe in your hands—dangerous too. You cain't get hurt by a cotton sack—'cept for maybe your back and your pride. Fallin' on a sharp hoe can bring some serious hurt." Simp made a good point.

"Hey, Mrs. Strom, Mom wants to know if she can borrow a cup of sugar." Hutch startled me as he suddenly appeared behind me.

"Sorry Meryl. I didn't mean to scare y'all. I forgot to get sugar while I was out lookin' for work today. Mom said to tell you we'll pay you back tomorrow, Mrs. Strom."

"Of course I can loan y'all some sugar. Meryl, can you get Hutch a cup of sugar?"

I reached for the cup, but instead Hutch opened the screen door and followed me into the kitchen. As soon as we were alone, he whispered, "You want to go to the movies with me in Kennett this Saturday night?"

"Grandma has never let me date, yet."

"Well, ask her," he persisted.

"You ask her," I shot back while scooping sugar.

"If she says yes, do you want to go? I want to take you to see 'God's Little Acre.' I heard it was good. Michael Landon, you know, Little Joe Cartwright from Bonanza plays in it. I don't know a lot more about it, but thought you'd like anything he was in."

I was familiar with handsome Michael Landon's character on Bonanza. We'd gone to Lyla Gain's cottage a few times in the evenings to watch it with her on her television. Lyla was Sid Carson's cook and house keeper. Bonanza was one of Grandma's and my favorite programs.

"Yes, I'd like to go if she lets me. But I'd wait until she's alone to ask her if I were you," I whispered back.

"We're gonna go have supper now, Mrs. Strom," Katty's voice blared from the porch. "I still cain't believe Carl Chaffin let that bunch of …I can't even think of a decent word to call them…come back to his farm." Katty grumbled all the way to their house. Simp grunted periodically, while Sadie followed silently.

"Now's my chance," Hutch whispered again.

"Better choose your words carefully," I cautioned.

"Thanks for the sugar, Mrs. Strom. Mom said to tell you we'd like to come over and sit on the porch a while with you and Meryl after supper, if it's okay?"

"We'll be here. You know you're welcome any time."

"Well…uh…okay…uh…see you later then. See you Meryl," Hutch hesitated, then carefully jumped the ditch so as to not spill the sugar. I figured he needed to find a little more courage before approaching Grandma.

"Meryl, surely you don't have another poem to write or some other kind of homework tonight—do you?" Grandma didn't wait for my answer before heading for the kitchen to start our supper. Her banging pots and pans reminded me of the noisy utensils affixed to the sideboards of the Boone's truck as it struggled past me on my walk home. That Army had a way of locking his eyes with mine that made me cringe.

Hey, why was I worrying about the Boones? I had just been asked for my very first date. I wasn't sure what Grandma would say, but as far as chances went, Hutch has an edge since she likes him so well. Time would tell.

"Meryl, did you ever say if you had homework or not?"

"No—no assignments today. Tomorrow is all about

assemblies, awards, and recognitions. I still wonder why Mrs. Tyree wanted the poems. Since we didn't read them in class today, now it'll be six weeks or longer before we find out how we did."

"Well, go on and set the table and put ice in the glasses. We'll get supper over with." I suspected Grandma was now lost in her matchmaking world. She probably hadn't heard a thing I said about the last day of school or my poem. By the way she was rushing with supper, I figured she was more interested in playing cupid later.

"Grandma, I know as Christians we're supposed to love everyone. But it's hard to love people who don't act right and are different," I said once I joined her in the swing after supper.

"Yes, it is," she agreed.

"How can God love the unlovable? Especially if we can't fix them?" I was thinking about the Boones.

"First of all, our job is not to fix people. We're not the Potter. We can't put people on the wheel. That's God's job. Ours is to direct 'em to the Potter and let Him fix 'em."

"Does God love everybody and everything?"

"The Bible gives examples of God lovin' people in spite of themselves. But he doesn't love sin. In fact it says He hates it. We don't have to love or tolerate sin either. We're not required to love people's sinful ways. There's a time when we can help others, and sometimes the only way we can help 'em is to pray and get out of God's way."

"Like when you've tried to fix—I mean help Daddy?"

"Yes, I admit it. I've tried to fix your daddy. But I learned a long time ago God is the only one who can fix him. All I can do as far as Larson's concerned is to pray."

"I don't hear y'all singin' tonight. Thanks for the sugar Mrs. Strom. I'll pay you back tomorrow. Hutch forgot I told him to get sugar while he was out today. I don't know where that boy's mind has been here lately." Mrs. Conner came alone.

"Now, I'm not gonna worry over a cup of sugar. Where is Hutch?"

"He's comin'. I made some peanut butter cookies with the sugar we borrowed. He's waitin' for 'em to come out of the oven and is bringin' a few over for us tonight."

"Well, you can for sure forget about returnin' the sugar since you made the cookies for us. Meryl, why don't you put on a pot of coffee," Grandma directed.

## Chapter Forty-Seven

HUTCH WAS SITTING on the porch, his back against the post when I poked my head out to ask how everyone liked their coffee. Grandma and Mrs. Conner wanted theirs with cream. Hutch and I liked ours black.

"Another thing we have in common," Hutch said quietly as I handed him his coffee before sitting and leaning against the post opposite of him.

"You must have left out pretty early this morning," I said accepting one of his mother's cookies and ignored another remark about our common ground.

"Ya noticed, huh?" He smiled.

"Umm—not really—did you find work?" In my haste to sway the conversation, I revealed that I'd checked out his driveway as I left for school. I didn't want him to think that I was keeping up with his comings or goings.

"I saw you walkin' with two other girls this mornin' in the school yard."

"How did you see me this morning? Were you looking for me?" Now it was his turn to be exposed.

"Well—um—I saw you on my way to Doodlum Switch."

"Really? But Doodlum Switch is in the opposite direction of the school."

"I—had to pick up somethin' at the Big Store first."

"The school is beyond the Big Store," I said, suspecting that he had purposely driven by in search of me. His face turned red.

"Guess I just got turned around. Anyway, I saw you with two other girls."

"Those were my friends, Polly and Darla." Hutch had clearly made it a point to come looking for me. He would have been going out of his way to come past the school to get to the Big Store or Doodlum Switch. And how in the world could anyone get turned around in Muddy Ox? It's not big enough to get lost or turned around in.

"I start Monday mornin' at the Raymond Huff farm on the other side of Doodlum Switch," Hutch added.

"Meryl starts Monday for the Bertram's. She works for 'em every year." Up until then Grandma had been sitting quietly with Mrs. Conner. Obviously, both were eavesdropping.

"I asked Carl Chaffin and Mr. Bertram first. Their fields were closer, but they already had all the hands he needed for now. They said if I'm still around come pickin' time, maybe they'll need me then." I hadn't considered Hutch might not stay for picking season.

"Carl Chaffin has his fields full for sure. He's let a large family from Eastern Kentucky come back and work for him. It's a mom and dad and a whole passel of children. He shares 'em with Asa Bertram in his field a lot," Grandma exclaimed.

"And how many children would be in a passel, Mrs. Strom? Is that who the Simpson's were uh…talking about when I was here earlier?" Hutch had likely heard the term passel before but wanted to tease Grandma.

"I'm not sure how many of anythin' makes a passel. No one knows how many children that family has neither."

"Why don't people simply count 'em?" Mrs. Conner asked the obvious.

"Simp says the children are so rowdy they never stay still long enough to get a good count." Grandma quoted Simp's exaggerated but mostly factual observation.

"Guess I'm glad Chaffin's field was too full to need me then." Hutch laughed.

"Y'all gotta over-look Katty. She speaks her mind regardless. She has a problem with one of that family's sons. He seemed to be a little too fond of Sadie to suit her and Simp when his family worked for Chaffin last fall."

"Sadie's young to have a boy settin' his cap for her, I'd think," Mrs. Conner observed.

"She turned thirteen her last birthday. She seems younger because Katty has always sheltered her so," I added.

"A lot of girls are married by age fourteen," Mrs.

Conner said.

Oh Lord, I didn't want Hutch's mom to get on the topic of girls marrying young and me have to argue Hutch down again.

"Sadie's a young thirteen. Katty likes it that way," Grandma explained.

"Hey Mom, I think Jasper just pulled into the driveway," Hutch announced. He had a good view of their yard from where he was sitting.

"Yes, that's him all right. I'll run on. Mrs. Strom, we'll come and sit with y'all another time. Hutch, stay a while if you like," Mrs. Conner rushed home.

"She knows he'll come lookin' for her if she doesn't go. She probably wanted me to stay until she saw what kind of mood he was in first." Hutch sounded disgusted.

"You don't like your stepfather. It shows." Grandma saw the strain on Hutch's face.

"I don't like how he controls and treats mom sometimes. Hey, Mrs. Strom can I ask you a question?" Now my face became strained.

"Yes." Suspicion lingered in Grandma's voice.

"Can I take Meryl to the movie show Saturday night?" Hutch must have taken her by surprise. She took forever to respond.

"If you take Meryl Jean anywhere, it will be durin' the day. She doesn't go places at night."

"All right, if I'm not workin', can I take her to the

Saturday matinee? If I have to work, can I take her Sunday afternoon?"

"Oh no—she can't go to no show on Sunday. That's the Lord's Day." Grandma was driving a hard bargain, but Hutch was determined.

"All right then—Saturday?"

"You mean you'd skip work to go to the movie show?"

"Not normally, but if she can't go on Sunday, I might have to do it just once."

"If she goes, she'll have to be back before dark. You understand that?"

"Yes ma'am. I'll be certain to have her back before dark."

I felt as though I was on an auction block silently watching the two of them go back and forth over me. However, I was flattered that Hutch fought so hard to persuade Grandma to let me go. Again, he could be thankful that she'd had taken such a liking to him, or the gavel might not have been pounded in his favor.

"Well, I guess she can go if she wants to. Meryl, do you want to go?"

"Yes," I finally got to have a say.

"Okay then. Hutch, why don't you sing us a song before you have to go home?" Grandma put him on the spot, but he obliged with a beautiful rendition of *Teen Angel*. It was obvious Grandma had never heard that song before as she listened soberly.

When Hutch finished singing about a girl who perished because she'd run into a fiery crash to get her boyfriend's high school ring, there was a long silence.

"You sang that real nice, Hutch. The songs of today sure are sad, aren't they?"

"Yes, some of them," Hutch agreed.

"A popular song when Omar and I was a courtin' was, *A Pretty Girl Milkin' Her Cow*.

The words went something like, *this song would have never been wrote if the girl had been milkin' a goat*, but those were different times." Grandma laughed.

"Well, you caught me by surprise, and it was the first song to come to my mind, Mrs. Strom." Hutch teased.

"I think I like *Teen Angel* better, Grandma." I laughed.

"Well, he sang his song real good anyway," Grandma repeated.

"Thank you, Mrs. Strom, and thank you for letting Meryl go to the movies with me. Guess I'll run on home. Got to get to Doodlum Switch again in the mornin'." Hutch reached over, gave my hand a slight squeeze, and was off.

"I tell you. That's a nice boy." Grandma praised Hutch a while longer. I heard her talking, but wasn't tuned in. I was remembering the soft squeeze.

"Makes me think about when your Grandpa Omar came around trying to court me. You're already three years older than I was when Omar and I got married."

"He's only taking me to the movies on a date. I don't have any thoughts of getting married now. You and I have talked about that."

"Oh, I know. And I'm glad your head's on straight about school. Just seein' you and Hutch together brings back memories. That's all."

It was hard to think of Grandma ever being young or being anything but—Grandma. The moon glowed behind the willow tree as the two of us sat quietly.

Grandma started to hum, then added words, *"Amazing Grace; how sweet the sound; that saves a wretch like me; I once was lost but now I'm found…"*

I harmonized with "*was blind; but now I see.*

"I think its bedtime," Grandma stood after the last line of our song.

"Thanks for letting me go to the movies with Hutch."

"I think his mind was set to take you on a date any way he could get me to agree."

"Well, thanks for agreeing." I smiled.

Later, Grandma was crawling into bed as I passed through her room. "Meryl, what's the movie that Hutch is wantin' to take you to see?"

"He said it was called, *God's Little Acre*. It has Michael Landon from Bonanza in it. You know, Little Joe Cartwright? Remember we watched it at Lyla's?"

"That little Joe Cartwright sure is handsome. So it's

a cowboy movie about God?"

"I don't know other than its called *God's Little Acre*."

"That's good that he's taking you to see a movie about God…he's such a…"

"…good boy," I finished her sentence. "Nite Grandma".

I had a hard time getting settled down to sleep. I couldn't believe I was going on a date. Tomorrow couldn't come soon enough for me to tell Polly and Darla my news.

# Chapter Forty-Eight

In case Hutch asked whether I checked to see if his car was in their drive again, I wanted to truthfully tell him I hadn't. It was hard not to look since it was my nature to be curious. I'd left for school in time to tell Polly and Darla about my date before first bell.

I didn't hear a car approaching until the tires crunched the gravel behind me. I was surprised to see Hutch once I turned around. He must have read my mind to see the question mark above my head, by my facial expressions.

"I asked your Grandma if I could take you to school. I figured you might not accept my offer without her approval, even if we have spent a few evenins' together on your porch…and star-gazin' while layin' in the grass in your yard."

"You left out the part about us having an audience of two very attentive older ladies."

"Well, one of them happily agreed I could take you to school today. Gonna get in?" He reached across the car, opened the door, and I slid in.

"You can drive around to the parking lot on the west side of the school and let me out by the bell, if you like. The car drivers park there out of the way of the busses."

"Okay…so are you happy that we're going to the movies?"

"I haven't been to the movies since before we moved to Muddy Ox, before—my mother died. Yes, I'm happy."

"Well, are you happy you're goin' with me? Your Grandma took so long to answer; I was afraid she wasn't gonna let you go."

"It probably had as much to do about her being home alone after dark as about me going to the movies. And yes, I'm happy to be going with you."

He smiled broadly.

"If she'd had somethin' against movie goin', I was prepared to come up with somethin' else—if I had to. I just wanted to take you somewhere."

"That's sweet. Thank you. She questioned me about the movie last night. But she was glad it was a movie about God."

"To be honest, the title is *God's Little Acre*, but I don't know how much it is about God. I just heard it was a good movie."

"Anyway, because God's in the title, she agreed to it."

"The movie starts at one in the afternoon. You think we can leave earlier? We can drive around Kennett a little bit and get to talk without our usual audience."

"Just as long as we're back when she requested, I think Grandma will be okay. If she's said you're a good boy once, she's said it a dozen times."

"And don't you think I'm a good boy, too?"

"Yes, but I don't have to hear it over and over again."

"If it makes you feel better, my mom thinks you're a sweet girl, too. And she loves to hear you sing. So do I."

"Thanks. Tell your mom thanks, too. What time should I tell Grandma we're leaving?"

"Six in the mornin'?" I gasped before I caught him laughing. "Just jokin'—how 'bout ten-thirty?"

"That's more like it." I smiled.

"I just want time to get to know you better, that's all."

"Like I said, I think Grandma won't mind so much about what time we leave, as much as she minds when we get home."

"So six is good?" He laughed and reached across me to open the door again.

"Ten-thirty will do just fine. Thanks for the ride. I gotta' run. See you later." We waved as he drove away. Now, I could tell Polly and Darla that not only did I have a date; I got a ride to school—with a boy.

I think they suspected something by the broad smile across my face. "You look happy. Are you really glad it's the last day of school? Surely not. It'll be six weeks or more before we'll see one another again." Polly's face was sad in contrast to mine.

"No, there is something else going on with her. Let's hear it Jean. What's up?" Darla knew I couldn't be happy about school being out. We three loved school. And, as for me up until now, school was the only social life I had—other than socializing in the cotton field and at church.

"Guess who has a date?" I couldn't hold it in one more minute.

"You? Who with? You mean your Grandma's really going to let you date? Is it someone from your church or someone here at school? Who is it?" Polly and Darla took turns shooting questions. They knew about the short leash Grandma kept me on.

"His name is Hutcheson Rydell—Hutch for short. You all don't know him. He's eighteen. He moved here with his mother and stepdad from West Arkansas. They live next door. He has a car, and he and his mother have been joining Grandma and me on our porch for the last few evenings. Grandma likes him. She really likes him. I've heard over and over about how much she likes him."

"Well, don't you like him, too? And why haven't you told us about him before?" Polly pouted.

"Yes, I like him. There wasn't much to tell before now. He asked Grandma last night if he could take me to the movies in Kennett, tomorrow. She said yes, as long as we got home on her time schedule, which is before dark."

"He wants to date you really bad to agree to that," Darla said as the first bell rang.

"We'll talk more during assembly," Polly promised, heading off to her home room. Mr. Vondell dismissed us immediately after roll call to go to assembly.

"I hate that you and Polly don't have telephones, Jean. We'll have to wait six weeks to hear about your date," Darla moaned on our way to the gym. Her father was a minister. A telephone was a necessity for them. She and Coop could talk every night as long as her father didn't need their phone for church business.

"I'm shocked that your Grandma let you go to the movies. I also figured your church would be against it. Our church is," Polly said once the three of us got settled down on the bleachers.

"The movie is about God so Grandma is fine with it. The opportunity has never happened before, so I'm not sure about the church."

As they continued to ask questions about Hutch, I realized how little I knew about him. After all, wasn't that why he wanted to leave earlier; to find out more about one another?

"This is exciting, Jean. I hope you have loads of fun," Darla said as I walked them to their busses.

"I haven't told you this yet. He gave me a ride in his car to school this morning."

"We could have met him?" Darla was disappointed.

"How tall is he? What color hair and eyes does he have?" Now, the normally low key Polly was full of questions.

"Let me think. The top of my head probably comes up to his chin. He has dark hair and—I don't know what color his eyes are. I've never looked at him that closely. Guess I'll find out tomorrow. Remember, I only met him three days ago."

"And he's already asked you out on a date. He really likes you, Jean," Darla gushed.

"We have a few things in common. Like he was thirteen when his dad died, and that was how old I was when I lost my mother. We both love to sing. He sings real well. We love to star-gaze, and we each like our coffee black."

"Sounds like you know a lot after all for only knowing him three days." Polly laughed.

"Guess you can learn a lot while sitting together on the porch and stargazing while lying in the grass together." Yes, I baited them and knew it would make them gasp.

"Wait a minute. You were lying in the grass with him?" They asked in unison. I knew then for sure I had their full attention.

"Not to worry. His mother and Grandma were only a few feet away and within earshot. And believe me—there's not a doubt they were listening."

"Oh," The girls said again in unison.

We hugged each other, then had a group hug, then hugged individually again. Polly and Darla got on their separate busses and waved. I watched them leave until all I could see were two tiny yellow dots in the distance.

Taking one last glance behind me, I thought how quickly the school grounds had become empty and silent. Only the ghosts of laughing children and smiling faces of friends remained.

## Chapter Forty-Nine

"YOU BEST LISTEN to me, Army Boone." The bellow of Katty's angry voice scattered the ghosts and brought me to reality, even though she was a distance away on the sidewalk in front of the Green Fly.

"Don't you be hangin' around our place now that you and your—family are back here in these parts. Sadie, you come with me. We're going home." Katty grabbed Sadie's shoulder, causing her to wince as she pulled her away.

"But Mama," Sadie whined.

"Don't you, but Mama me. And don't you be talkin' to the likes of that boy. There ain't nothin' about that family I want you messin' with. And don't you dare be wantin' him to come around our house again. You're not to have anythin' to do with him or…" The rest of Katty's speech became muffled and faded in the distance. Her feet pounded the ground and her head bobbed as though it was loosened from her neck. Sadie was probably lectured their entire way home.

Army didn't say a word, nor did he move from the stump he was perched on near the entrance of the Green Fly Diner. Again, his eyes found mine as I passed. I tried to break his stare, but it was as though his eyes had me locked within their power. Finally, I was able to turn my head and loosen his spell. An eerie feeling crept over me as I walked faster and faster until I was all but running to get home. Katty and Sadie were leaving our yard as I turned down our lane. Grandma waited in the swing when she saw me coming.

"What did Army or Sadie or both of them do now?" I asked, assuming that Katty had given Grandma a full report.

"I tell you Sadie don't know what's good for her. You'd think she'd know her mother's temper by now, but she don't act like she cares or is afraid of her a'tall," Grandma huffed.

"So what happened? I couldn't hear except for Katty yelling at Army and fussing at Sadie as they left."

"Evidently, Sadie had slipped away from Katty again while she was payin' her bill. There she was, big as life, talkin' to Army when Katty came out the door of the diner. Of course, Katty had one of her mad fits. No tellin' what she said to that boy," Grandma said shaking her head.

"The only part I could hear was Katty threatening Army if he came around their house again. And of course, she ordered him to stay clear of Sadie," I added.

"Katty said she couldn't hear much of his and Sadie's conversation, but she did hear Army saying something about, "your mama and my mama and the law."

"He said that? Did Katty hear anything Sadie said back to him?"

"No but Katty was mad as a wet hen, thinking that Army was trying to threaten her, in Katty's words, with his pipe-smokin mama."

"Whew! How red was Katty's face this time?"

"Blood red. Of course them trottin' home so fast didn't help. I'm tellin' you, Army's 'pipe-smokin-mama' better bring her entire clan with her if she thinks she's gonna get the best of Katty Simpson," Grandma laughed.

"I was wondering how long it would take them being back, for the problems to start. Hey, did Hutch come and talk to you about me this morning?"

"Yes, he did."

"And…?"

"He asked permission to take you to school. I told him that you'd left early, but he might catch up with you. Did he?"

"Yes. He wants to leave for Kennett at ten-thirty tomorrow."

"What time does that movie start?"

"He said it starts at one o'clock, but he hoped we could ride around Kennett a little bit before it started. Maybe he wants to get a Coke or something before the movie."

"Guess it's okay. Do you want to go that early?"

Grandma asked.

"I already told him yes, if it was all right with you."

"It's fine as long as you're back…"

"…before dark. I know." I laughed.

"How was your last day at school?"

"Sad. I won't get to see Polly and Darla or any of my other friends for at least six weeks. Six weeks seems like forever."

"Just think. After you graduate, you may not see most of them ever again."

"I try not to think about that, but it's true." I put my hand up against my forehead and mocked Scarlett O'Hara in *Gone with the Wind*. "I'll think about that tomorrow."

Grandma looked puzzled. Then it dawned on me; she probably didn't know about *Gone with the Wind* or Scarlett O'Hara. I was certain she'd never read the book. She'd read the Bible and heard it preached many times. However, she'd probably never read a novel in her life. The McCrady girls having the names they had and being named after the *Gone with the Wind* characters held no connection for Grandma. In addition to never reading a novel, I knew for a fact that she'd never stepped foot inside of a movie theater. Her world was so disconnected from the world I knew.

"I was just being dramatic, like an actress." Rather than going into the whole story, I let her think I was being silly. Besides, if I quoted Clark Gable's famous last lines of the movie and she found out they actually cursed in books and on screen, she might change her mind about me going to the movies at all. Some things were to be thought about 'tomorrow' and some things, especially in this situation, were best not to be brought to mind at all.

"Getting in practice for your movie I guess?" she smiled.

"Something like that," I mumbled.

"Hello ladies," Hutch said as he jumped the road ditch between our houses. I welcomed his coming. He arrived in time to help change the subject.

"I thought I'd check to see if you asked your Grandma about us leaving at ten-thirty?" He was talking to me but was looking at Grandma and smiling.

"I did and she's okay with it."

"Good. I'll pick you up right at ten-thirty then."

"What's your mother doing, Hutch? I haven't seen her all day?" Grandma asked.

"She's not feeling well. She has a headache. She gets them pretty often here lately." There was something about Hutch's answer that seemed evasive.

"Hope she gets better. Tell her to let me know if she needs me," Grandma offered.

"I will. Thank you. It looks like it might be going to storm after while. Sometimes a change in the weather will give her headaches. We won't be coming over later if she doesn't get better," Hutch said as he stepped off the porch.

"We won't be out on the porch if it's stormin' either. Even if a good electrical storm does put nitrogen in the ground and pretties up the grass, I don't want to be sittin' out here on the porch during one," Grandma said.

"I'll tell mom what you said Mrs. Strom, and if I don't see you tonight, I'll see you at ten-thirty tomorrow, Meryl." He gave us a wave after reaching his porch.

"Did you pick up on his tone when he was talking about his mother?" I was wondering if Grandma saw or heard the same thing I did.

"Yes, I did. It's true I didn't see his mother outside today, but I did see his stepfather stomp out to his car and drive off in a huff. From the way he slammed the car door before he sped away, I figured they must a had a spat. That coulda had a lot to do with his mother's headache."

"Oh," I said.

"When Hutch came and sat with me after he got back from taking you to school, he said that his mother didn't like his stepfather's rambling ways. I gathered they argued about it often. Hutch said he tries to stay out of it. He confessed him and his stepdad don't see eye to eye a lot a times. That boy sure thinks a lot of you though."

"He told you that?"

"He didn't have to. I can see it. Maybe we should get supper over with in case it storms, and we end up havin' to light an oil lamp to keep from sittin' in the dark."

I sat on the swing for a few minutes after Grandma left for the kitchen. So Hutch comes and talks to her while I'm at school. That was interesting. The wind picked up and limbs of the willow tree swayed harder. Bad weather was surely approaching.

The storm arrived a little before we got supper over with, but luckily our electricity stayed on. Once the kitchen chores were finished, Grandma took to her chair in the living room and began sorting quilt pieces. A few claps of thunder were so loud they shook the windows while bolts of lightning lit the sky. It was frightening.

"It'll be okay," Grandma said when she saw I was anxious about the storm. "A good electrical storm is good for the soil. The grass will sure be pretty and green in the morning. As long as it's not a tornado, I'm not afraid of storms."

"How can you not be a little afraid of storms?" I asked.

"When your uncle Paulie was about three, he was outside one day when there came a sudden hard rain. I guess it was the first time he'd ever been caught out in the rain like that. It scared him so bad he started screamin' and runnin' to the house. Omar and me and his brothers laughed at him. We thought it was funny. My mother, after seein' the fear on Paulie's face scolded us for laughin'. She ran to meet him, sat him on her lap and told him how God sent the rain so the flowers could grow, and the little ducks would have a pond to swim in. When the storm was over she showed him the rainbow and said that it was a sign from God that the storm was over. Her sweet voice calmed him and her patient way of explainin' things took the fear of rain storms right out of Paulie—and me too. My mother was wise," Grandma boasted.

I had to admit her mother's story calmed me too.

Then Grandma shared memories of her and Grandpa Omar's courtship, as she called it. "My mother let Omar, along with my four sister's beaus come courtin' one night. We cleaned the house and fixed food all day. But even though there was a table full of food, we all ate like little birds. Back then, it was customary for a young lady to want her beau to think she hardly ate at all.

"Well, it come time for the men to go out and smoke. Most men smoked pipes or cigars back then. While they were outside, we starvin' girls started grabbin' food with both hands and gobbled it down. Little did we know they were watchin' us through the windows." She threw her head back and laughed."

"What was wrong with eating in front of the men? In your pictures, you and your sisters were all thin. It was your supper, wasn't it?" I was confused.

"People had their own ideas about what made a lady be lady-like in them days. A lady never showed her ankles, never let her face get all sunburned, and ate like a bird."

Hearing her story, I remembered how in *Gone with the Wind*, Mammy fed Scarlet so she wouldn't eat heartily in front of Rhett Butler and the other men. She also laced her corsets so tightly she could barely breathe, much less eat. I realized that Grandma didn't need to read *Gone with the Wind* or about Scarlet O'Hara—she lived it. Once we went to bed, the sound of the soft rain hitting our tin roof lulled me to sleep. If it stormed anymore that night, I slept right through it.

## Chapter Fifty

AFTER TRYING ON everything in my closet several times, I decided on my pleated, rose colored, skirt and white buttoned-down blouse. Hutch arrived precisely at ten-thirty. I'd just powdered my nose when I heard Grandma tell him I was nearly ready. He remained standing in the doorway. As I walked into the kitchen, I heard Grandma try to persuade him to sit several times. But I was sure he didn't want to take away from our date time. Nor did I. She'd have us on the clock once we rolled out of the yard.

It was a little awkward at first. I didn't know if I should sit next to him or stay on my side of the car. He didn't know if he should play the radio or leave it off. We talked about his mother's headache, the storm the night before, and how green the grass was because of the lightning.

He finally broke the ice by telling me I should scoot closer so he could hear me better and then complimented me on my outfit. We chose to leave the radio off for the time being. I slowly slid over next to him. He kept both hands on the steering wheel since he'd promised Grandma he'd drive safely. Her words probably echoed in his head.

"I was going to take you to the movies at Tommie's Drive-Inn until your Grandma said we had to date in the daytime."

"I've heard the girls at school go on about Tommie's. It seems like most of them end up there on date nights; that would have been nice. Right now though, I am happy to have a movie date with you no matter what time of the day it could happen."

"Me too," Hutch took his eyes off the road long enough to give me a wink.

"I used to love to go play on the swings during intermission when I went to the drive-in with my parents." He gave me a surprised look.

"I was a child, when I went to the drive-in with my parents."

"I was wondering," he teased.

"Well, I'm not promising that had we gone to Tommie's, that I wouldn't have wanted to swing during intermission. I might have asked you to give me a push to get me started."

"I'm your guy. I'd a done it—if you'd asked. Hey, have you ever had a donut from Causbie's Bakery? They're the best."

"No, I haven't." I smiled.

"You want one?"

"Depends, will we be getting coffee to go with it?"

"Black of course?" he teased again.

"Of course, wasn't that one of the things we have in common?" By this time, we were more comfortable and most of the awkwardness was gone. We found a picnic bench at the park to enjoy our donuts and coffee.

"This is nice. And yes, these have to be the best donuts I've ever had." They were tasty. Although, I think the magic of a first date made them even better.

"I told you they were good. Hey, this proves it doesn't matter what you do or where you go, it's who you're with that makes it work. The park would be just a park, if I wasn't here with you," Hutch said.

He was right. We were having a fun time just riding up and down the streets of Kennett and eating our donuts in the park.

"So, did your mother really have a headache or was something else wrong?" I caught him off guard. He washed his last bite of donut down and took a deep breath.

"She had an argument with my stepfather. He wants us to leave here already. Mom likes Muddy Ox and where we live in Silver Leaf. She loves your Grandma. And my job is supposed to start Monday."

"Oh…you would be going with them?"

"Honestly, I've been giving that a lot of thought. I eventually want to join the Army, but…right now, I like where I am." His eyes held mine until I blushed and looked away.

"Mom needs me though. My stepdad leaves when

the mood strikes him. She needs me to be there for her when he isn't," he continued.

"Oh…well, y'all are still here. Guess she's decided to stay."

"Yesterday she decided to go and today she decided to stay. Come tomorrow or the next day—who knows?"

"Oh…" I didn't want Hutch to move away. Our friendship had just only begun.

"Anyway, let's talk about you. You have one more year of school—then what?"

"I'm not sure. College maybe. But we don't have money for college. If not college, I'll get a job somewhere. Maybe I'll go back to Illinois or Michigan. My half-brother lives in Michigan. He'd love for me to live closer to him."

"Now, that's new. I didn't know you had a brother. I thought you were an only child."

"Half-brother—he was twenty-two, married, and on his own before I was born. I was raised an only child."

"If you went to college, what would you want to end up doing?"

"Teach, I guess. I've been in the F.T.A program throughout high school."

"What's F.T.A.?" Hutch questioned.

"Future Teachers of America."

"Oh…hey, we better get to the theater," he said checking his watch. "We want to get a good seat and some popcorn—want some?"

"I'd love popcorn if you'd like some. I remember movie popcorn was the best."

"Let's go then. We'll find our seats, and I'll go get our popcorn," Hutch said as he opened the car door for me again.

The line had already formed before we arrived. The closer we got to the marquee; I noticed the pictures on the billboard gave no indication our movie had anything to do with God—except the title.

"I heard it was a good movie. That's all I know," Hutch defended when I brought it to his attention.

He went for popcorn while I waited in our seats. I scanned the packed theatre to see if there was anyone there I knew but recognized no one.

"You sitting here all by yourself, little lady?" Hutch whispered in my ear when he returned with our popcorn and drinks.

"My date is supposed to be back soon, but you can join me if you like," I flirted. Hutch grinned and slid into the seat next to me. The movie began immediately. The first half was interesting, but toward the end I couldn't believe the raciness of that flick. A couple of scenes made me very uncomfortable, especially sitting next to a boy and us seeing the same steamy scenes—at the same time. Hutch never said a word, as if he saw nothing.

Michael Landon played the part of an albino. His character was made up to be anything but handsome.

After about twenty minutes into the movie, Hutch discreetly slipped his arm around my shoulders. I sat frozen but was thrilled. When the scenes became too illicit, I looked away from the screen and made small talk with Hutch. I probably would have tried talking with the person on the other side of me, had I known them. I couldn't have told anyone a word Hutch and I said to one another during our small talk. I was so nervous and embarrassed. I'm not sure if my mind and mouth were even engaged.

We darted out of the theater as soon as the credits began to roll. I presumed that surely Hutch didn't know beforehand about the raciness of that movie. However, I was not about to ask. I wasn't sure I actually wanted to know.

## Chapter Fifty-One

"IT'S STILL EARLY. Let's go to McCormick's. I've heard their food is some of the best in Kennett," Hutch suggested when we reached his car.

I was ready to go anywhere as long as we got away from that movie theatre. The only way God had a part in the plot of that production was that the land owner had promised to give Him the proceeds if oil was found on a particular acre of his farm. Problem was that the man kept moving the acre all throughout the story. He feared the albino, Michael Landon, might luck up on oil and he'd be forced to keep his promise to God. That was the subplot. The actual plot was mostly about how many men could have their way with Darling Jill. Grandma would not have approved.

"Yes, McCormick's…," I quickly agreed. Funny, but a few hours prior, I'd hoped someone I knew would have seen me on my date. At this point, I hoped not a soul saw me watching that movie. McCormick's had a buffet, or you could order from the menu. I think I ordered a hamburger and fries. I couldn't tell you what Hutch ordered.

"Hey Jean." The familiar voice approaching our

table belonged to Cilla Royal.

"Cilla—hi. Hutch, this is Pricilla Royal, better known as Cilla. She's a friend from school." Hutch shook her hand.

"This is my boyfriend, Timmy Bennington," Cilla said.

"Nice to meet you," Hutch shook Timmy's hand.

"Want to join us?" I asked.

"Oh, Jean, we'd love to but we're meeting Tara, Mattie Lynn, Carla, and Patty Ann here with their boyfriends. We're all going to Tommie's later. Want to go with us?"

"Oh…thank you anyway, but we have to leave as soon as we're finished. We have to get back home—before—umm Grandma needs me." I couldn't believe it. Had I not had a curfew, we could have gone to Tommie's with the cool kids.

"Maybe we can do it another time. Maybe even double date?" Cilla said. As if double dating with Cilla and her friends could have really happened. I knew that time would never come, although it sounded good. But Grandma would have never agreed.

"That'd be great. Let's do it sometime," I played along.

"We're going to try to grab a table big enough for everyone. See you later, Jean. It was nice meeting you, Hutch."

"Later," I replied, but she didn't hear me.

"She seems nice," Hutch said after we were alone again.

"Yes, I love Cilla. She's so funny. There's never a dull moment when she's around. We've been in class together since eighth grade." I was glad Cilla had other plans and didn't join us though. I was afraid she might have asked where we'd been. I didn't want to tell anyone I had seen that racy movie.

Briefly, I wondered if Cilla and Timmy were at the movie too, and we hadn't seen one another because it was so dark in there. Then I figured she probably wouldn't have gone to two movies in one day, and they were for sure going to Tommie's.

"Hutch, I want to thank you for today." I think he could sense I didn't enjoy the movie, but I honestly did enjoy being with him. To me, having donuts and coffee at the park together was the nicest part of the day.

"Believe me when I tell you—the pleasure was all mine." I did believe him. Hutch didn't hide that he liked me. I liked him too.

I waved to Cilla and her table full of friends on our way out. Hutch came around and opened the car door for me instead of reaching across the seat. All in all—despite the movie, it was a wonderful first date. I slid next to him this time without his prompting. He turned the radio on but turned it off again. Instead, he sang Elvis songs to me most of the way home.

"Look, that's the family that Katty was so upset

about the other day." I said as we passed by the Boone's shotgun house after we turned onto the gravel road leading to Muddy Ox. The younger ones had resumed their positions on the roof, and Mrs. Boone was rocking and smoking on the porch as usual. Their truck was on jacks, and Mr. Boone's legs and feet extended from under it.

"Which one is the guy Katty thinks is after Sadie?"

"He must not be there, right now. At least I don't see him if he is," I answered as I scanned the yard.

"It's a couple of hours before dark. Have you ever seen the place they call Five Points?" I was amazed at Hutch's knowledge of the area. He knew about places and things I didn't know existed in the almost five years I'd lived in Muddy Ox.

"How is it you know so much about everything around here and about all the places to go and where to eat in Kennett?"

"This is not the first time we've lived in these parts. My stepdad's a rollin' stone like your dad, remember? It's only the first time we happened to move next door to you."

We passed our lane and turned left onto the blacktop by Chaffin's store. After about a mile, he turned left again, onto another gravel road.

"What's Five Points?" I asked.

"It's where five roads intersect. It's rare to find a crossroad with five roads leading from it." It seemed

Hutch was on a mission to show me things I'd never seen, along with extending our date to the last minute. After about four miles of dust and gravel, there it was.

"When I first saw this, I felt like Five Points was like life. There are many choices, and it's up to us to choose the right one," Hutch said thoughtfully.

"Hey, that's deep. I'm impressed."

"Guess I'm feeling philosophical today. You must bring that out in me." He laughed as he made a U-turn and headed home. He parked in his driveway, and we walked hand in hand to where Grandma was waiting in the porch swing.

"Did y'all have fun at the movies?" Grandma asked. We looked at one another. He said yes, and I nodded my head.

"We got donuts and went to the park before the movie. And then, we went to McCormick's afterward. We had a great time. Grandma, the next time we go to Kennett, we have to get a donut at this bakery called Causbie's. You will love them."

"Well, I'm going to go check on mom. If she feels like it, we may see ya'll later. Bye Meryl. Thank you, Mrs. Strom, for lettin' her go with me." Hutch slowly slid his hand over mine as he smiled slightly and left.

## Chapter Fifty-Two

"Y'ALL GOT HOME before I started supper," Grandma remarked.

"That's okay. I'm stuffed. We had donuts in the park, popcorn in the movies, and hamburgers at McCormick's."

"Donuts and hamburgers too?" Grandma asked.

"Yes, and we shared popcorn and a coke at the movies," I repeated.

"I'll rustle up some leftovers for me, then. Oh, by the way, I made strawberry shortcake in case we have visitors again tonight." Grandma smiled.

She stood to go inside but was brought to a halt by the blare of the fire whistle. "Been a while since we heard that—wonder where the fire is? Sounds like it's gettin' closer."

Almost immediately, we heard a ruckus from next door. "Simp run, Hurry. Grab a bucket," a frantic Katty was yelling as she scurried off their porch. "Where's Sadie? Simp, have you seen Sadie? Saaa...deee!"

Suddenly, we saw fire and smoke rolling through the roof of their toilet. I needed a second look to believe that their toilet was actually on fire.

"Mama, Mama," Sadie yelled as she came running through the yard. A relieved Katty held her tightly for a second then shooed her over to the safety of our porch. Simp and Katty furiously dipped water from their rain barrel. I grabbed our bucket to help when suddenly the bucket was snatched from my hand.

"Meryl, you and mom stand back," Daddy yelled while yanking the bucket. By this time, a low-hanging tree branch next to the toilet had burst into flames.

"Daddy, where did you come from?" Blinking again to believe it was him.

"Y'all stay back, I said. Them limbs could fall any minute," Daddy ordered.

"Grab the hose," Darby yelled as soon as he and the other firemen arrived.

"Okay, turn the water on," Obe directed.

This time the tank was filled to the brim. Within minutes, the fire was out and the hose was being rolled back onto its spindle. I hadn't noticed Hutch had also come to help.

Katty and Simp sat on the edge of their porch with Sadie safely tucked between them. Darby appeared with an old rusty coffee can containing the remains of several partially burned rags. "Simp, here's where the fire started. Had coal oil in it, too."

"Darby, who in this world would set fire to a old outhouse?" Simp questioned.

"If not for these rags and can, I'd guess maybe

someone was careless with either a match or cigarette. But this right here says it was no accident," Darby answered.

"None of us smoke so it startin' accidental is out of the question. It's just plain meanness to set a toilet afire," Katty spouted disgustedly.

"What other reason than mischief or meanness could be going on here?" Obe questioned.

"It's suspicious that 'em Boones are back and now so are the fires. There ain't been no fires since last fall—right 'fore that bunch left town," Katty grumbled.

"Have you seen any of 'em around here lately?" Obe asked.

"No, but Katty saw that boy, Army by The Green Fly yesterday. As far as I know, none of 'em have been around here. Sadie, has that Army kid been here and you didn't tell us?" Simp asked since he was reluctant to trust Sadie concerning Army.

"No—he hasn't been here," Sadie blurted.

"What was he sayin' about me and his mama up at the Big Store yesterday, Sadie?"

"Nothing Mama—I mean he was sayin' somethin', but you grabbed me away 'fore he got to finish." Sadie's answer was evasive.

"The town's a buzzin' about 'em bein' back," said Darby.

"Meryl and me saw them at their house, on our way back from the movies today." Hutch spoke up from behind the group.

"But we didn't see Army anywhere," I quickly added.

"You and Meryl back from the movies?" a shocked Daddy asked.

"Daddy, this is Hutch Rydell. He lives next door with his mother and stepfather. Grandma let him take me to the movies today." The toilet fire was out, but I needed to stop another spark before it got any hotter. Daddy was home. So was his hot temper.

"Good to meet you, sir." Hutch extended his hand. Daddy hesitated, but I was relieved when he finally met Hutch with a manly handshake.

"Guess, I oughta get home more often," Daddy said half serious and half joking.

Grandma was quiet. I figured she was waiting to see how things played out.

"We're gonna go put the truck up. Hope we find the culprit soon, Simp. And hope it's not the start of another mess of fires like last year. Glad to see you back, Larson." Daddy greeted and shook hands with Darby and the crew before they left.

"I'd planned to build us a new outhouse. Guess I'll be doin' it now and not later."

"Simp y'all can use our toilet 'til your new one gets built," Grandma said before she left to scrounge up enough leftovers to feed a hungry son.

"Mom, whatever you got in your refrigerator will

do. You know me, I can eat anything." That was the truth. Daddy wasn't picky at all with food. If he was hungry, he'd put most anything in his cast iron belly. He appeared sober, too. I would have hated for him to be drinking when he met Hutch for the first time.

"Thanks for helping us put out the fire, Larson. Y'all go on to your supper. We'll probably have to take you up on that offer of your toilet, Mrs. Strom," Katty said.

"But we won't be usin' it for long. I'll start us one soon as I can."

"Now Simp, I said for you to use it as long as you needed to." Grandma repeated.

"Mom said we might be over later, if the invitation still stands."

"Sounds good, Hutch. I've made a strawberry shortcake. Y'all need to come help us eat it," Grandma offered to Hutch as he was leaving.

"I'm home now, Mom. We won't be needin' help eatin' nothin'," Daddy grumbled as he followed her into the kitchen.

"Oh, Larson, you know I can stir up another cake in a blink if we need one."

Grandma shoved a pone of cornbread into the oven. I peeled potatoes to fry, and we warmed up yesterday's beans. Daddy had a few questions as we busied around.

"How long's our new neighbors been livin' next

door?"

"Just a few weeks now, I think. We only actually got acquainted with them earlier this week though. Meryl, make a pitcher of tea. We'll have coffee later with our cake. How about that Larson? I didn't know you were coming home but baked a cake anyway."

"Mom, you already said why you made the cake. So…how long have you and that boy been datin', Meryl?"

"Today was our first date," I answered sheepishly.

"Larson, I told him right away that she couldn't date at night. He was happy to oblige. He's a nice young man. So polite and good to his mama. I think you'll like him."

"Never mind about me, Meryl, do you like him?"

"And he wants to be a mechanic," I threw that in for good measure before answering Daddy's question. "Yes, I like him. Daddy, you do know I am seventeen now, don't you?"

"Now, he's got to be a good guy if he wants to be a mechanic. And yes, I know how old you are, baby. I was there when you was born," Daddy answered sarcastically.

Grandma and I simultaneously looked to see if Daddy was joking again. Maybe he'd had a drink or two, after all. He was taking my dating Hutch a little too calmly.

## Chapter Fifty-Three

I T WASN'T LONG after supper that Hutch and his mother joined us on the porch. Grandma never brought up Mrs. Conner's headache and surprisingly, no one mentioned my date with Hutch…as of yet. I was glad for a lot of reasons—avoiding questions about that movie being the main one.

Daddy and Hutch hit it off well. Their conversation went from Daddy's job in Florida to Hutch's desire to be an auto mechanic. Daddy also shared some of his Army experiences. I was happy to do more listening than talking during all of that.

"Hutch said all that commotion goin' on over here today was that the Simpson's outhouse caught fire. Well, I never," Mrs. Conner exclaimed. "Who in this world but for mischief, would want to burn down a toilet?"

"Simp and everyone else was wonderin' that same thing. Katty thinks it's the Boones since there was a fire and now they've returned from Kentucky. She don't like 'em. She really don't want their son, Army around Sadie." Grandma's expression said as much as her words. Mrs. Conner nodded as if she understood and agreed.

"Did any of 'em over there do anythin' to rub the Boones the wrong way?" Daddy asked, motioning toward the Simpson's house.

"Katty don't make no bones to Army about not likin' him. She ordered him out of their yard once and had another run-in with him at the Big Store yesterday."

"Well Mom, there you go," Daddy concluded.

"That aint enough to give 'em reason to set fire to their toilet, or cause any of the other suspicious fires we've been havin' if they're the ones doin' it. And to burn our house, too? We sure haven't done anythin' to cause a body to do that," Grandma replied.

"Hmm…well, I hate to leave good company, but I think I'll go to the blacksmith shop. Maybe they'll know more than y'all do about them hillbillies. Some people say if you want to know what's happenin'—ask a woman. Askin' them boys down at the shop could work even better. They seem to know all and see all."

Hutch turned to me after Daddy left. "I like your dad. I think he likes me too. You never said he was coming home."

"I didn't know. We never know when he's coming. I wish he'd stayed here tonight. I guess it doesn't matter though. He'd be getting with his buddies eventually."

"You don't like his—buddies?"

"They're guzzlers. Daddy will probably come back tipsy."

"I picked up on that something was wrong. You

were too quiet," he teased.

"Hutch, I think we need to go home now. My headache's coming back. Y'all can talk again tomorrow," Mrs. Conner said.

Hutch followed his mother's lead and escorted her home after briefly holding my hand. We washed the dishes and went to bed. I knew Grandma would sleep lightly until Daddy's return. He'd managed to set her worry wrinkle in place again.

I lay quietly and replayed the events of the day. I could officially say I'd had my first date. Cilla even ran into us at McCormick's and saw us. Then it hit me. I wasn't nervous for Cilla to see me eat. Neither was I uncomfortable to eat with Hutch. Wait until I tell Polly I got past eating in front of people. Why wasn't I uncomfortable? It must have been because of Hutch. I felt safe to eat in front of him, so I also felt safe in front of Cilla. My mind played a scenario of going to the Green Fly, ordering food, and eating at a table instead of hiding on the back porch. That image was too strong. The old fear was back. I hadn't gotten past it completely—not yet.

I must have been dead tired. I never heard Daddy when he came home. Even his snoring hadn't awakened me. I dressed for church and tip-toed past him on my way to the kitchen.

"What time did Daddy get home?" I whispered as I slid into my chair.

"Around one o'clock. He didn't seem real drunk," Grandma whispered back.

"That's good. Maybe he'll go talk to Asa when he wakes up."

"He keeps saying he's going to. That's Larson though. He does things on his time and not anyone else's," Grandma said as she took a pan of biscuits from the oven.

"True," I agreed while lathering my biscuit with butter.

Once she finished her breakfast Grandma went to ready herself for church. I cleared the table and put our dishes into the pan to soak. Grandma said to leave them and not take a chance on waking Daddy. Also, we needed to be ready when Effie and Jake arrived.

Their arrival came sooner, rather than later. I barely had time to brush my teeth, fix my hair and powder my nose. Of course, Effie saw Daddy's car.

"Was that Larson's car in your yard, Mrs. Strom?" We hadn't reached the end of the lane before Effie's inquiry began.

"Yes, he's home for choppin' season. What have you heard about what they found out about the Simpsons' outhouse catchin' afire?" Grandma changed the subject to throw Effie off track about Daddy. Effie probably had all the facts concerning the fire. Hardly anything got past Effie Walby.

"Well, first of all I couldn't believe a body would

want to burn down a toilet? But it was strange' for an anonymous person to call for the fire truck. Now that was suspicious for sure," Effie added.

"An anonymous person called for the fire truck? I hadn't heard about that." Grandma was surprised.

"Only someone with somethin' to hide wouldn't say who they was on a call like that," Jake grumbled.

"That's what I thought too. They said it sounded like a child, but it could'na been Sadie. The Simpson's don't have a phone," Effie reasoned.

"That's right. Besides, Sadie was on their front porch. I think that's where Katty said they found her," Grandma recalled.

"What I heard was that they couldn't find Sadie at first until she come runnin' from the direction of their front porch." Evidently, Sadie's whereabouts had been up for discussion by Effie knowing every little detail. At least people weren't saying Sadie came from the direction of the outhouse. I was glad to hear that.

"Didn't Mrs. McCrady say who came to use her phone to make the call?" I questioned. A known fact was that if you lived in Silver Leaf and you needed a phone, you could always use Mrs. McCrady's.

"That was another odd thing. She said the call didn't come from her house. So…is Larson goin' to try to work for Asa again?" Effie let the mystery rest and worked her way back to Daddy.

"We'll see. I'm sure he'll try if he can." Grandma's

answer was brief.

"You know Asa's got a new tractor. Does Larson know that?"

By this time, Grandma's patience had worn thin. "Asa aint the only farmer around here, Effie. Even new tractors need things done to them from time to time. If Asa don't need 'im, I'm sure Larson'll find someone who will." Grandma's tone told Effie to drop it. She wasn't hateful—just to the point.

"So you're a senior now, Meryl. Are you goin' to college after you graduate? I've noticed that boy, Hutch sittin' on y'alls porch a lot. I hear he's a nice boy—good to his mama and all. You're seventeen now, ain't ya? A lot of girls are married with a couple of kids by seventeen." Effie finally took a breath. It was clearly my turn to be probed.

"Yes, I'm a senior. I'm not sure about college. I am sure of one thing. I'm not getting married and having kids for a long time—if ever. Yes, Hutch…and his mother come over and sit with Grandma and me occasionally." By duplicating Grandma's tone, I guess I was a little short with her, too. But surely Effie had some business of her own to tend to. She didn't have to dig into everyone else's—especially mine.

"Didn't I see that boy, Hutch…?"

"Effie, I want to get your Dutch Girl quilt pattern, if you don't care. Quiltin' time's about here." Grandma interrupted Effie before she could quiz me any more about Hutch.

"You can get the pattern any time you want. That boy's dad is never home. Do you think…?"

"I'd like to get a pattern for Jacob's ladder, too." Grandma blindsided her again.

"I have a real pretty pattern for Jacob's ladder. I'm makin' a top usin' that pattern already. Come over, and I'll show it to you. You can have both patterns if you want 'em."

Grandma managed to keep the conversation about quilts and patterns going until we arrived at Hayti church. I was relieved. I definitely didn't want Effie to get started about my date with Hutch. Was it possible that Effie hadn't heard about my date? Could that little tidbit of information slipped by her? Probably—or it would have been her first question.

The conversation on the way home was about the song service and the youth.

Jake always had a lot to say about the youth. He and Effie were kind and generous people, but his desire to control things and her need to know everything about everything was to a fault.

"There's Larson, sittin' in your porch swing now. Looks like that boy, Hutch, is with 'im," Effie announced. "Hello Larson. Welcome home," she said as soon as the car stopped.

"Thank y'all for lettin' us ride to church. Effie, I'll be over tomorrow to get your patterns. Y'all have a good afternoon. Bye." Grandma wiggled out of the car as to not give Effie a place to wedge in with more questions, especially ones directed to Daddy.

Hutch and Daddy nodded as the Walby's drove off. I was equally bothered and pleased to see Daddy and Hutch together and so deep in conversation. Hopefully, they were discussing mechanics. However, a part of me feared I might have been the topic of their conversation instead. I politely greeted them but didn't linger before going to change from my church clothes. When I came back into the kitchen Daddy was sitting at the table and Hutch was gone. Daddy's expression was unreadable.

"I see you were talkin' to our neighbor," Grandma remarked as she started dinner.

I found an apron and began washing leftover breakfast dishes.

"How long did you say he's been our neighbor?" Daddy quizzed.

"About three weeks now, but like I said, we haven't been visitin' with 'em that long. I thought I'd fix salmon patties and fried potatoes. We also have that pot of beans left over from yesterday. How's that sound?"

"Mom, you know I'll eat most anythin' that don't eat me first. So…you haven't known the guy very long, but you let him take Meryl to the movie show in Kennett?"

Grandma stopped her cooking to look straight at Daddy. "Now, Larson, first of all, I'm a pretty good judge of character. Second of all, Meryl's seventeen now. Most girls start dating at fifteen and sixteen. Some of 'em are married way younger than that around these parts. Anyway I figured you trusted me to do right by her or you wouldn't have left her here in my care. You, of all people, should know I wouldn't let Meryl do anything I didn't feel good about." Daddy had definitely offended her.

"I'm not saying that mom. It's just in the short time that boy and me was talkin', it's clear he's serious about Meryl."

"Serious." I broke in.

"It's not hard for one man to read another one, Baby," Daddy added.

"I thought y'all might be talking about fixing cars or tractors or something. Anything but me. There's nothing serious about it. We went to the movies—that's all. Did he tell you he was serious about me? Anyway, I only just like him. I really just met him. End of story," I said defensively. I'd never thought of Hutch as a man. He was the boy next door.

"Larson, you don't have to worry. He's never had anything to say about Meryl but good. Why, he's come over in the mornings and sat with me on the swing a couple of times and watched her walk to school. He always talks about how pretty he thinks she is."

"He's came and talked to you about me when I wasn't here, Grandma?"

"Why, yes, there's nothing wrong with that either. One of those times was that mornin' when he asked me if he could drive you to school. He's just a…"

"I know Grandma. I agree. But it's embarrassing for him to talk to you and Daddy about me like I don't have a mind of my own. Daddy, all I'm thinking about is graduating next year. I went to the movies with Hutch. We like to sing together. That's it. Okay?"

"Mom, those salmon patties are sure a smellin' good." Daddy changed the subject with a compliment to Grandma's cooking but was still eyeing me. He dropped the topic of Hutch and me for which I was thankful. However, I feared it wasn't finished.

"Meryl, if you'll get a bowl for the beans, I'll get the cornbread, and we'll be ready to eat."

Salmon or any kind of fish for that matter wasn't to my liking, so I was glad to find a bowl for the beans. I'd be happy to eat just beans and cornbread. I was also glad for Daddy's mouth to be full so he couldn't talk anymore about Hutch and me.

"That was good, mom," Daddy said as he pushed back from the table. "I sure have missed your cookin'. I think I'll run by and see Asa now. By the way, 'em fellas at the blacksmith shop didn't have nothin' good to say about that Boone bunch neither. They also thought it suspicious that they're back and so are the fires. 'Course, no one has any proof of anythin'—yet. I'll be home later."

"Son, don't stay out late, especially if Asa has work for you. He'll probably want you to start early…"

"I won't. I'll probably be home in time for supper—maybe." Daddy was out the door before Grandma could give him any more argument.

## Chapter Fifty-Four

WE CLEANED THE kitchen in silence. After putting the last pot away, Grandma left for her Sunday nap. Finding it difficult sometimes to sleep during the day, even on a Sunday afternoon, I opted to work on another skit for church. Hutch's car was backing out of their driveway as I plopped into the swing. He and his mother headed toward Doodlum Switch. Sometime later, I had been so absorbed in my skit that I didn't see Daddy's car approaching. Instead of pulling into the driveway, he stopped on the lane even with the porch. Someone was in the back seat.

"Hey Baby, come get in the car. I've been telling Gullet here about your cookin'. I want you to cook us a chicken dinner." Daddy must have been drinking the entire two hours he'd been gone. His eyes were blood red.

"Let me tell Grandma first, Okay?" I knew she would object.

"Naw…she's probably asleep, don't wake her up." Bet Daddy knew she'd object also.

"But Daddy, if she wakes and I'm gone, she'll be worried."

"I said come on and don't wake her up," Daddy said sternly.

"Let me put my notebook in the house first, Okay?"

I quickly scribbled a note to Grandma and tossed it on the kitchen table before getting into the front seat of the car. I wanted to trust Daddy, but this didn't feel right. The stench of liquor was over-powering. Daddy and his friend were clearly drunk. Grandma once described Gullet as a '*woolly-booger*'. To her, that meant smelly, long-haired, unshaven, and unbathed. I agreed with her assessment once I was inside the car.

"Did you talk to Asa yet?" I asked trying to cover my nervousness.

"He wasn't home. Guess they went visitin' since its Sunday."

Daddy turned down the gravel road that Hutch had taken to Five Points the day before. He made a sharp left, barely missing the ditch to take a field row alongside a corn field. The car jolted to a stop inches from a set of rickety steps leading to the raggedy porch of an unpainted shotgun shack. I followed as they staggered through the ripped screened door and crossed a bare wooden floor into the kitchen. There was a small cook stove, a tiny refrigerator and a wooden table with three cane-bottom chairs.

After pitching a sack of groceries onto the table, Daddy pulled up a chair and dropped down. Gullet lit the gas cook stove for me and grabbed two pint jars from a lone cupboard that angled crookedly on the wall. He plopped heavily into a chair across from Daddy.

"Go 'head, baby, rustle us up a chicken dinner," Daddy said pouring whiskey from a pint he slipped from his pocket for the two of them. "Gullet, my little girl here can cook up a storm, just like her grandma."

I spooned several scoops of lard into a cast-iron skillet to heat and found a sharp butcher knife for cutting up the chicken as I'd seen Grandma do many times.

"She's pretty and knows how to cut up a chicken too, Larson?" Gullet slurred.

"Yeah, she does. After dinner, I'll have her sing for us. She can sing as good or better than any of 'em you hear on the radio these days."

I knew Daddy was showing me off—his pride and joy. And, he would have snapped the neck of anyone he thought had inappropriate intentions toward me, but I cringed to hear the drunken Gullet call me pretty.

"Meryl—Meryl Jean Strom, you come on out here," A desperate voice yelled from outside. I peeked through the dirty window and saw Grandma walking so fast she kicked up a trail of dust behind her. By the time she reached the steps, she was completely out of breath.

"Meryl, come on. Come on right now," Grandma panted from beyond the screen door.

"Mom, she's frying up a chicken dinner for Gullet and me. I was tellin' Gul…"

## MERYL JEAN ANOTHER WHIRLWIND

"No she aint! She aint cookin' dinner for either of you. Meryl, put that knife down and come on home with me—now."

"Now Mom, I told Gullet how good you taught her to cook."

"Larson, Meryl's coming with me. Y'all are drinkin,' and this is no place fittin' for her. Meryl, come on. Simp's waitin' for us at the end of the field road."

Daddy wanted to argue his case more but decided against it. I dropped the knife, reminding them that the burner was still on, and followed Grandma to where Simp was waiting. They'd have to finish cooking their own chicken dinner. She had Simp park far enough away to avoid a confrontation had Daddy tried to have one. I'd never seen Grandma so mad. She waited until we reached the car before speaking. Her voice shook. Her pale lips quivered.

"Meryl, what on earth were you thinkin' to go with them? You knew they were drinkin."

"He didn't give me a choice, Grandma. You know how Daddy does," I argued.

"Why didn't you wake me up?"

"He wouldn't let me. I barely had time to scribble that note. Daddy didn't know I did that. He's going to be mad when he comes home."

"I don't care. He can get mad all he wants. I'll not let him take you off to be a cook for a couple of drunkards—daddy or no daddy."

"Grandma, I didn't want to go. But he made me."

"Well, I won't have it. I just won't have it."

"Mrs. Strom, don't blame Meryl. You know she's right. She had to go if Larson made her. You know how he is," Simp came to my defense.

"Larson and me are sure goin' to have it out when he comes home."

"You'd better be careful, Mrs. Strom. You know he's got a mean temper."

"I know Simp, but this cain't happen. I'm gonna protect Meryl no matter what."

Grandma's jaw was set, and her brown eyes were snapping. At that moment, I believe she would have fought a bear or Daddy—if that was what it took.

It was past nine that evening when Daddy came home. Grandma and I were sitting on the porch. I was glad Hutch and his mother hadn't come to visit. Matter of fact, his car was still not in their driveway. Daddy staggered onto the porch but didn't linger.

"I'm going to bed. Got to get up early in the mornin'." Neither of us said a word as he walked past us to his bed.

Although Grandma didn't confront him then, I knew she would when she felt the opportunity was there. We gave Daddy time to fall asleep before going to bed ourselves. A clap of thunder sounded in the distance as we stood to go inside. More rain meant no work in the fields for me tomorrow. But it also gave

Daddy longer to sober up before approaching Asa for a job.

"Hoo—Hoo," screeched a hoot owl as Grandma reached for the door. She scowled at him with the expression she'd held for Daddy all evening. His wings flapped in the wind as he flew away. Daddy probably did himself a favor by going to bed. Even his strong will might not have been enough to match the determination of my Grandma.

## Chapter Fifty-Five

"It don't matter, Larson," Grandma argued as I entered the kitchen come morning.

"Mom, there wasn't nothin' wrong with me takin' my own daughter to Gullet's for her to fix us a meal. I am proud how good she can cook now, and I wanted to show her off. Meryl, did you feel like you were in danger?" Daddy asked as I mutely slid into a chair.

"You don't see it as doin' nothin' wrong, Larson?" Grandma ignored his question to me. I was surprised how well she was holding her ground.

"Look, she's still my little girl, and I can take her with me to a friend's place if I want to," Daddy added with a little edge to his voice.

"You're right on one count but wrong on the others," Grandma said placing her hands palm down on the table and meeting Daddy's eyes. His jaw was twitching, a sign of his anger and frustration as Grandma continued.

"Yes, she's your daughter but she ain't no little girl no more. She's nearly grown. Remember, you left her with me to raise her as right as I know how. The way I see it, she had no business over at that house with two drunks even if one of them was her daddy." I'd never heard Grandma talk to Daddy or anyone else that boldly. She was so mad her lips had paled again.

Daddy's face reddened, his fists clinched, and his biceps pulsed. I half expected him to turn the table over in a rage. Instead, it was as though—if he had any—his better judgment kicked in. He released his hands and the color returned to his white knuckles.

"So you're sayin' I can't take my daughter where ever and whenever I want?"

"Yes, Larson, I am. Meryl's well thought of in this town. People love and respect her. You cain't ruin her reputation by takin' her places no respectful girl should go. Ain't that why you brought her to me 'cause you realized you'd started to do that? Weren't you takin' her to sing in them honky-tonks in Illinois after Edna died?" Grandma's voice was a bit softer as she pricked a nerve in Daddy at the mention of Mama's name.

"She had those fellas' in those joints cryin' like babies," Daddy boasted.

"I'm sure she did. God has given your daughter a beautiful voice. But that Godly gift nor your sweet little daughter don't belong in any honky-tonk or a drunkard's den. You know I'm right. You can take her where you want as long as it's decent with decent people."

"Baby, were you afraid to be with me and Gullet?" I guessed Daddy was hoping I would refute Grandma's protest and get him at least part of the way out of hot water.

"I wasn't really afraid, Daddy, like I wasn't really afraid when I was with you in the taverns. But I didn't want to be in either of those places. It didn't feel right. I love being with you—just not in places like that," I answered meekly.

The muscles in his arms and his jaws flinched again. I hadn't said what he wanted to hear. However, he saw he was fighting a losing battle. Rather than take his case any farther, he sidestepped the situation as usual and changed the subject.

"Guess, it's a good thing it rained last night. Asa won't be busy in his field this mornin'. Is breakfast 'bout ready? Think I'll go talk to him right after we eat."

Daddy knew this would put Grandma back into her nurturing roll and calm her bristles. History was made that morning. Daddy saw how far his usually passive mother would go to protect me—even if it was him she had to battle.

I watched the tires on Daddy's car throw mud and gravel when he drove away as though they were spitting the last angry words that earlier he had to silently surrender.

Surely, Asa would need Daddy somewhere. Like Grandma had said, even new tractors needed servicing—sometimes. The kitchen felt different after Grandma's clash with Daddy that morning. Grandma even looked different. I think she was proud to have stood her ground. She almost looked taller as if her backbone had gotten stronger and her countenance was one of peace.

"You were amazing Grandma. I've never seen you so mad or determined. I also have never seen you walk so fast as you did yesterday in that field road leaving Gullet's house. You were sure huffing and puffing down that dirt path."

"I don't think I can remember when I've moved that fast myself. It was madness mixed with fear that gave me the power to do it. I've never been any madder than I was when Effie told me she saw you get in the car with your Daddy and that—that Gullet."

Oh no—Effie saw me drive away with Daddy and Gullet. That would be another topic of gossip in whatever crowd she was a part of until something bigger came along.

"Is Gullet really his name? Who would name their kid Gullet?" I had to ask. The question had bothered me for some time.

"No, his name is Stanley. I knew his mother well. She died givin' birth to her tenth child when Gullet was only two years old. Rumor was, Gullet, uh…Stanley, had to be watched continuously as a child 'cause he'd put anythin' and everythin' in his mouth. His dad said he was like an old turkey and didn't care what he put down his 'gullet'. After that, everyone started calling him

Gullet, and the name stuck. People were prone to saddle their children with nicknames back in the day."

"Well, it might be cute when they're little, but it's hard to take a grown man named Gullet very seriously. If and when I have a child I'm not going to let anyone give him or her a nickname—for sure not one like that."

I'd no sooner spoken those words than Hutch pecked on the screen, and Grandma bid him in. "Did I just hear you say you planned to have a child one day?"

"Not anytime soon, but if I do, I don't want my child to have a silly nickname."

"Well—Hutch is my nickname."

"That's part of your name—Hutcheson. We're talking about Gullet. Grandma said people gave him that nickname as a child, and it's stuck. Gullet is a pitiful nickname."

"My stepdad said he heard that he was called that because it didn't make him any difference how strong the whiskey was; he would throw it down his gullet anyway."

"Just think, would you want a banker, a lawyer, a teacher—a president, named Gullet?" I exclaimed.

"That's really stretching it—President Gullet?" Hutch couldn't resist teasing me.

"Hey Hutch, what are you up to this mornin'? Guess you couldn't work neither 'cause of the rain?" Grandma knew I was getting aggravated, so she broke in.

"Not up to much, Mrs. Strom. Meryl, can we talk?" Hutch's expression changed.

"Okay," I answered but stood in place.

"I mean, can I talk to you in private?"

"Oh…Uh…y'all can go out onto the swing. Don't mind me; I'll get the kitchen cleaned up," Grandma said, as she shooed us out the door.

I followed him to the swing. Grandma made enough noise with the dishes and pots and pans that hopefully our talk would remain private.

"What's wrong? You look serious."

"I'll just get to the point. We're moving to Arizona. My stepdad has family there and prospects of a job. I need to go to look out for Mom. Meryl…she needs me."

"Arizona? That's—that's a long way." I'd only been north as far as Michigan and south as far as Florida. I'd never been west of Lake City, Arkansas where my mother's side of the family lived. I had no idea how far Arizona was, but it seemed a universe away.

"Yes, it is. It's really far. It's sure too far from here—from you."

"Well…" I stumbled for words.

"Meryl, marry me and go with us."

A loud crash came from the kitchen. "Sorry, I dropped the iron skillet. Like I said, don't mind me. Everything's okay. Y'all Go on with your talking." If I'd had any doubts about Grandma's eavesdropping, my doubts were confirmed.

"Marry you? Hutch, I've got another year of high school. I'm only seventeen. I've, I've—I've…got to see what Mrs. Tyree thought about my poem." I was reaching for excuses. Giving my poem precedence was only greater proof of my immaturity.

"Your poem?" Hutch was totally confused.

"Never mind about the poem. Hutch, you're a sweet guy, but I'm not ready for marriage. I've only had one date, and that was you. I don't know what I want to do after I graduate. I don't even know what I want to do after supper tonight."

"Marry me, and we will figure it out together."

"Hutch, I really, really like you, but I have so many things I've never done yet. I haven't traveled anywhere other than when we followed Daddy from job to job or visited family. I've never had a job other than in the cotton patch. I've never had a second date or a—first real kiss." At that point, I realized I had composed an entire new list of 'nevers'. Only these 'nevers' were more in the category of expectations than dreads.

I was so floored by Hutch's marriage proposal that I hadn't noticed Daddy pulling into the driveway. His foot was on the first step as Grandma opened the screen door to meet him on the porch. I don't know if I felt rescued or invaded by the two of them.

"Asa told me I could start today if I wanted. He needs the oil changed in his tractor and his other equipment serviced before the next plowing. I think I'll grab a little nap before dinner and then go."

Grandma gave a sigh of relief. "That's good news, son. I feared Asa might not need you this year with him already havin' a field full of help.

"None of 'em knows a thing about mechanics. 'Sides, Asa and me go way back, Mom."

It was as though they'd forgotten that Hutch and I were still there—until they turned and saw us sitting silently in the swing staring at them.

"Uh…Larson, let's go inside and let Meryl and Hutch finish talking. Does your hair need trimmin' or maybe the hair in your ears? Do you need any clothes washed?"

"Mom, I'll be gettin' grease all over everythin' anyway. What I have on now will do fine. And no, I think the hair in my ears is okay. So Hutch, where'd you say you're workin'?" Daddy dragged up a chair and lit a cigarette. Grandma's hint flew right over his head.

Hutch stood. His face had fallen, and his shoulders were slumped. I definitely wasn't prepared for what came next. "I guess I won't be working around here after all, Mr. Strom. It seems we'll be headed to Arizona as soon as my mom can finish packin'. I was really hoping to get to stay around a little longer but—well—guess it's not meant to be."

I stood to tell him good-bye. Before I knew what happened, he bent and kissed me right in front of Grandma, Daddy, and—God. Nearly every emotion in existence ran through me at that moment. I feared what

Daddy would say or do, embarrassed for Grandma to witness it—and thrilled to have had my first real kiss.

"It's been a pleasure to know you Mrs. and Mr. Strom," Hutch said, his eyes remained locked with mine. "Maybe I'll be back in these parts again someday. Meryl, guess you can cross that last never of yours off your new list now."

My heart was still pounding as I watched him jump the road ditch for the last time. I had mixed feelings. I really cared for Hutch. He obviously thought he loved me. Had our time together been at a different time in my life, I might have given him the answer he wanted. But at that moment, I'd given him the only answer I could.

Daddy took his nap. Grandma absentmindedly wiped the already cleaned kitchen table again. "I think I'll rest a while too and catch up on some Bible reading." Grandma was clearly disappointed that I'd closed the door with Hutch. She probably wished I'd at least left it cracked a little.

I stood by the kitchen window and inched back the curtain to watch Hutch leaving with his family. He paused to glance toward our house before slamming his trunk shut. His car trailed behind his parent's until it was a blur—then disappeared completely. I felt conflicted. Was I feeling remorse, anxiety, emptiness, or closure? I couldn't decide. All I positively knew, was a small part of my heart went with him.

## Chapter Fifty-Six

I WAS STILL staring through the window pane when I heard Katty's startling scream, "Simp, Simp, grab a bucket. Sadie—where's Sadie?" Her shrill voice cut like a sharpened hoe blade into my moment of confliction and confusion. I ran to the porch to see what was happening.

"Mama, Mama," Sadie cried as she burst into Katty's arms.

"Meryl, tell your Daddy to come help. It's the Simpson's house that's afire this time," Grandma yelled as she ran past me toward Simp and Katty's.

The whistle grew louder as the fire truck approached on the same gravel road that had carried Hutch and his family away only moments before. Daddy jumped to his feet, grabbed our water bucket, and raced out the door. I joined Grandma, Katty, and Sadie who were now standing at the edge of our yard.

The blaze was quickly extinguished. Several of the men huddled to discuss the cause. We four ladies inched closer to hear. "It melted the asphalt siding off the back of the house and scorched some of the wood but that's all. It should be an easy fix, Simp. Glad we got it out when we did," Darby said, joining their huddle. He had something in his hands.

"What'd ya' find, Darby?" Katty asked as she broke into the huddle.

"It looks like pieces of an old nail keg. What's left of a leg and bib of some overalls are still in it. And it smells like coal oil. Simp, is this your keg? I think here's where it started."

"No. I never seen that nail keg before. I buy my nails by the box. I bought a box of 'em last week at the Big Store to fix the chicken pen. I'd never buy nails by the keg lessen I was a buildin' somethin' big like a house or a barn maybe."

"Simp, this helpin' y'all put out fires is gettin' to be a habit." Daddy joked. "Here's the bottom ring and some more pieces of that keg?" Daddy did a little investigating on his own.

"There's writin' 'on some of these pieces," Obe announced as he joined the huddle with more parts of the keg.

"What's it say?" Simp probed.

"It's scorched pretty bad. But maybe I can make it out. Har…t…ck." Darby said.

"Har…t…ck?" Katty muttered.

"Gen…ore?" Maybe General…General ore…General Store? Obe's conclusion was more of a question than an answer.

"t…ck…t…ck…" Simp read.

"Kentucky," Daddy shouted.

"That's it. The last word's Kentucky. It says General Store and Kentucky. But what's Har?" Darby asked.

"Harlan, Kentucky," Katty groaned. "I know about Harlan, Kentucky. My mama was from there, least that's what I was always told."

"Your kin come from Kentucky, Katty?" a puzzled Grandma asked.

"I never knew my mama since her and my twin died while she was birthin' us."

"Katty, you were born in Kentucky?" I was surprised since she loathed the Boones and seemed to equally loathe Kentucky because they came from there.

"Yes, but I don't like to talk about it," Katty confessed.

"What's so wrong with Kentucky?" Sadie asked.

"Nothin's wrong with Kentucky. Kentucky's all right. It just holds bad memories for me—that's all. Them Boones being from there brought me a lot a bad memories."

"Well, I'm thinking this sure points to them. They're the only ones 'round these parts that has a connection to Kentucky; 'cept for what we now know about Katty. And we know she wouldn't set her own house afire," Darby said.

"There ain't been any suspicious fires around here since before they left last fall—right, Darby?"

"That's right, Simp," Darby agreed.

"Now they're back and so's the fires. These last two was aginst us," Katty added.

"First our toilet and now our house. They sure don't like us for some reason," Simp concluded.

"I'll go with y'all to Clete's office and tell him what we've found here. It's the Sheriff's place to investigate this now. I'm jest a volunteer fireman."

"You're right, Darby. It's the law's job to talk to those gun-packing Boones," Simp agreed.

"Sadie, you stay here with Mrs. Strom," Katty ordered.

"I wanna' go too," Sadie protested. Katty and Simp gave in to her, as always. They left following Darby toward Clete's office. All the rest of us could do now was to wait.

After going home, Grandma and I took to the porch swing. Daddy pulled up a chair and reached for another smoke. With the excitement of the fire over, the memory of Hutch's leaving returned and with it, an ache in a place of my heart I never knew existed.

"The Conner's and Hutch sure left in a hurry," Grandma said sadly.

"He said his stepdad had family in Arizona and a job prospect there," I said softly.

"I didn't know you two were that close." Daddy was probably questioning the kiss.

"We were friends. He—he just kissed me goodbye," I downplayed the scene.

"It sounded to me like you might have been more than just friends. Didn't he ask you to marry him and go away with him?" Grandma unintentionally revealed she'd been listening.

"I thought you were too busy cleaning the kitchen to hear anything we said."

Grandma started to fidget, and Daddy nervously cleared his throat. "He did what? He asked you to marry him and wanted to take you to Arizona? Why you're too young to be thinkin' about marriage."

"That's what I told him. I really liked Hutch, but I'm not thinking about marriage now."

"You don't need to be marryin' at seventeen years old," Daddy repeated.

Grandma started to debate the marrying age again, but I interrupted. "Well, he's gone, and I'm still here. So that's that." I wanted to stop talking about it. I was struggling with my own conflicting emotions.

Trying one of Daddy's tactics when things got sticky, I changed the subject. "I'm glad you're getting to work for Mr. Bertram. Daddy, that's good. I wonder how Clete, I mean Mr. Oller will feel about confronting the Boones?" There, they had two subjects. Surely they'd latch on to one of them.

"I bet Hutch only went out of loyalty to his mother. I tell you, that boy loves his mama." Grandma wasn't about to drop it, so I used another of Daddy's tactics—I left.

Stretching across my bed, I tried to relive the kiss. It happened so quickly, and I was stunned. One thing for sure, it was more than just a 'truth or dare' kiss.

I didn't remember falling asleep or how long I'd slept. If I'd had a dream, I couldn't remember that either.

*"Meryl…"* I was startled awake.

Rising to my knees, I peered through the window above my bed. Was Hutch back? Was he outside my window? It sounded like his voice. I stepped onto the front porch and looked toward their house. Their driveway was empty. It must have been a dream, but it sure sounded real. I curled back down on the bed.

I knew I'd made the right decision. It wasn't about Hutch. There was nothing wrong with him. It was me. I was too young, too immature, and actually too self-centered for a serious relationship. My goal was a high school diploma and a life beyond what either of my parents had settled for. I was not ready for marriage. Hutch didn't know it, but I did him a big favor by saying, "no."

*"Maybe I'll be back to these parts again someday."* That's what he said before he left. I reached for my diary. Reading the list of new anticipated 'nevers' that I'd shared with Hutch earlier, I slowly drew a line to cross off the last one—*I've never had a real kiss.*

## Chapter Fifty-Seven

"CLETE BETTER MAKE it clear to that bunch to stay away from us. I won't be threatened by the likes of them. That's for sure," I heard Katty's angry threat.

Katty and Simp had returned. I put my diary aside and rejoined the group on the porch.

"That must have been some meetin' with Clete Oller. Y'all been gone a long time," Grandma said.

"We stopped by the Big Store to pick up a couple of locks for the doors. Whoever it is that has it in for us, Boones or otherwise, may try to get inside the house to pull their next tricks. They'll need a crowbar to get past these," Simp dangled the over-sized locks.

"Well, tell us. What happened?" Grandma asked.

"Don't know yet—Clete said he'd go talk to 'em and get back to us. He was drivin' away as we left." Katty's nature wasn't to let others fight her battles. I suspected if she'd had her way, she would have personally confronted the Boones.

"Y'all can trust Clete. He'll get to the bottom of this." Clete had gotten Daddy out of some sticky situations before. Daddy spoke from experience.

"Well, I don't know what in the world they have it

in for us about. Yes, I ran that Army kid off that day, but I'd be willing to say I ain't the only one in these parts that don't want that hooligan hangin' around." Katty was right. Army had a sneaky way about him that put people on edge. Actually, he was more than sneaky—he was almost evil.

As if on cue, the sun's glare on the red light atop Clete's patrol car preceded his arrival as it turned onto our lane and stopped even with the porch. "Y'all best stay here in the car 'till I say you to get out," Clete said to the pair in the back seat. After he stepped away, we saw his passengers were Army Boone and his mother.

"That sure didn't take long," Katty said, peering around Clete to make eye contact with her offenders. "I cain't believe you brung 'em to us though. I don't want nothin' to do with that…that bunch a…," she began.

"Hold on Katty. I told ya he'd get to the bottom of it. Let Clete talk," Daddy urged.

"Wasn't real hard, Larson. They wasn't hidin'. I cain't take a lot of credit. I persuaded Mrs. Boone and Army to come and tell y'all what they told me. By the way, her name is Zettie. Her husband's name is Orville, just so you know.

"They were gonna try to be closed-mouthed about everythin'. But when I showed 'em what was left of the nail keg and pointed out that it was clearly from Kentucky, they were more cooperative."

"Clete, I don't like 'em, and I don't care to

know 'em by their first names neither," Katty said in her loud whisper. Mrs. Boone looked at Katty in a way that left no doubt that she'd heard.

"Katty, you don't have to like 'em but you need to hear what they got to say. Zettie, here, 'fessed up purty dern quick when she saw I was about to take her kid to jail."

"So it was Army then?" Simp asked.

"Like I said, y'all need to hear his mama's story," Clete repeated.

"All right, let's hear it," Katty grumped.

Clete led the pair from his car. Grandma sent Daddy and me for three more kitchen chairs, which were set in the yard to keep a distance between them and the Simpsons. When Katty gave her a look of disgust, Grandma reminded her that it didn't matter about how different the Boones were; we were still the same people and it wasn't right to keep company—invited or otherwise, standing in the yard.

Katty huffed in resentment, but the chairs were brought just the same.

"She'll be offerin' em a glass a tea next," Katty grumped to Simp in her loud whisper.

"Can I get y'all something to drink?" Grandma gave Katty another look of disapproval and continued with her offer.

"What made you want to set fire to our home?" Simp barked, getting straight to the point before the

Boone's were even seated. Clete remained standing and on guard.

"…and our toilet?" Katty added.

"I…," Army began as he made eye contact with Sadie, who had yet to speak.

"It was my doins'. I made him do it," a defiant Zettie interrupted.

"Well, I put the keg there and set the fires," Army argued with his mother.

"Shut yer mouth, Army. They're a talkin' jail for you," Zettie warned.

"I don't care, Mama. I'll go to jail for ya if I have to. I ain't scared of 'em or no jail neither," Army sneered and jutted his chin toward our group.

"I said shut yer mouth, Army Boone. Don't say another word," Zettie snapped.

"Why in the world, 'cept for pure meanness would you set a toilet afire—much less a house?" Katty screeched at Army.

"I told ya. Twas me 'at made 'im to do it." Zettie yelled, staring Katty down.

"You…why you pipe-smokin', tobacco-spittin', excuse of a mother." Katty's face reddened and her fists clinched. She was seconds from losing what little control she had.

"Ya had it comin'," Zettie snarled angrily, her jaw jutted as she met Katty's glare.

"Had what comin'? What'd I do to deserve my toilet

and house bein' set afire by the likes of you? Do you have any idea…?"

"Ya kilt her!" Zettie screamed.

Katty flinched as though the wind had been knocked out of her.

"Better get her out'a here, Clete," Simp knew Katty was near exploding.

"Killed who? I ain't never killed nobody in my life. You're a crazy woman." Katty regained her stamina and stood as tall as her five-foot fame would allow.

"Katty never killed nobody. You put your son up to settin' a person's house afire 'cause you have a false claim aginst 'em? What's that teachin' your kid?" Simp yelled.

"Yer little girl was in on it too," Zettie sneered smugly.

Katty dropped her fists and turned to Sadie. "Tell us that's a lie, Sadie," Katty begged.

"Sadie is that true?" Simp's voice cracked.

Katty and Simp dropped to their seats. The look Sadie and Army shared confirmed Sadie's involvement.

"He made me. He said if I didn't go with him or I told people about him startin' the fires, he had somethin' awful to tell Mama. Somethin' that would kill her. I didn't set any of the fires. I was just with him," Sadie screamed through tears.

"Why you little bas…" Katty was back on her feet, her fists clinched again and aimed at Army, before Clete stepped in.

"Now, Katty, let's not make this whole thing worse by me having to charge you with maulin' another person's youngun'."

"Clete, it'd be worth the charges," Katty said through clenched teeth.

"I've known Katty Simpson for many years. She's never killed anyone. She might let her anger get the best of her sometimes but it's not in Katty to kill someone," Grandma defended.

"Sadie, why didn't you tell us he was threatenin'—blackmailin' you?" Katty turned to Sadie again.

"I was scared. I didn't know what he was gonna tell you, but whatever it was, he said it'd give you a heart attack and you'd die," Sadie confessed. It was obvious her fears of losing the most important person in her universe was why she was so easily manipulated by Army.

"All right you little blackmailer, tell me. Tell me what you threatened my daughter with. Nothin' you got to say can cause me no harm." Katty called his bluff.

"No, Mama, No," Sadie screamed, proving her belief to Army's evil claim.

"Sadie, don't worry. It's all right. He cain't hurt me."

Army started to respond to Katty, but his mother interrupted before he could say anything. "Well, I will. You kilt yer mother and yer sister," Zettie screamed.

"My mother and my sister died during childbirth,"

Katty snapped.

"That's why it's yer fault," Zettie yelled again.

"How can that be Katty's fault when she was bein' born too? Katty was a twin." Simp couldn't believe his ears.

"'Twas yer fault. You got born just fine, but you kilt both of 'em. You shoulda died 'stead of bein' born first and causin' 'em to die." Zettie was now on her feet. Her hands were on her hips, and she was the one spitting words toward Katty.

Katty was strangely without words. Her once red face was now as white as a ready-to-be-picked cotton patch.

"You can't blame Katty for that. A baby can't help how and when it was born. Why everyone in these parts knows how Katty's mother died tryin' to birth her and her twin. How can you blame Katty and her only a baby?" Grandma was stunned.

"You shoulda been the one to die. You—you—kilt my mama," Mrs. Boone screamed.

"Your mama—you mean Katty's mama don't you?" Daddy questioned.

"She was my mama, too. She had me when she was twelve years old. This woman and me don't have the same daddy but our mama was the same woman. I never met my daddy or my mama. Don't even know what they look like. The State took me away 'cause Mama was a child having a child, with no means of support. I always knowd who she was though. I thought I'd go to her someday and tell her I was her daughter but Katty here kilt her 'fore I could do it."

"So it's you—you're the one? I'd heard rumors that Mama had a child out of wedlock. I never wanted to believe it." Katty's voice was unusually soft. Sadie wrapped her arms around her mother, while Simp stood with his hands on Katty's shoulders.

"Yes, it's me. I'm the one. The throwed-away-bastard-child. I heard you settled over in these parts. My husband come here for the work and to get away from coal minin'. I come to see my mama's killer and make you suffer. And by the way, my middle name is Rose. She named me Zettie Rose—after her. Who'd she name you after?"

Katty's eyes narrowed, and her lips tighten over gritted teeth. Clete stepped in just in time. "Look, you and your son have broken the law many times over. Settin' fires and causin' property damage, blackmail-in'…"

"Spyin'," Simp added to Clete's list of crimes.

"Spyin' too—and if I tried, I could probably come up with a few more things. I'm afraid that even though this is a—a family thing, y'all have made it criminal. They can press charges, and I can arrest you," Clete reached for his handcuffs.

"We—I ain't gonna press charges," Katty said in her new soft voice.

"We ain't?" Simp was shocked and confused.

"What do you mean, Katty? These people have committed a crime toward y'all." Clete couldn't believe his ears.

"My mama must a loved her to name her Rose after herself. I cain't send somebody my mama loved that much to jail."

"I won't press charges neither," Grandma followed Katty's lead.

"You neither, Mrs. Strom? Well—if y'all don't want to press charges, I guess it's your choice, but the school and Big Store might. Army, why did you start those fires?" I was glad Clete asked Army that question. I was wondering the same thing.

"I told Army to do that so people would think it was yer Sadie that was startin' the fires," Zettie Boone shouted.

"But why my house? We weren't involved in any of this," Grandma asked.

"Because if people didn't believe it was Sadie's doins', they'd think it was her," Army said, pointing to me.

"You could a killed me and my family—and my friends? Maybe you need to go to jail after all," Katty was reconsidering while angrily shaking her finger at the Boones.

"I didn't wanta kill you. I wanted to punish you. It wasn't fair for you to live so good when I lived hand to mouth all these years," Zettie said, with disgust.

"If you'll give it some thought, you'll realize I was left without a mother or sister, too. My daddy had to work and leave me with one and then another. We moved to the Bootheel when I was still a kid. I pulled a cotton sack just like he did. Simp and me married when I was barely fourteen. We worked hard to have what little we have now, which is hardly nothin' by some people's standards. You don't know about people 'til you've lived their life, too." Katty's own words slapped her in the face. "Guess I wasn't bein' fair in your case neither. I didn't like you 'cause of how you looked and acted—and 'cause you're from a place that holds nothin' but hurtful memories for me."

Zettie held eye contact with her as Katty continued. "I'm sorry you had such a life and hated me for it, but I didn't cause any of your sufferin'. Now, go—out of my sight."

"Hey, Clete, let's take a walk. I want to talk to you about a dog," Daddy said, resorting to his familiar line when he had something up his sleeve. I could almost hear the wheels turning in Daddy's head as soon as they rounded the corner and got beyond hearing.

## Chapter Fifty-Eight

"Now, would y'all like a glass of tea or something?" Grandma asked again, still trying to be hospitable.

"Can I have one of yer biscuits I heard people 'round here talk so much about?" Army asked to everyone's surprise.

"Okay, I think there are a few left, I'll go get you one," I offered. I returned from the kitchen with biscuits and tea for Army and his mother. Everyone was silent while they savored them. I looked from one to the other, and then to the Simpsons, trying to imagine each one's pain and what evil seed that had caused it.

"Samplin' one of Mrs. Strom's biscuits, I see. They're the best. Y'all come get back in the car. I'll take you home 'til I can do a little more investigatin'," Clete said once he and Daddy returned.

"Wait," Katty mumbled as she pulled something from a small tobacco sack she had pinned to the inside of her dress. "Here—you can have this," Katty's hands trembled. "This is a picture of my—our mama. At least you can see now what she looked like."

Zettie Boone studied the picture for a second, gave

Katty a twisted smile and slid it into her britches pocket. I supposed that smile was her way of thanking Katty—without words. Army and his mother chewed on Grandma's biscuits as they rode away.

"I cain't believe you gave her your mama's picture, Katty. You've carried it 'round your neck in that sack ever since I can remember." Simp looked at Katty as though he was looking at a stranger.

"I got more pictures like that. Maybe it'll be enough to make her go away, and we won't have to lay eyes on the likes of her again. That woman and me may have the same blood, but that's where it ends. Anyways, I didn't do it for her. I did it for my Mama."

"Larson, what'd you say for Clete not to take 'em straight to jail?" Simp asked.

"I suggested that it seemed like whatever threat they was before, was gone now. Also, he could pick them up later, after he found out if the school or Big Store wanted to press charges or not. If nobody presses charges, y'all don't want everybody 'round here smellin' a stink that don't need to be stirred anymore, do you?" Daddy flicked his cigarette butt into the road ditch and rejoined us on the porch.

"Maybe Larson's right. Simp, let's go home. I want to get somewhere quiet, and jest think 'bout this and then push it all out of my head again." The trio left, Katty and Sadie arm in arm with Simp following behind.

"Now that sure was a strange turn of events. Katty

must feel awful to discover the people she had such disgust for, were actually her blood kin," said Grandma.

"And Army and Sadie are cousins?" I questioned in disbelief.

"Goes to show things are not always what they look like. We thought Army was hangin' around Sadie 'cause he was sweet on her. Now we know, he was puttin' the fear in her all along," Grandma concluded.

"He was setting her up to be blamed for the fires—and me too," I added.

"Yes, but even if it was lookin' that way, me and you never wanted to believe that Sadie was the firebug. And no one ever thought it was you, Meryl."

"Well, I didn't know about any of this stuff until right before I came home from Florida."

"How'd you find out about it then, Daddy?"

"Ugh…I got my ways."

It aggravated me for Daddy to be so evasive. "Well, if we could have reached you, we'd have told you ourselves," I pouted.

"Take heed, Larson. You need to keep in touch with us when you're away." Grandma warned Daddy with one of her louder-than-words-expressions.

"Guess you're right, Mom. With this Boone stuff goin' on and Meryl havin' her first date and then gettin' a marriage proposal, why I'm liable to leave and next time have a son-in-law when I get back home."

"We don't need to get started on that again. We

settled that." I said quickly.

"I know, I'm just teasin' you, Baby. I'm proud of all those little ducks you have lined up for your future. Your old Daddy is proud of you in everything you do."

"Me too," Grandma agreed.

"But now, I need to take a little ride. I won't be long." Daddy reached for his hat.

"You're gonna be back for supper ain't cha' son?"

"Mom, I wouldn't miss it for nothin'. Why, word is gonna be spread all the way to Kentucky about how good your biscuits are. I'm proud of my two girls more than ever now," Daddy winked as he walked to his car.

"Today's been like a day and a half," Grandma sighed as she was kitchen bound."

As I remained in the swing, my mind wandered to Hutch and his parents. How far had they made it towards Arizona? Would I ever see Hutch again? And I wondered how Katty felt to discover she had a living sister, even if she was reluctant to claim her? Would Daddy make it home for supper—sober?

Grandma and I finally ate. Daddy's food was set on the stove and covered with a clean dish towel as usual. We might have returned to the porch, had it not been for the mosquitoes. I cringed at the thought of having to fight those dreadful things in the field the next day. There wasn't a cloud in sight. I was sure the field would be dry enough to chop.

"Larson better get on home if he's gonna feel like

workin' in the mornin'." If the events of the day weren't enough, Grandma was going to bed with her worry-wrinkle firmly in place again because of Daddy.

Headlights shone down the lane as we were about to lock the door. Daddy had made it home. His supper was placed on the table by the time he walked through the door. I didn't detect any sign he had been drinking. He devoured his food and hugged us goodnight without any explanation of where he'd been. Grandma put his dishes in the pan to soak and I wiped the table, giving him time to settle into bed.

After checking the doors once more, Grandma turned out the lights. Daddy's snoring began immediately. I crawled into bed, settled into my sleep nest and was out soon after my head hit the pillow.

AFTER BREAKFAST THE next morning, Daddy checked the oil in the car and added water to the radiator. The slamming car hood was my cue to grab my bonnet and hoe so we could leave for the field. Grandma handed me our dinners, twist-tied in Wonder Bread sacks, on my way out the door.

The Simpson's house was quiet when I looked their direction. It was unusual not to see or hear anything of them. Katty did say she had some things to think about. I glanced at the empty driveway where Hutch's car usually parked and was reminded again of our eventful yesterday. I needed to do some thinking myself.

The cotton field was buzzing about the Boone's absence when we arrived. "You'd a thought someone would'a heard all the pots and pans a clanging when they left, but I guess they didn't. Cain't believe they left without sayin' a word," Mrs. Bertram seemed partly annoyed and somewhat ecstatic they were gone. Yes, she'd need to find more workers, but the field would surely be less chaotic without their brood running through it.

"That's the strangest thing I ever seen. Why, I bet they didn't even get done unpacking before they packed up and left again," Asa said, still scratching his head.

"Maybe they had to get back to Kentucky in a hurry for some reason. Maybe they found work somewhere else. Who knows?" Daddy said as he started to climb onto the tractor but paused when he saw Clete's car approaching.

"Do you know anythin' about the Boones leavin'?" Asa quizzed Clete before he was completely out of his car.

"What? No, I don't. You mean they're gone? They're who I'm here to see."

"They went back to Kentucky, we're a guessin'. Their truck's gone, and the house is empty," Asa reported.

"Is that a fact?" Clete mumbled.

Asa was still mumbling under his breath as he left to see if anyone's hoes needed sharpening. Clete walked over to Daddy who was leaned against the tractor with his arms crossed over his chest.

"Did you talk to the school officials or the Big Store owners to see if they wanted to press charges?" Daddy asked, reaching into his pocket for a smoke.

"I never got around to it. Wiley Bunkus and Clave Taylor got into a fight over property lines again. They fight like that every time they get dog drunk. By the time I got those fellas settled down, it was too late to talk to anybody about anythin'."

"You know, Clete, as far as everbody knows, the fires are still a mystery. Do you have any idea about which one of 'em Kentucky hills or hollers 'em Boones headed for?" Daddy asked quietly, looking down to the ground and kicking dirt clods.

"No, can't say I do," Clete replied as he stuffed his hands in his pockets and glanced at the sky.

"So if there ain't no charges aginst 'em, why would you want to go a lookin' for 'em? A hornet's nest is best left alone—don't you think?"

"Makes sense, Larson. What do you think about it, Sis?" I had been standing quietly while leaned against my hoe handle and listening to their exchange.

"I guess if the Boones are gone, they took theirs and

maybe a few other people's problems with them," I replied.

"You got a pretty smart little girl there, Larson."

"Yeah, and she can cook pretty good too. You might want to clear it with her Grandma though before you get her to cook you a meal."

Clete looked bewildered as he tipped his hat to us before getting into his car.

"So, you didn't know anything about this?" I asked Daddy once Clete was gone.

"Aw…well…havin' been pressed aginst a brick wall with a rock bein' rolled t'ward it myself a few times, I couldn't stand by and do nothin'. Even if it was their own doins', I could see how 'em folks hadn't been nothin' but misunderstood in a lot a ways—'specially 'round here."

"I figured as much. Daddy, your mind works like a mousetrap."

"Takes a mind like that to know one, little girl." Daddy smiled. "Maybe, I wanted to help rid Muddy Ox of the ruckus they brought to it. Maybe I saw that kid Army, had all the odds stacked aginst him. Truth was, I jest plain didn't like 'em much. Before long, I'm gonna be about three states away. I didn't want to go and leave that bunch at arm's length of the two people I love the most in this world." Daddy looked me straight in the eyes.

"So how did you do it?" I had to know.

"Well, everybody knows that Tommy Mac Brown makes the best moonshine in the Bootheel. I couldn't think of any two fellas that'd appreciate a jug or three of it any more than Wiley Bunkus and Clave Taylor. Seems I was right.

"Then, I dropped in on our Kentucky neighbors. I convinced 'em there was money to be made in places other than 'round here where it looked like they'd worn their welcome out. I told 'em that even if Clete didn't have your Grandma and Katty pressin' charges aginst 'em, the Big Store and the school might. I also told 'em how Clete was a pretty understandin' guy, but he was still the law. Since they'd bent the law and broke it off in the ground so many times, it'd be good for them to go while the gettin' was good—while 'em and Army was on this side of a pair of iron bars. Would you believe that lil' tuff guy Army, still wanted to say he didn't care 'bout goin' to jail? I told him he'd best keep his mouth shut 'til he'd lived enough life to know what he was scared of or not."

"And did he?" I asked.

"He didn't like it—but he did. Man that kid's got a stubborn streak. I told 'em I knew for a fact that Clete would be havin' his hands full of some other problems that'd probably keep him busy for most of the night. And, since Mrs. Boone had dealt with Katty and got that out of her craw, it was time they made tracks. That is, after they tied all 'em pots and pans down so they wouldn't get every dog in town a barkin' when they left."

"Evidently, they listened. No one seems to have heard them leave," I said.

"Hey Jean…" Tara called as she arrived to the field. I handed Daddy his lunch and watched as the tractor blew a trail of dust in the opposite direction of Clete's car that had left only moments before.

"Whew, I was almost late. Grandma Bertram would fuss at me until noon if I was late for the first day in the field," Tara said as she grabbed the row next to mine. She was the only McCrady grandchild left to work for the Bertram's now. Scarlet and Melanie had graduated, married, and moved away. That was the pattern for most. They either married and moved away or moved to find work or go to college—but moved was the operative word. Very few graduates stayed in the Bootheel. The Bootheel wasn't what they wanted away from—it was the cotton patch.

"Okay, let's get movin'. Tara Gayle, you and Jean hurry and get your talking over with, so you can do some chopping," Emmy Bertram barked.

The putting of Daddy's tractor faded in the distance. Only the sound of hoes slicing through the rich gumbo dirt on our half-mile rows remained.

Our work day had begun.

## Chapter Fifty-Nine

BY ELEVEN O'CLOCK we'd chopped our rows back to the wagon for the third time. I stopped for a dipper of water while Tara left in search of a thicket to go to the bathroom.

"Hey, how about sharing that dipper there, young lady?" I turned and was face to face with a boy I hadn't seen before.

"It's all yours," I said, handing him the dipper.

"I'm Wade Wilson." His name rolled off his tongue like butter and honey.

"Meryl Jean Strom, but most everyone calls me Jean. You just getting here?"

"Yeah, we worked in Charley Wagner's field 'til about an hour ago. It got done, so he sent us over here. He said Mr. Bertram lost a bunch of his hands today."

"Wow…news travels fast. Yes, a family moved away —unexpectedly."

"Guess that explains it. You live 'round here?" He dropped the dipper into the bucket and leaned against the wagon. His muscles flexed as he crossed his arms over his chest.

"I live with my Grandma in Silver Leaf. How about

you?"

"We came up from Mississippi a couple a weeks ago. Mr. Chaffin put us up in one of his houses on the other side of number eight ditch."

"We?" I asked.

"Yeah, that's my Ma and Pa, four brothers and my sister on 'em rows over yonder." An unruly curl fell across his forehead as he adjusted his hat.

"That's eight hoes swinging. I bet Mr. Chaffin was glad to see y'all coming."

I guessed Wade to be around eighteen or nineteen. His brothers looked as though they were between the ages of sixteen and twelve and his sister was about ten or eleven.

"I 'magine he was," Wade's smile revealed a deep set of dimples. "We weren't sure he'd take us on. We were lucky to get his house, even if it is too small for our bunch."

"Well, I know for a fact a larger shotgun house of Mr. Chaffin's right down the road became empty last night. It's by a smaller ditch called Seldom Seen."

"Thanks, I'll tell that to my Pa."

"Ready to start another row, Jean?" Tara reappeared. Her eyes were squarely on Wade.

"This is Tara McCrady. The Bertrams are her grandparents."

"Wade Wilson," he smiled and tipped his hat to Tara. He brushed back the curl again, only to have several others fall in its place.

"I was telling Wade about the shotgun house down the road being empty. Their family of eight is cramped into one of Mr. Chaffin's little houses across Number Eight Ditch."

"The shotgun house is empty? Don't the Boones live there?" Tara questioned.

"Guess you hadn't heard. They left sometime in the middle of the night."

"But didn't they just get here?"

"Your Grandpa told us they were gone, and the house was empty before you got to the field this morning."

"You kids gonna stand and talk all day or are you gonna find another row to hoe," Emmy shouted from midfield.

I expected Wade to grab a row by Tara, but he chose the one by me instead.

"So you and Tara are school friends? What grade are y'all in?"

"This will be our senior year." I made sure my hoe never missed a lick. Mrs. Bertram still had us in her sights.

"Are you a senior too, or have you already graduated?" Tara asked.

"I dropped out. We move around too much for me to keep up with school."

"Oh—I see," Tara's tone was disapproving.

Wade was another product of families who followed the harvest. With that large family, following the harvest was probably the only way they could survive.

"Hey Pops, Jean here says Mr. Chaffin had a bigger house come empty last night. It's on this side of Number Eight right down the road a ways." Wade's father and mother met us as they were chopping their way back down the field.

"Go talk to 'im, Horace? We sure could use a bigger place," Wade's mother urged.

"I'll talk to 'im come dinner time, maybe. Yer right. A person cain't cuss a cat in that little place we're in now 'thout gettin' hair in their mouth."

I didn't know if Wade's father meant to be funny with his homespun, Mississippi drawl, but I struggled to keep a straight face. I'd never heard that expression before.

"We'd better speed up guys if they're meeting us coming back down the field. Mrs. Bertram will be yelling again soon," I urged.

"I'm surprised the Boones left but am glad they did. The field is a lot quieter without all of those kids running through it," Tara said.

"The whole town will be quieter," I answered before remembering my personal challenge to be more tolerable of those who were—different. "Wherever they went, I hope they find good work and do better for themselves." Tara shot me a puzzled look.

"What's people do for fun in this town?" Wade asked.

"You don't do anything much in this town for fun. Kennett, Hayti, or Caruthersville are the closest places to find something to do for fun," Tara responded.

"What's there?"

"They all have movie theatres and skating rinks. Kennett has Tommie's Drive-in. Just about all us kids go there on date nights," Tara explained.

Wade got quiet. I figured he was contemplating which of those places was best for a date with Tara. We'd almost caught up with his parents, so we could take it easier.

"It's dinner time," yelled Mrs. Bertram. Wade sauntered over to their pickup truck where his mother divvied out their dinners.

Tara and I found a shady spot near the wheel of the wagon. She pulled a ham sandwich, cut diagonally to make two precise halves from her brown paper bag. I snatched a fried bologna biscuit from my recycled bread sack. Given a choice, I would've chosen offerings from Grandma's kitchen over Tara's or anyone else's any time. Afterward, she munched a Twinkie, and I enjoyed a fried peach pie before stretching underneath the wagon to rest.

"That Wade guy is cute, don't you think? I love his dimples," Tara swooned.

"I think he likes you." Boys liked Tara, the petite,

bouncy, blonde cheerleader.

"He was certainly interested to hear where the dating spots were," Tara said giggling.

"Where do you think he'll take you?"

"Probably Tommie's. It's the favorite spot." Tara beamed with confidence.

We pulled our bonnets over our faces. Drifting off to sleep wasn't a concern. Her Grandmother was better than an alarm clock for calling us back to the field. However, our red blood was a dinner bell to the blue steel-billed mosquitoes that were determined to rob us of our would-be naps.

Between slapping my oppressors and the caws of the crows also having their noon meal in a cornfield nearby, I gave up on a nap. I sat up in time to see Wade's dad talking to Carl Chaffin, who'd driven by to survey his crops. After a brief handshake, Mr. Wilson rejoined his family. By their smiles, I gathered they'd been given the larger house. I couldn't imagine eight people sleeping and moving around in one of those one bedroom huts.

"Okay y'all—let's hit it again," Mrs. Bertram bellowed.

Tara and I reached for our hoes before seeing them in her Grandfather's hands, as he walked toward us.

"Your Grandma said she thought you and Jean might do a better job at keepin' up if your hoes were sharper," Asa Bertram said sternly, as he handed over our hoes.

"Okay—thanks, Grandpa."

"Thank you, Mr. Bertram," I echoed.

Wade waited by the wagon until Tara and I had chosen our rows. This time, his row was next to Tara's putting her row between Wade's and mine.

"Thanks for telling us about that house, Jean. We'll be moving into it tonight."

"You're welcome," I said, leaning around Tara to respond.

"Hey, Grandma was right. This sharp hoe does…"

Looking to see what made Tara stop mid-sentence, I was sickened by the sight of blood oozing from her leg.

"Oh Tara—you cut yourself. Mrs. Bertram, hurry. Tara's been hurt!"

I could only yell, but Wade sprang into action. In seconds, he'd wrapped his shirt around Tara's leg, swept her up, and carried her back to the shade of the wagon.

"Tara Gayle, don't you know better? I thought I taught you the dangers of a sharp hoe. Honey, are…are you all right?" Mrs. Bertram got the scolding part out of the way before asking if Tara was all right. She might have also regretted having Mr. Bertram put such a sharp edge on her hoe. Her grandchildren meant the world to her, but because the accident scared her so, scolding was her first reaction. Sympathy had to get in line.

"It's bad, Grandma," Tara sobbed.

"Asa, you'd better run her to Doc Fonsworth. She

may need a stitch or two."

Wade swooped Tara up again and into the passenger seat of her Grandfather's truck and they sped off.

"Son, you'll need a shirt in this heat," Mrs. Bertram said to the shirtless Wade.

"Tell you what, ma'am, if it sets well with you, can Wade and his mama go pack our things, so we can get moved tonight? By the time he went to the house all the way across Number Eight Ditch to get a shirt and got back, there wouldn't be much day left anyhow. The rest of us will stay and work. We'll all be back to work in the morning."

Calculating the distance, Mrs. Bertram agreed to Mr. Wilson's suggestion. Wade drove off with his mother, but not before giving me a wave and a smile. I was glad Mrs. Bertram agreed. He'd have burned to a crisp without a shirt. Besides, it was—distracting.

I was in awe of how quickly Wade came to Tara's rescue. He was her hero, wrapping his shirt around her leg and gracefully lifting her to safety. I could only daydream of such. I noticed how muscular for sure he was without his shirt. He could have probably lifted me, but I would have felt awkward.

I'd better make sure I kept my mind on where my hoe landed. With Wade gone, it would probably have taken two of those other scrawny guys in the field to help me if I had an accident. How embarrassing. No— there'd be no accidents for me, for certain.

With all the excitement, I hadn't noticed the clouds rolling in. *Boom*, came a loud clap of thunder with a crack of lightning in the distance. We immediately vacated the field. No one chopped during an electrical storm where hoes became lightning rods.

"Oh well, more days are ahead. Lord willing, tomorrow will be better," Mrs. Bertram sighed and shook her head at the day's turn of events. She was not happy.

IT WOULD TAKE the rest of the season for Tara to heal from her twelve—not one or two stitches. She couldn't risk infection by returning to the field. Luckily, her closet wouldn't suffer even if she did. Her parents would see that she had new school clothes.

## Chapter Sixty

THE SUN DRIED the dirt to keep it from clumping on our hoes the next morning. Yesterday's rain wasn't a gully washer but kept us out of the field the rest of the afternoon. The Wilsons finished moving and were ready to work early the next morning as promised.

I felt awkward when Wade paired with me without Tara. We talked about Tara's accident, his rescue, and his family's happy move. We both complained about the Johnson grass that seemed to have sprouted overnight.

"This house sure is better. Ma and Pa have their room. My sister shares a room with my two younger brothers, and I share a room with the other two.

"Bet you miss Tara not being here."

"Why would you say that?" Wade stopped and looked at me.

"Oh—I don't know. I guess I thought since you were asking her about the fun places for dates, you were thinking about asking her to go to one of them with you."

"Nope, I was thinkin' about asking you." I was glad Grandma had made the bib of my bonnet large enough to cover my face. I was surely blushing.

"Me—I thought—well Tara is—I never thought about you wanting to go with me somewhere." I stumbled and mumbled, not knowing how to respond.

"Tara's cute all right, but you're not too bad yourself. Anyways, I don't mind girls to be a little—full figured." I got his point when I followed his eyes below my chin.

I wasn't sure I was pleased with his left-handed compliment. I definitely wasn't happy with his *full-figured* remark. I didn't like that he was looking at my—full figure so intently. It was one thing for a guy to look, but he needed to keep his comments to himself. It was another thing to blatantly make such a remark to a girl—to me.

I felt uncomfortable with Wade's boldness. On the other hand, I was flattered he thought I was worth the attention. I think he even almost said I was cute too.

"Hey, is everything all right here?" We both flinched at the sound of Daddy's deep voice. I couldn't believe the transformation Wade made before my eyes. The sharp tongue that all but insulted me a few seconds before became smooth as butter again—like it sounded when he first introduced himself to me.

"We're fine Daddy. Wade, this is my Dad. Daddy, this is Wade Wilson. He and his family moved into the Boone's shotgun house last night." Muddy Ox would probably never see them again, but that old shotgun shack would forever be the Boone's to me.

"I'm glad to meet you, sir. I've been admiring how you handle that big tractor." Wade's words were so sugary they could have sweetened a glass of tea. He extended his hand for a shake and Daddy obliged.

"You the fella that helped with the Bertram's granddaughter? You did good, kid."

"Was glad to help if I could. I've been chopping here with Jean for the last couple days. It's made the time go faster for sure. You have a nice daughter, sir."

I had to look at him twice to convince myself that he was the same flirty guy who had just brazenly referred to me, Daddy's Baby, as *full figured*. Daddy wouldn't have been so cordial had he known how Wade was sizing me up—literally.

"Well, gotta' get back to plowin'. Take care of her, too, Okay? Y'all chop fast as you talk to keep Emmy Bertram off your backs."

"Oh, we will. Sir, you can count on me to take care of your daughter," Wade answered with his condescending voice.

Daddy grinned before disappearing on his tractor behind the sun's haze.

"I'm not likely to cut myself with a hoe as Tara did. And I do pretty well taking care of myself," I spouted after Daddy left.

"Never mind that, I was just getting on his good side. You want to go to Tommie's Drive-Inn with me Saturday night don't you?" He said, reverting back to his normal tone.

I swallowed hard and replied without thinking of how it would sound, "My Grandma won't let me date at night."

"Thought you were a senior?" Wade nearly laughed before seeing I was serious.

"Yes," I answered with annoyance.

"If Grandma don't let you date? What about your dad? Don't he have a say?"

"He leaves things like that mostly up to her. I've dated, just not at night. I didn't say I hadn't ever dated."

"So everyone you've dated has took you places in the daytime?"

"Yes." I skirted the details, everyone only being Hutch.

"Well, have you ever thought of slippin' out without them knowin'?"

I had to look him straight in the eyes to see if he was serious. Was he really suggesting I sneak out of the house? The thought of it sent a chill through me. If Daddy ever caught me sneaking out of the house—I didn't even want to think about the repercussions. Worse, Grandma would lose trust in me. That would hurt more.

"No—I've never thought of that—and never would," I added sharply.

"Well, ask if you can go to Tommie's with me. I've met your dad, and he likes me. Maybe he'll get *Grandma* to change her mind."

I didn't appreciate his tone when he said get Grandma to change her mind. But it would be fun to go to Tommie's. I couldn't believe Wade Wilson asked me for a date. I couldn't help being unsure of him though. I'd ask Grandma. If she said no, I could tell him I couldn't go and get out of it gracefully—even if I would be somewhat disappointed.

"I'll ask her. But I can't promise what she'll say."

We chopped the rest of the afternoon without either of us mentioning Saturday night again—until quitting time. After Emmy announced it was six o'clock, Wade leaned close and whispered, "Don't forget to ask Grandma. And don't take no for an answer, okay? That's my motto—don't take no for an answer. After all, you *are* seventeen years old."

I didn't need him to remind me of my age. That got on my nerves. Actually, a lot of things about Wade got on my nerves. He was definitely full of himself along with being two-sided. But he did ask me on a date without clearing it with my Grandma or Daddy first.

"All right, I'll ask and tell you tomorrow."

During the ride home, I rehearsed in my mind how to approach Grandma. I'd never felt so giddy, unsure of myself, elated—or scared. I knew if I told her about our entire conversation, she'd not hesitate to say NO.

## Chapter Sixty-One

TIRED, HOT, AND hungry, I propped my hoe near the screen door before going inside. I couldn't wait to rid myself of the grime from the field. After supper, I figured I'd approach Grandma about the date.

However, this night my most important date would be with a pan of hot water and Epsom salts to soak my sore, battered feet. The afternoon sun had baked the muddy gumbo clods creating rock sharp edges that poked through my thin sole tennis shoes. Maybe Grandma had cardboard somewhere to make inserts for my shoes, as she had before.

"Effie was over today and said that poor McCrady girl will be laid up with her leg for the rest of the season," Grandma began.

"She sliced her leg something awful. That's for sure," I agreed.

"Meryl, I hope this is a lesson for you. Remember how I warned you about a sharp hoe before you ever started choppin'?"

Of course, I remembered. The mental picture of crippling up and down a cotton row with a sliced leg was branded in my mind. I was sure Tara had also heard that warning from Mrs. Bertram many times. But Tara's accident probably had to do less with what she'd been taught and more with being overruled by a pair of dreamy brown eyes and dimples you could get lost in.

"That boy you were choppin' by today did a good deed for that girl. Asa said the doc told him the shirt tied around her leg kept her from losin' a serious amount of blood," Daddy said, chewing his words and food alike.

"Yes, Effie went on today about that boy and his shirt too," Grandma added.

"Pretty nice fella, far as I can see," Daddy added.

"Effie said the family was from Mississippi. She also said the Boones packed up and left in the middle of the night leavin' that shotgun house in a mess." Grandma bounced from one shared fact of Effie's to another. The messy house was new knowledge.

"Yeah, Asa told us when we got to the field this morning," Daddy said casually.

"Guess they scrambled after Clete went to talk to them."

"No Mom. Clete said he had to go break up another fight 'tween Wiley Bunkus and Clave Taylor. The Boones left before he got to 'em."

"And, Larson, you didn't know anything about that or have anything…?" Before Grandma could pin Daddy down, Simp knocked on the door.

"Katty sent me over with this cobbler. She said she

stretched a jar of apples to make two cobblers. So she made y'all one, too, Mrs. Strom."

"That woman is bent on feedin' us if we're here or over there. Katty's somethin' else." Grandma tried to sound annoyed but was clearly pleased. "You tell her thanks. Is she doin' okay after the shock of yesterday?"

"Awe, you know Katty. She might get knocked down, but she don't stay down. Anyhow, we hear they left town. If we're lucky, that bunch'll stay gone," he grumped.

"Might be wise of 'em," Daddy agreed.

"We were just talkin' about them leavin'. It seems they left shortly after that boy and his mama was here yesterday." Grandma looked suspiciously at Daddy again.

"Well, it cleared up some things for Katty that she'd always wondered about. I think she's okay now though. Don't reckon she'll grieve over family she never knowd she had."

"Especially if family wants to do you harm," Grandma added.

"I'm gonna run back home now and leave y'all to yet supper. I plan to hit the bed early tonight. That hot sun can sure take a lot out of you."

"Thanks again, Simp. Tell Katty I'll get her dish back tomorrow."

"That cobbler sure looks good, Mom. I'm claimin' that corner right there," Daddy announced.

I put on a kettle of water to heat while we cleaned the kitchen. After enjoying a bit of Katty's cobbler, I grabbed the cane bottom chair so I could sit and submerge my feet in the soothing Epsom salts bath. Daddy could have my place in the swing tonight.

"Let me have your shoe," Grandma had the cardboard and scissors ready to cut inserts. I didn't even have to ask.

"Meryl, why do you wear them flimsy things out in the field?" That was the first time my unobservant father had noticed me not wearing those hideous boy shoes.

"Where's what I got you for Christmas? Those flimsy tennis sho…"

"I don't want to ruin those good shoes," I interrupted quickly before Daddy could insist that I wear the oxfords to the field.

"Grandma, I want you to think about something, okay?"

"About what?" She might have thought I wanted support concerning my shoes.

"Since I am seventeen now and a senior, if I got asked out on a date and someone wanted to take me to the drive-in movies, could I go?"

"Well I let you go with Hutch to the movies didn't I? Sure, you could go, if it was a nice boy and you got home before dark again."

"It's the drive-inn. Drive-ins are outdoors and they

only show movies at night."

"Now, Meryl Jean, you know I don't let you go anywhere at night. I don't want to be staying here by myself after dark or hafta bother Simp and Katty to stay over there. They've already been too good to us. Besides, people say more mischief usually goes on after dark. It probably does at the movies too."

"Mom, I'm here now. You wouldn't be stayin' alone."

"You're here in town, Larson, but can I count on you bein' home? Bein' at the blacksmith shop is not the same as bein' here with me." She was right. It was rare Daddy stayed home with us any night.

"If I say I'll be here with you, Mom, I'll be here."

"Larson, you're willin' for her to go out at night—alone—with a boy?"

"I'm guessin' it's this boy that come to the McCrady girl's side when she got hurt. If it is—I met him in the field today. He's a all right fella far as I can see. Meryl, is that the boy that asked you to the drive-in movies?"

This was becoming easier than I'd worried. Daddy's rising to my defense was promising. If he was willing for me to go and vowed to stay home if I did, Grandma could actually agree.

"Yes, he wants to take me this Saturday night."

"Hutch was willin' to take you to the movies in the day time."

"Grandma, Hutch is gone. Wade is here. And he

wants to take me to the drive-in."

"I say it's okay," Daddy argued.

Grandma was outnumbered. She gave in for me to go as long as Daddy would stay with her until I got home. I didn't think she was actually afraid of the dark, but she'd never been alone at night since age fourteen, after she married Grandpa Omar. It was probably more about dread than fear.

"Larson you say you met him, and he's a good boy?"

"As far as I could tell, Mom."

Neither of them asked me what I thought about him. It was scary how he turned on the charm for Daddy when only seconds before he openly commented on my bust-size. Crazy as it was, I still wanted to go in spite of the obvious red flags.

"All the kids go to Tommie's Drive-in on Saturday nights. I'll be there with a bunch of my friends from school." I wanted to finally get to be with the cool kids, and I felt like Grandma would feel better knowing it was a group.

Anyway…I was Larson and Edna Strom's daughter. I was pretty sure I could handle myself.

## Chapter Sixty-Two

MY FEET WERE now pink and wrinkled and the water was cold. Grandma worked on my cardboard inserts while we talked. I should be able to walk without a limp tomorrow. I was excited to tell Wade I could go to the drive-in with him. Going to the cotton patch was taking on an entirely different purpose.

"Good night. Thank you, thank you," I said as I hugged Grandma and gave Daddy a peck on the cheek before going inside. Snuggling into bed, I played in my mind how I'd tell Wade I could go. I'd act casual and not too excited that it was actually going to work out.

Wade didn't have to know he was only my second date. Maybe I was overreacting to his comment and his personality change with Daddy. It'd be okay. Cilla and Tara and the others would be there with their dates—maybe even Darla and Coup. But not Polly since her church frowned on going to the movies.

I had a restless night, punctuated by a haunting dream. Wade's face and eyes flashed in my head. Then soft images of his dimples and cunning smile appeared as if on flash cards. Suddenly, his face went blank and became an abstract of someone I felt I should know but couldn't quite recognize. Before I knew it, I was running through the same cave from my previous dream, when Mama was chasing me. Suddenly, I saw a ghostly form sitting on a big rock near the curve of the cave. I came to a dead stop. I should've been frightened but somehow felt at ease. Inching closer, I saw the back of an angelic like form.

"Hello," I said quietly.

"*Meryl*," it said, turning to face me. As before, I faced—my mother.

"Mama, it's you. Why did it take you so long to come to me again?"

"Meryl…"

"Yes, Mama, what is it?"

"Beware."

"Beware of what? Mama, what should I beware of?"

"*Beware–Beware…don't make me ashamed of you.*" I reached for her and cried after her, but she was gone.

"Wake up, Meryl," Grandma was shaking me. I was calling for Mama as I sat up in bed.

"Honey you were dreamin' about your mama again. You were callin' for her over and over."

"Oh Grandma, it was like before, but this time she wasn't chasing me. She was sitting on this rock, waiting for me. She warned me to beware and not make her ashamed."

"It's okay. It was just a dream. Go back to sleep

now, honey. We can talk about it in the mornin'. I promise that your mother was never ashamed of you. Find peace in that and go back to sleep. Mornin' will be here all too soon."

I heard the familiar squeaks of bedsprings in between Daddy's snores as Grandma climbed back into bed. He was snoring so loudly my cries never woke him.

If Grandma and Aunt Jackie are certain Mama was never ashamed of me, why do I keep dreaming she's saying she is or could be? The final thing I heard was Katty's cats hissing and howling. Their fight ended. Sleep returned.

I WAS THE last to make it to the kitchen table the next morning. Daddy was on the porch putting on his boots and having a smoke while I finished breakfast.

Pulling my hair back into a pony tail and dabbing my nose with a puff of powder, I rushed to the car and we off to the field. It was probably a waste of time to powder my nose. It'd be sweated off in no time.

Riding with Daddy got me to the field a little earlier than the rest. I found a spot under the shady side of the wagon to sit and wait for the other hands to arrive. Trying to reclaim some of the rest that had been stolen by my dream the night before, I hugged my knees to my chest and propped my head on them before hearing voices approaching.

"She's unbelievable," Wade said to person whose voice I didn't recognize.

"Yeah, I didn't think there were many like her still around," the stranger replied.

Was Wade referring to me? Did he actually call me unbelievable? How thrilling.

"You can tell she's never been out much. She's never been allowed to date after dark—unbelievable," Wade laughed.

"Are you jokin'? Who only dates in the daytime?"

"Meryl Jean—Jean is green," Wade chanted.

"Green behind the ears and every other way too, I bet. Are you sure you want to waste your time with her?" the stranger questioned.

"Oh, it won't be wasted. She'll be so happy I even asked her out, she'll be putty in my hands," Wade bragged.

"That other girl's the cute one. You know the one you carried out of the field that day? Why don't you try her?"

"Yeah she's a looker. But she's used to guys asking her out. The fat one will be so happy that someone like me gave her a second look she will be—grateful, if you know what I mean."

My stomach churned to hear their sick laughs at my

expense. My ears and face burned from embarrassment—and anger.

"Mornin,' Mrs. Bertram. This is Calvin Burns, a friend of mine. Can you use another hand in the field today?" Wade addressed Emmy Bertram with the same phony voice he'd used with Daddy, as she approached the wagon.

"You know how to use a hoe?" Mrs. Bertram asked.

"Yes, ma'am," Calvin said in a tone matching Wade's.

"All right, it'll be startin' time here in 'bout ten minutes. Pay's $6.00 a day. If you're okay with that, then grab a row and keep up," Emmy quipped.

"Yes, ma'am," Calvin mockingly saluted her once her back was turned.

"People say her bark is worse than her bite, but she's a tough old bird. I wouldn't want to cross her," Wade whispered when Emmy got down the field a ways.

"Tough for sure. What a…"

"Hey Wade, have you seen Meryl?" Daddy startled them.

"Meryl, no we haven't seen her. I…I didn't know y'all were here yet," Wade stuttered.

"She rode in with me," Daddy scanned the field again. "But I don't see her now."

"Here I am, Daddy. You looking for me? I've been sitting on the other side of the wagon resting before starting time." When I appeared from behind the wagon, it was time for Wade and Calvin to get red-faced. And—it had nothing to do with the sun.

"Oh, there you are. Thought I'd let you know, Asa's sendin' me to Kennett for a part for the plow. I should be back by dinner."

"Okay, thanks for letting me know. Hey, Daddy, if you're going to Riggs's Farm Supply, and you have time, can you pick me up a work shirt? Try to find me a—green one—if you can. I like green."

Daddy had an odd expression. I'd never asked him to buy an article of clothing for me before. Plus, he wasn't likely to find a green work shirt. Most were blue.

"You want a green work shirt? Okay, if I see one. I'll be in a hurry though. What size you want?" Any other time, I would have been embarrassed to talk clothing size in front of anyone, especially a boy who had asked me on a date. This time, I welcomed it.

"Get me an *extra*-large one," I emphasized extra.

Daddy was dumbfounded but said if he found an extra-large green work shirt, he'd get it for me. I shot Wade and Calvin a look that could kill as soon as Daddy drove off. Their faces reached an even deeper shade of red.

"Meryl, I—uh did you ask your Grandma if you could go to the movies with me Saturday night?" Wade asked trying to move past the fact that I'd possibly heard his and Calvin's conversation.

"I did. And she said yes. Daddy's okay with it, too." I pretended to be overjoyed.

"Good, want me to pick you up around five? We can cruise Kennett before the movie starts," he said giving Calvin a smug look.

"No—I don't think so," I said, stopping them in their tracks.

"Uh…you don't think so?"

"Grandma and Daddy said I could go, but I'm saying I don't want to."

"You don't want to go?" he questioned.

"I know it's an opportunity of a lifetime for a nice looking guy like you to want to take a fat girl like me out anywhere. I probably should be *grateful*. But you know what? A piece of putty like me doesn't want to waste her time on two-faced, smooth-tongued—you. Maybe you should find another desperate *green* girl to prey on."

"Meryl—we were just joking around. You know how us guys do." Wade stumbled, struggling to pull out of his trap.

"Yeah—Wade said he thinks you're unbeliev…" I quickly stopped Calvin.

"Oh, were you going to tell me how unbelievable Wade thinks I am? I already heard how you two can't believe girls like me still exist. Well, guess what? You're looking at one."

"Time to get a move on," Mrs. Bertram yelled.

"Y'all best be finding rows somewhere else other

than beside me. Daddy filed my hoe really sharp this morning. We wouldn't want to have an accident like Tara had."

"Are you threatening us?" Calvin challenged.

"No—no threat. It's a promise," I said staring him down.

The two of them silently found rows, over by Wade's family.

I pulled my bonnet bib down as far as it would go and chopped faster than usual, not looking anywhere but down at my row for the rest of the morning. I didn't want to give either of them the satisfaction of knowing they'd hurt me or have them see the tears that took turns trickling down my cheeks.

I tried not to think about their cruel words. Calvin actually couldn't hurt me. I hadn't cared about him, but I'd allowed myself to buy into the fairytale that the handsome, heroic Wade could like me.

Suddenly, my mother's words from the dream the night before struck me full force. *"Meryl, beware. Don't make me ashamed of you."* For the first time since she'd died, the warmth of my mother I had so sorely missed seemed to embrace me. She was with me in spirit after all and was looking out for me.

I realized the two dreams I'd had was Mama warning me not to fall prey to a shallow guy—or guys like Wade. They only wanted to steal my innocence and self-respect as Mama's was stolen when she believed the lie of a Wade-like fellow herself at age thirteen. My mother wanted more for me. So did I.

I wiped the tears and held my head high as I chopped alone the rest of the day. Actually, I wasn't completely alone. I knew God was with me—and so was Mama.

## Chapter Sixty-Three

I ONLY WENT through the motions during supper. Using the stale excuse of having a headache, I went to bed earlier than usual. All I wanted to do was get somewhere away from having to think, talk, or smile. I couldn't decide if I was more hurt or angry after hearing exactly what an insignificant human being Wade Wilson thought I was. I had succumbed to my old habit of using the weapons of embarrassment, shame, and humiliation for self-punishment.

How could I be so gullible? *"Meryl Jean, I thought you were smarter than that."* I kept repeating to myself. I wanted to erase the day's events and surrender to complete, escapable, dreamless sleep.

Finally, refuge came with no disturbing dreams about car-crashes, Wade, or Mama. An early morning thunderstorm and the hard rain pounding our tin roof was a welcome sound as it partially broke through my sleep barrier. I'd dreaded going to the field and facing Wade and his sidekick after yesterday's ordeal. At least now, nature had given me a reprieve before I had to face that humiliating emotional whirlwind. I rolled over, pulled the sheet over my head, and sank back to sleep.

## MERYL JEAN ANOTHER WHIRLWIND

"Well, there you are finally. I was beginnin' to think you were gonna to sleep 'til noon. How's your headache?" Grandma said as I curled next to her in the swing.

"Headache—oh it's better. Where's Daddy?"

"Obe McDougal picked him up early this mornin'. Said he needed help with puttin' brakes on his work truck. There's a couple pieces of jowl and some biscuits left. You just need to fry you an egg or two if you're hungry."

Not having completely recovered from Wade's verbal kick to my stomach the day before, I grabbed a cup of coffee and rejoined Grandma on the swing. "I'm not hungry right now. Maybe I'll fix something later."

"Sure you're not sick or comin' down with somethin'?"

"No, I'm fine. I promise."

"This is one of the wettest springs I can remember. So many rains has caused the choppin' to get behind for most all the farmers. Oh well, that's how things go here in the Bootheel," Grandma rambled, but I felt her watching me from the corner of her eye.

"I'm glad it rained. My pay day will suffer, but I dreaded going to the field today."

"I'd a thought you'd be looking forward to working alongside of that new boyfriend of yours. I've heard it said some of the best courtin' there is, takes place out in the cotton field."

"Didn't you ever court in the cotton field, Grandma?"

"No, I went from being my mama's little girl to being Omar's wife. No cotton field courtin' for me."

"Well, just so you know, Wade is *not* my boyfriend." Hearing my tone, Grandma shifted in the swing for a better view of my face.

"I figured y'all goin' to the movies and all, that you considered him a boyfriend like you did Hutch."

"I've decided not to go to the movies with Wade after all. And there is no comparison to Wade and Hutch."

"What went wrong? It sounded like you were looking forward to it the other day. Your Daddy even likes the boy—he said."

"Daddy doesn't know the real Wade. He's like two different people. Wade was trying to get on Daddy's good side, so y'all would let me go."

"But isn't he the one who helped Tara McCrady after she about cut off her leg with the hoe?"

"It was a bad cut, Grandma, but her leg was never in danger of being cut off."

"Well…Effie…"

"Effie wasn't in the field. I was standing next to

Tara. It was a bad cut, but some people don't do anything but exaggerate. Besides, anybody out there might have done what Wade did. He just happened to be on the row next to her." A tear slid down my face.

"Meryl, you're crying. Was that boy disrespectful? Does your Daddy know?"

"No, Daddy doesn't know anything about anything. Wade hurt my feelings, that's all. It wasn't so much what was done, as it was what he said when he didn't know I was listening. I don't want to get Daddy involved. You know how he gets."

Grandma was quiet for a second, probably imagining a scene between Daddy and Wade.

"Believe me. Wade Wilson is not the nice guy he wants people to think he is."

"I'm sorry honey. But it's better to find out now than later."

"Remember the dream I had of Mama chasing me?"

"Yes, I remember."

"Remember how she wasn't chasing me that last time but was sitting and waiting for me to get to her? I feel like she warned me about Wade in both of those dreams. Do you think it's possible Mama could be looking out for me from the grave?"

"Some folks think that's possible. I can't say yes or no. I know this; if she could, your mama would. You don't think your Daddy oughta know this boy disrespected you?"

"No, I took care of it. It'll be okay. Wade knows I see him now for what he is. He never really liked me anyway. He'll find another girl to take to the movies, I'm sure."

"Alright but promise me if he says or does anything else you don't like, you'll let me know. Don't keep things like that to yourself, Meryl."

As I started to reassure Grandma that I would confide in her should another situation arise, an old Ford truck seemed to appear from nowhere and stopped on the lane alongside the porch. The words Potions and Elixirs of Life scrolled on its splintered sideboards were barely legible. Rust covered what looked like a once, dark blue finish.

The driver remained at the wheel while a bone-thin woman got out and stood by the passenger door. She appeared very old, by her wrinkled face and bent frame. Her eyes were clouded, as one who was blind or partially blind. The narrow lips of her drawn mouth exposed a few stained and jagged teeth, as she spoke in a scratchy, low voice. A few sprigs of more silver than black hair peeked around the dark scarf draped over her head.

"Are you Alice Strom?" The mysterious woman asked but kept her distance.

"Yes…I am Alice Strom," Grandma stepped off the porch toward her. "How do you know my name?" I remained in the swing but could clearly hear their conversation.

"I have a message for you." She extended her skeletal, withered, hand.

"Do I know you? Are you from 'round here?" Grandma stepped closer.

"Who I am is not important. I have something to tell you." Taking Grandma's hand in hers and turning it palm up, she began tracing the lines.

"I don't believe in fortune tellers." Grandma partially withdrew her hand.

"Alice, I don't claim to be a fortune teller, but I do have a message for you." The old woman didn't loosen her grip.

Grandma started to pull away again but stopped. "I don't have any money."

"I'm not asking for money. I have something to tell you." She repeated.

"How do you know anythin' about me?"

"I know you're a good woman and mother, Alice Strom. You have five sons. They are fine, strong men. But—one son causes you more trouble than all the others. He will break your heart, Alice. But he can't break your spirit. Don't give up on him." The old woman gave Grandma an eerie smile before returning to the passenger seat. As they drove away, she repeated from the open window, "Don't give up on him."

Grandma stood bewildered for a moment before rejoining me in the swing. "Well, if that ain't the strangest thing I ever…"

"You've never met that woman before?"

"No—never."

"I tried to get a look at the driver, but y'all blocked my view. What I could see of him was shadowed. He was dressed all in black, wore a wide brimmed hat, and his nose was so long and sharp it about touched his chin. I couldn't see his face or eyes because he never turned his head. Grandma, he almost looked like a statue. He gave me goosebumps." It was mid-morning, but it was still dark and gloomy from the earlier rain storm, making it more difficult to see the driver.

"I never tried to see him. I couldn't take my eyes off of her."

"What or who do you think she was, Grandma?"

"She said she wasn't a fortune teller, but she had something to tell me. Money wasn't what it was about. She didn't ask for any. Right now, I'm not sure if she delivered a good message or an evil one. Guess time will tell."

"Well, everyone in this town knows you're a good woman and mother. Most everyone knows you have five sons. And for sure, everyone knows Daddy has control of your worry wrinkle. She could have talked to practically anyone and found out what she told you."

"That's true. I'm not going to let it worry me. She did me no harm. It was in the least—strange. Meryl, if we're to think it's possible your mother is watching out for you from the grave, maybe we could believe this woman was sent with a message for me about your daddy. Anyway, if it's real, somethin' will happen to prove it."

"We sure are getting our share of rain these days," Katty said as she and Simp arrived, breaking into our fog of confusion and startling us.

"Oh, Katty, I didn't hear y'all come up. Rain? Yes we are. I don't know what in the world the poor farmers are gonna do about their crops this year."

"There's still time to replant. It's early in the season if it'll jest stop raining so much now," Simp said.

"Did y'all see that old truck over here a few minutes ago?"

"Truck? No, I didn't see no truck, did you Simp?"

"No, didn't hear no truck neither," Simp added.

"Wonder why we didn't see or hear it? We were on our porch," Katty continued.

"Come to think of it Grandma, I never heard it coming. It was just—there. Did you hear it drive up?" It felt spookier to me the more we talked.

"No and I didn't notice which way it turned when it got to the corner down there neither. It's almost as if it just—disappeared. Now, that is a mystery."

"What are y'all talkin' about, Mrs. Strom? What happened?"

"Katty, this rickety, old, truck stopped by the house and a woman, so thin that she'd have to stand twice to make a shadow, got out and said she had somethin' to tell me. She looked like a fortuneteller. She sure held my hand and traced my palm like one."

"Was she a fortuneteller? I don't like fortunetellers," Katty said. Her eyes grew wide.

"She said she wasn't. She didn't ask for money, like fortunetellers usually do."

"She sure sounds like one to me—tracing your hand like that," Katty huffed.

"Who sent her with the message, and what message did she have for you?" Simp questioned as he walked over to the lane. "You say there was a truck? It didn't leave no ruts if there was. Shoulda been fresh ruts here if it just drove off," Simp confirmed.

"You're right. How can that be? With all this rain, it should have left ruts," I agreed.

"She never said who sent her. She just said I'm a good woman and out of my five sons, I had one who causes me more trouble than all the others. Then, she left. Oh…and she said I shouldn't let him break my spirit."

"She sure needn't feel like she told you anythin' special. Anyone 'round these parts could a told you that." Katty snickered.

"It was the way she looked and how she talked that made it different. You know me. I think fortunetellers and witches and the likes are devilish."

"That makes two of us. By the way, where is Larson?" Katty grinned.

## Chapter Sixty-Four

IF I'D HAD an inkling I was right about Wade, my perceptions were confirmed once I arrived at the field come Monday. I heard Calvin's laughter before I saw him with Wade. A blushing, but less than attractive, girl was chopping a row of cotton between them. She was thin and somewhat shapely but didn't look as though boys would stand in line to take her on a date. Did Wade with his good looks and cunning ways think *homely she* would be *grateful* that *handsome he* would give her his attention?

My guess was—yes.

I wanted to take her aside and warn her about those two Casanovas. But anything I said would have been regarded as envy or jealousy. I hoped she'd see through them. Also, her mother was alive and well and in the patch with her. I prayed if the girl was blinded by brown eyes and dimples, at least her mother would have 20/20 vision.

"Hey Baby, I forgot to tell you, that clerk at Riggs Supply said they never have carried green work shirts—only blue ones," Daddy said as he passed on his way to the water bucket.

"That's okay, Daddy. I have enough shirts anyway." He looked baffled.

Asa approached and started talking to Daddy about the equipment as they walked away. Poor Daddy was at such a loss at times. If he'd noticed Wade and Calvin had moved on to another conquest, he never said. He also never mentioned my skipping the date.

As expected, Tara's injury kept her out of the field the rest of the season. Wade and his family left to work elsewhere, as the need for them dwindled in our field. He and I never spoke again. Despite the field being full of people—I happily worked alone.

I expected Daddy would be making plans to move on too when his job with Asa slowed down—but he didn't. When he wasn't hanging out at the Blacksmith Shop he mingled with another pack of drunkards and do-nothings over around Five Points. Talk was there was everything from gambling, to moonshining, to chicken fighting, to prostitution going on there. Grandma's name for them was, *that rough bunch*. She'd say, "You put a rough bunch of drunks, slow minds, and fast tempers together and stir in a mess of bad women, and you get nothing but—trouble." Grandma was right.

One Sunday afternoon, we were abruptly awakened from our day of rest naps by Katty and Simp banging on our kitchen door. "Mrs. Strom, Mrs. Strom. Are you awake?"

"We—we just woke up," said a groggy Grandma as she bid them inside. More steps pounded on the porch as Effie and Jake followed Simp and Katty through the door. The four of them stood wide-eyed—their faces drawn.

"You'd better take a seat, Mrs. Strom," Jake Walby suggested.

"And don't get upset now, ya' hear?" Simp added.

"Goodness Gracious! What on earth are y'all talkin' about? What's wrong?" By now, Grandma, at their urging was sitting. I stood silent, fearing their message.

"Oh…it's Larson. He's been KILLED!" Grandma screamed. After all, what else could warrant such caution from the four of them?

"No—no. He's not been killed," Katty assured.

The color briefly came back to Grandma's face as she gave a sigh. However, her sigh became a groan and the color once more disappeared at hearing Simp's next words.

"Mrs. Strom, Larson has killed Wiley Bunkus."

Grandma slumped as though the life had been sucked out of her.

"Larson's tellin' it was self-defense," Katty added quickly as she rubbed Grandma's hands while Effie patted her shoulders. They were so concerned with my seventy-four year old Grandma they had forgotten Larson's daughter was also present. No one had to ask me to sit. Luckily, the chair I dropped into was directly in line with my body, or I might have hit the floor.

"Oh, Meryl Jean. Honey, it's gonna be all right. You be strong now. Your Daddy will be okay." Effie came to my side after noticing my reaction. Her words sounded muffled, as though they were coming through molasses.

All I could think about was that Daddy's temper had finally gotten bigger than he was—something Grandma and I had constantly feared would happen. How could Effie know Daddy would be all right? He'd killed someone. For Heaven sake. How could that ever be all right? Self-defense or not, Daddy took a life. My brain couldn't make my mouth speak. They were saying there were witnesses, but a man was still—dead. This was real. Wiley's face would never show another expression, his eyes never see again. His heart would never make another beat—all from the hand of my very own father.

"Where's Larson now?" Grandma finally found her voice.

"They've taken him to the Caruthersville jail," Simp answered.

"Oh…Oh…" Grandma put her hand over her heart again. "I can't stand to think of my son in jail—behind bars. I need to go to him." Grandma's voice was barely a whisper.

"Now listen. Jake and Simp talked to Clete. They'll be checkin' Larson into the jail, askin' him questions, and gettin' him settled. They'll also be busy gettin' statements from witnesses. We'll take you if you insist, but you might should wait 'til mornin'."

"Okay Katty, can we go in the mornin' early?" Grandma took my hand in hers.

"Just say a time, and we'll do it," Simp reassured.

"Right after breakfast if that's okay," Grandma said.

The two couples hugged and patted us and searched for words of comfort, until it almost became awkward. Effie was the first to suggest they go. The kitchen became a chamber of silence once they left. Silently and robotically Grandma and I moved to the swing, our normal place of comfort and solitude.

"The dream—Meryl, remember the dream I had 'bout your Daddy?"

"Which one, Grandma? You're always dreaming about him?"

"The one where he was so small. As big and fierce as Larson can be, he's small and helpless right now. I've heard jail cells are cramped, and when their broken enough, a person's spirit might almost shrink down to nothin' inside of one." Grandma was dazed.

"They said it was self-defense. We always worried he could kill a person over us or to protect someone else. But I didn't think it would be in self-defense. Why would Wiley ever try to take down Daddy?"

"Whiskey has a way of makin' people feel like they're giants while it shrivels their brains to the size of a pea. Somethin' that small don't have room for good sense and reasonin' in it." Grandma's simple explanation was vivid.

Supper was a blur that evening. We gleaned leftovers. Neither of us felt like cooking nor were we very hungry. Grandma's night prayers reminded me of a sermon we'd heard about how God would hear our moanings and groanings if words wouldn't come. Her prayers that night brought reality to that scripture.

I had seen Wiley Bunkus a few times and only up close once when he was riding in the car with Daddy. The best I remembered, he was tall and lanky. His sharp, chiseled, ashen grey facial features appeared cold and stone-like. A protruded Adam's apple moved up and down his long neck when he talked or swallowed. According to Jake and Simp, witnesses said Daddy's fist broke that neck with a single blow.

*Lord, please help us. My daddy took someone's life.*

## Chapter Sixty-Five

THE USUAL FORTY-FIVE minute trip to Caruthersville seemed to take twice as long today. Grandma sat clutching a change of clothes for Daddy but eventually laid them between us in the back seat. The rest of the way she wrung her hands, until her knuckles looked raw. We had no clue of what to expect. Neither of us had been inside a jail before. I'd only heard stories of people who'd been thrown—actually thrown—into them.

Simp let us out in front of the jail and found a shady spot to park and wait. We awkwardly entered the heavy doors. His glistening badge seemed to supersede the face of the uniformed man sitting behind a desk. This ordeal caused by Daddy was something no mother should have to ever go through. Daughter—either.

"Ma'am, I hate to ask, but can you empty your purse?" The jailer asked in an apologetic tone.

"Empty my purse? What on earth for?"

"It's procedure, Ma'am."

"All right," Grandma obediently emptied her purse. When her pocket Bible fell on top of her lace handkerchief, he told her it was okay and let us to proceed.

Daddy was sitting on his bunk, the cell door wide

open. Grandma cried softly before pulling herself together. I also couldn't hold back tears. We were truly as uncomfortable as we looked, sitting nervously on the stools the jailer brought us.

"Mom, you gotta' believe me. I didn't mean to kill Wiley."

"So you're admittin' it son? Why did you kill him?"

"Daddy, they're saying you broke his neck."

"Baby, Mom, listen to me, Wiley was drunk. We were all drinking, but you know I can hold my liquor." Daddy's boastings of holding his liquor held no merit for me now.

"You must a not held it so good this time, son." Evidently Grandma shared my lack of merit in his claim. Daddy normally would have come back with a snide remark. But this time, he chose to continue with his side of the story. "We was jokin' and laughin' and a rollin' dice. Out of nowhere, this woman, Wiley's sometimes girlfriend, come up behind me and kissed the top of my head. She said it was for luck."

"Sometime girlfriend, I thought Wiley was married," Grandma interrupted.

"Yeah, but…well…that was Wiley's problem. Mom, I didn't even know that woman. I still don't know her. Anyhow, Wiley got mad and started mouthin' off. I didn't pay him no 'tention. Can you believe the idiot kicked my stool out from under me? When I stood up, he was in my face with a knife in his hand. Y'all know I don't carry no weapon."

"Well, it was self-defense then—right?"

"Yes Baby, I tried to talk him down, but he was so drunk and green-eyed jealous that he lunged at me with that knife. I hit him once—and I guess that's when I broke his neck."

"I don't understand Larson. If it was to protect yourself, then why do they have you here in jail?"

"Them shysters runnin' that operation over there hid the knife so that when the law come they could call it a killin'—cut and dried."

"Why would they say you were a killer if you had to defend yourself? Again, I don't understand, son."

"Listen Mom, they was doin' everythin' at that place. They was moonshinin, chicken fightin', gamblin' and it's practically a full-fledged whorehouse. If the law started pokin' around and saw what was goin' on, 'em people would be the ones in jail."

"So why didn't you just tell Clete all of that, Daddy?"

"I did tell Clete after he got there. But by the time he showed up the first cops that come had me arrested, cuffed and sittin' in their patrol car. They didn't know me and wouldn't listen to my side. Mom, it was my word against all the others. Them cops only saw a dead man and—me."

"Dear God, Son." Grandma held her heart again.

"Listen, that bunch over at Five Points are dumb as

dirt but they was smart enough to put their knot heads together and stick to the same story. Anyone who knew Wiley knew he was always flashin' around that big pearl handled knife of his. But those big-shot cops didn't know Wiley, me, or none of the rest of that bunch.

"Wiley was the only one that could tell the truth—and he was dead. Naturally, they called it murder. And with 'em hidin' the knife to get rid of the evidence, everythin' and everybody pointed to me. 'Course, they could tell I was drinking pretty heavy too. I told Clete how it went down. I know he believes me, but his hands are tied without that knife."

"Wiley had several kids too didn't he?"

"Yes, Mom, he did. I know you're thinkin' that was no place for me, but Wiley sure had no business there with a family at home."

"Lordy me, Larson. You might as well a been in Sodom and Gomorrah."

"Wasn't that bad. But yes, there was better places I could a been."

"So what's going to happen now?" I asked.

"Clete said I'll have to stay here at least 'til I can go before a judge, and that may take a while. He also said he'd try to find Wiley's knife." Daddy was cautiously hopeful.

"I hate you being here in jail son, but I don't have the money to get you out."

"I know, Mom. Don't worry. Clete talked to 'em.

They know I'm not a murderer, even if I did have to be a killer. There is a difference you know—don't you?"

"We brought your clothes, Daddy," I said unclear how to respond to his last question.

"Simp and Katty were good to bring us here to see you. Maybe I can give 'em gas money, and they'll bring us back Friday. We better not keep 'em waitin' now though."

"Okay, Mom. But I just want you and Meryl to know I'm not guilty like in the same way I know people are gonna tell around."

"That's not entirely true, son. You did take a man's life even if you didn't mean to do it. And you was guilty of being in the wrong by just being there. See what followin' your own will has done for you?"

"I know. I know. If I had it to do over, I'd change a few things."

"I'd hope you'd change every bit of it," Grandma grumbled then hugged him a long time. He didn't know it, but I knew she was praying over him.

"Bye, Daddy. I love you." After giving him a hug, I followed Grandma.

She stopped abruptly and we turned to face him again. "Remember those words about doing things differently if and when you get out of here, Larson. And, by the way, you don't have a wife any more, but you have a child to think about, and she's standin' right here."

He stood mutely in the door of the cell as we left. Grandma couldn't have said anything that made a bigger impact than to remind him of how his actions had affected me.

"So was it self-defense?" Katty was bursting to ask when we returned.

"Larson says it was. He said Wiley was crazy drunk and pulled a knife on 'im."

"Only a fool'd pull a knife on Larson Strom, lessen they planned to eat it." Simp snickered.

"Well I don't think nobody'd ever accuse Wiley Bunkus of bein' very smart. So if that's it, why's Larson still in jail?" Katty spouted.

"Them *no-goods* hid Wiley's knife and stuck together to say Larson killed Wiley in cold blood. Clete's trying to clear him, but it's gonna take time."

"I feel sorry for Mrs. Bunkus and those kids. It also scares me that if Daddy hadn't defended himself, I'd be the one without a father right now."

"I've had to bury too many loved ones already, Meryl. I hope God lets me go first before I have to bury one of my boys."

"Now, Mrs. Strom, Meryl, y'all needn't be talkin' like that. Larson's still alive. You still have your son. And Meryl, you still have your daddy. Mrs. Strom, we don't want to hear no more talk 'bout you dyin'. I can't think about a world without you in it."

"That's such a sweet thing to say, Katty, but we're

not put on this earth to live forever. I appreciate your kind words. I also appreciate y'all takin' us today."

"We're glad to do it, Mrs. Strom," Simp assured.

"This may be a good time to say we may need you to take us again this Friday. I'll give you gas money, of course."

"Just let us know," Simp replied.

"I hope he's free by Friday. He will be if they find the knife," I said.

"Well, there's lot more horse's butts in this world than there are horses," Katty blurted out of the blue. We all looked at her in disbelief. That statement was shocking, coming from Katty. Not only was it a coarse remark, but it was also totally out of context to our conversation.

"Where'd that come from Katty?" Simp asked.

"Mr. Rudy Pylant. He said it this mornin' at the end of his 'Old Camp Meetin' Time' radio show."

"Mr. Rudy said that over the radio? Who was he callin' horse's butts? Is he even allowed to say that while he's on the air?" Simp was shocked.

"Actually, he didn't say butts. He called them what they was—asses.

"KATTY SIMPSON!" Grandma gasped.

"Well it's in the Bible, Mrs. Strom," Katty argued. "I don't think he knew he'd left his microphone on. He was talking about crooked politicians, but in this case, I think it can go just as well for a bunch of dishonestmoonshinin'-gamblin'-knife hidin'-no-goods, too," Katty snorted.

"Well, I guess you and Mr. Rudy are both right. Crookedness is wrong, be it politicians or like you said, a *bunch of no-goods*," Grandma agreed.

Simp took us to see Daddy the following Friday. It was two weeks before we asked them to take us again and even longer between the next times. Grandma didn't want to burden them. Plus, she didn't have the extra money for gasoline. I really wanted to believe Clete could clear Daddy by proving self-defense. However, months went by, and Daddy remained in the Caruthersville jail.

We found a little comfort when he was made the jail's trustee. That was common practice in those days for some inmates. Clete convinced the officials and judges of Daddy's self-defense claim, but they couldn't set him free without proof or unless someone posted his bail. He could come and go as he pleased anywhere in town, as long as he was back in his cell by 6 p.m. His cell door was never locked.

Finally, Uncle Bray came to Daddy's and our rescue. He couldn't stand to see his brother arrested for a matter of self-defense. Plus, he knew what the situation was doing to Grandma and me. After he showed up with a thousand dollars bail money, Daddy was a free man. At least he was out of jail—even if he wasn't yet cleared.

The weekend after he was released Daddy dropped by Chaffin's corner store for a pack of cigarettes. One of his false accusers was leaning against the Coke box. He was shocked to see none other than Larson Strom, who was supposed to be tucked away in jail, casually stroll through the door. This man knew the man who killed Wiley in self-defense. He also witnessed the power of his fist. He probably feared what Daddy might do to those who lied about him—namely him.

After calculating in his twisted little mind, the advantages of coming clean and saving his own hide, he sided up to Daddy, "Larson, I know where that knife is. I'll get it for you. Just don't let the others know I give it to you, okay?"

"That'd be a smart thing on your part," Daddy muttered through clenched teeth.

An hour or so later, a car stopped at the edge of our yard. Daddy approached the nervous driver, who remained behind the wheel. When he returned to the porch, he held the large, pearl-handled, switchblade knife that Wiley Bunkus had waved many times in the face of countless others and had threatened him with that fateful evening.

Daddy wasted no time getting the knife to Clete who wasted no time getting it to the judge. Unfortunately, for that witness, he was forced to testify to the claim of self-defense. The case was dismissed. Daddy was cleared of all charges. Uncle Bray was returned the bail money, and those in our small circle released a unified sigh of relief.

"Remember that fortuneteller-lookin' woman who told me I had a son who'd break my heart?" Grandma reminded me a few days later.

"How could I forget her? Does this thing with Daddy prove she was a good messenger or an evil one?"

"That remains a mystery. What she said was true though. Larson has broken my heart, this time and many times over. But, you know what? He still can't break my spirit and never will. I won't give up prayin' for him 'til God answers my prayers. I feel like the message was from God—even if the devil did bring it—if that was what happened."

"Maybe God is answering your prayers a little at a time. As far as I know, Daddy hasn't gone back to Five Points or hung out with any of those people anymore."

"The last I heard about that *bunch of no goods* was that the ones who didn't wind up in jail, decided to move as far from Muddy Ox as they could get. Some people joke they may have joined the Boones somewhere in the hollers of Kentucky. If they did, this time it's me sayin'—goodriddins." Grandma laughed.

"Me too," I agreed. We knew if Daddy wanted to, he could find another bunch like that to hang with, but at least it wouldn't be that group.

"As for Larson, a lesson bought was better than one taught."

"What exactly does that mean, Grandma?"

"I taught your Daddy time and time again to stay away from places like that, but I guess it took buyin' time in a jail cell to let him see for himself that jail was no place he wanted to be. He bought that lesson for sure."

"I never thought we'd feel at ease to know Daddy was at the blacksmith shop until we discovered there were worse places and worse situations he could be in."

# Chapter Sixty-Six

AT SCHOOL, I avoided talking about Daddy with my classmates. The few who knew about what happened at Five Points never brought it up to me. That was good. We were dismissed for picking season after only six weeks. I had to pick harder than I'd ever picked before. I wanted a year book, senior pictures, and there was cap and gown rental and invitations to buy. It was unnerving, exciting—and expensive.

I was glad my brother in Michigan insisted on sending me the money to buy my class ring. Brother said since he couldn't come that it would be a graduation gift from his wife, Willowdean, and him—and Mama.

That was heartwarming.

With Daddy's fiasco behind us, the Boones gone and never coming back, I could get on with the task at hand—graduating.

I still couldn't answer the question of what I wanted to do after graduation that had been posed to me several times. College seemed a galaxy beyond my reach. I wished the big dipper that Hutch and I lay on the grass and looked at would pour a stream of tuition money down on me. *Meryl Jean, are you going to be a dreamer your entire life? Things like that just don't happen.*

With a new cotton sack draped over my shoulder and sporting yet another new bonnet, I set off for the first day of my last season ever of picking cotton. Tara waited by the wagon. An ugly scar was the only physical reminder of her traumatic leg injury.

"Hey, Jean, are you ready to hit the field?"

Immediately, the roar of a mechanical cotton picker went whirring down the road by our patch. It was on its way to Carl Chaffin's field that adjoined Mr. and Mrs. Bertram's.

"No matter what kind of job I work at in the future, I'm always going to remind myself that—at least it's not picking cotton," I proclaimed.

"This might be the last year for you girls to have to pick cotton, but because of them things, pickin' cotton by hand could be endin' for all of us before long. Why, they can pick more cotton in a day than we can get picked in a week—and they don't have to stop and get a drink of water," Mr. Bertram grumbled at the mechanical contraption after overhearing our conversation. That was true. It was evident that the day of the field worker was quickly coming to an end. More and more mechanical pickers were seen daily.

"But look at the mess they leave. There's cotton strewn all over the field, especially at the end of the rows," Tara argued.

"Yeah, but the land owners still come out ahead,

considerin' how quickly they can get their crops harvested," Mr. Bertram replied.

"Well, Tara, you and I won't have to worry about it after next May—right? We'll be doing something different. I'm not sure what, but I don't see another cotton field in either of our futures." Tara and I shouldered our sacks and chose rows.

"What do you see, Jean?" Tara quizzed.

"College maybe, if I had the money, and if Grandma would be willing for me to go."

"Well, there are scholarships."

"Yes, but I don't see me getting one. My grades are good, but probably not good enough to get a scholarship," I sighed.

"There are all kinds of scholarships. You may not be at the very top of our class, but you make good grades. I've had too many classes with you not to know that."

"Yeah…well…maybe. So, Tara, what do you want to do after graduation?"

I didn't want to talk anymore about me. Even if by some stretch of the imagination, I could get a scholarship, Grandma's warming up to the idea of me going away to College was far-fetched. Moving to Kennett or Caruthersville was far away to her.

"Are you going to college?" I asked Tara.

"I've applied for a few scholarships. I'm hoping to…"

"Tara Gayle, how's that leg doin'?" Emmy Bertram

interrupted.

We were picking grab-rows. Stuffing three rows of cotton in our sacks would get them filled much quicker. We'd evolved into a pretty fair team once I perfected my skills. Mrs. Bertram didn't have to fuss at us as she once had. Still, the sound of her voice caused us both to jump.

"It's all well now, Grandma. This scar is the only reminder." Tara raised her pant leg to display her battle scar.

"I still can't believe after all the times I'd warned you about the dangers of a sharp hoe, that you'd let that happen to you."

Tara knew better than to try to dispel her grandmother's notion that she didn't *let* it happen to her. It just happened. Anyway, I knew Wade's good looks had blinded her, and she couldn't see the weeds on her row and where her super-sharpened hoe was going.

"Yeah Grandma, I've sure learned my lesson," Tara conceded.

"I'd a more expected Jean to do somethin' like that than you. She hasn't been choppin' as long as you have."

I opened my mouth in my defense but decided to follow Tara's lead and concede. I could almost hear Grandma whispering, "*A soft answer turns away wrath.*"

"I'm doing good now though, don't you think, Mrs. Bertram?"

"Jean, you're doin' really good to be as green as a gourd when you first come. Y'all pick it clean now, and don't miss any of that cotton underneath there," Mrs. Bertram said as she moved down the field. "Pick it clean. The gin don't pay as much for dirty cotton." Her voice echoed across the field.

Again, I'd been called green and was reminded of Wade's insults. As though Tara and I had been struck by the same brainwave, she said, "It was Wade that distracted me that day. I don't want to let Grandma Bertram know it though."

"Your secret's safe. But you didn't miss much not being in the field with Wade."

"Really? I thought he was a dreamboat," Tara swooned.

"He was a dream all right—a nightmare."

"How can you say that, Jean? I could have gotten lost in his eyes and dimples."

"I saw another side of Wade. He wasn't as he seemed. His smooth-talking southern drawl was how he wooed people. The next word out of his mouth could have been an insult or a lie."

"Well, I was only with him a short time. He actually talked to you more that day. I thought he sorta liked you. But I sort of thought he liked me too," sighed Tara.

"That was his deception. He didn't actually like you or me. He saw me as a desperate, easy, target. In two days after I turned him down for a date, he'd already moved on to another girl. He didn't talk to you as much because you were cute, popular, and could date anyone you wanted. His game was to prey on girls that he thought no one else would ask out, so they'd be *grateful* because he showed them attention."

"You—you—turned down a date with Wade? How do you know he thought I was cute?" Tara couldn't resist hearing if someone—even someone like Wade had complimented her.

"I overheard him talking to a friend when he didn't know I was listening. He said he passed you up because you were too cute and popular. He targeted me because I was overweight and *green*, he said. Your Grandma reminded me of that just now when she called me green as a gourd."

"The cad—how dare him. What did he mean you were green?"

"I told him Grandma wouldn't let me date at night. He knew I hadn't dated very much. By green he meant innocent, hadn't been around—you know, a virgin."

"And he thought I'd been around? I'm a virgin, too. Like I said—the cad. I don't care how cute he is, he's still a cad." Tara was appalled.

"It was more about popularity. He figured you'd be harder to win over. Since I was fat, he thought I'd jump at the chance to go with handsome him."

"Jean, you're pretty. The fact your Grandma won't

let you go out at night, and you hadn't dated much was why he targeted you, not that you were—not because of—you know, your size." I heard the words Tara hadn't said. I had a pretty face, even if I was fat. That was an overused line for fat girls, although Tara would have never said it.

"After Wade showed Daddy his fake, sugary side, Daddy persuaded Grandma to let me go to the drive-in with him. But, once I overheard him bragging to his friend about how green I was, I didn't want to go anywhere, at any time, with Wade."

"Good for you. You mean your Grandma gave in for you to date him at night?"

"Yes, but I figured out his intentions—night or day. Two days later he was wooing another girl. She was thin but, you know, homely. To Wade that spelled desperate."

"Did she go out with him?"

"I don't know. I didn't see either of them after that. Hey, it's almost dinner time. We can rest a while."

"Jean, don't you let someone like Wade destroy your confidence. So you're not thin. You're pretty, you sing beautifully and—you're you and that's a good thing."

"I'll admit the old inferiority feelings crept back in for a while. I still feel uncomfortable in certain crowds."

"Wade might have been drop-dead handsome then, but he's ugly to me now. He was right to pass me by. I'm glad he did," Tara decided.

After shouldering our sacks, we headed to the scales. We each had picked over one hundred and fifty pounds of cotton before noon. We laughed to think our anger toward Wade set our hands to picking faster. I only needed a hundred more to reach my two-hundred fifty pound daily goal.

We hit it hard after dinner. I needed every day's pay of seven dollars and fifty cents I could earn to add to my graduation fund. After a couple of hours, Tara and I carried our tightly packed sacks to the scales. Once they were emptied, we fell backwards into the wagon of cotton and began making the equivalent of snow angels. "I love the smell of freshly picked cotton like this, don't you, Jean?"

"Yes. There's not another smell like it," I agreed.

"Guess that is one thing we'll miss, right?"

A wagon of freshly picked cotton offered a sense of euphoria equal to that of snuggling into clean bed sheets, line-dried by the sun. Tara and I joked that it smelled even better off the stalks and emptied out of our sacks into the wagon.

While enjoying a few stolen moments of fun and rest, we overheard two women talking softly as they walked by on their way back to the field. They couldn't see us lying in the wagon and didn't know we heard them.

"Her poor family. The last thing they needed was another mouth to feed."

"That Wade Wilson has struck again. I'd heard he got another girl in the family way over around Turkey Trot. I hated it for sure when I heard it was that poor girl."

"Her Daddy told my husband they didn't want to make him marry the girl 'cause just 'cause you smooth out a couple of bumps in a road, don't guarantee the rest of the path will be easy. Besides, Wade Wilson wasn't the type to settle down and make a livin' for a wife and baby." Their voices faded but Tara and I figured out the rest.

"Now we know why that girl hasn't been back to this field. It was in the spring when he was siding up to her out here. She's probably showin' pretty good by now." I knew those women were talking about the girl I saw Wade flirting with that day. Poor thing, all she became was another notch on Wade Wilson's belt buckle. Thank you, Mama, for warning me in those dreams. That girl could have been me.

## Chapter Sixty-Seven

IT HAD BEEN a good year for cotton farmers and pickers alike, especially me. New outfits and ten more pairs of tennis shoes lined my closet. The last half of my senior year would begin in seven days. I was excited and anxious about what was ahead for me.

Because the temperatures were a little cooler and the sky overcast, I'd thrown my bonnet back. Head down, hands moving as fast as they could go, I never saw the huge spiderweb draped across the middle of the row until I was eye to eye with a half dollar sized yellow, black-dotted cotton spider. I let out a scream that could have given the spider and half the people in the field a heart attack.

"That was a granddaddy or maybe a grandmamma spider for sure," my rescuer said as he slammed the spider to the ground with a swipe of his hat, then ground it into the dirt with his boot.

My flesh crawled and my heart nearly pounded out of my chest until I noticed the brawny young fellow who had heroically come to my aid. Then, my heart pounded for another obvious reason.

"Thank you. I usually don't scare easily, but that

thing caught me by surprise," I said once I could speak.

"It was bigger than most, and so was its web." He agreed while clearing the web with another swipe of his hat.

"Well, thank you again. I'm Jean Strom," extending a hand to my hero.

"Melb…Mel Tarkington," he said, with a gentle, lingering handshake.

"I saw you when we started this morning. This is your first day in this patch, isn't it?" Our eyes still locked, I added, "…and your family. I saw you—and your family this morning."

"Yeah, we were pickin' for Emmet Tuttle, but his field got done. My dad heard that Mr. Bertram was still workin', so we came here."

"Oh…do you know Polly Evans? Her dad sharecrops for Mr. Tuttle."

"I think there was a girl they called Polly over there. I'm not sure."

"She's my friend from school."

"How is Muddy Ox School? I'll be startin' there Monday as a senior." He said proudly.

"So am I. I'm a senior this year too. So is Polly."

"Good, at least I'll already know someone when I start." He sounded relieved.

"You'll like Muddy Ox. I've been going there since eighth grade. We moved here from Illinois after my mother died. We live with my Grandmother in Silver

Leaf."

"We?"

"My dad and I."

"Isn't that your dad drivin' Mr. Bertram's tractor?"

"Yes, that's my dad."

"Melba, you gonna talk all day or you gonna use that cotton sack?" His father's voice echoed across the field, although he was only a few rows over.

Mel's face flushed red. Heroes didn't usually get reprimanded so blatantly. His handsomeness still outshined his embarrassment. But I felt bad for him.

"Sorry, if I got you in trouble," I whispered.

"It's all right. I'm used to it. It's not your fault. My dad looks for reasons to yell at me."

"Anyway, I'm still sorry. Thanks again—Mel."

Hmm, so Mel knew it was my dad driving the tractor. That was interesting. Evidently, he'd noticed me too. Maybe his rescuing me from that spider wasn't a coincidence. Yes, I heard Mr. Tarkington fussing at Mel's little sisters and his mother in only the short time we'd been in the field that morning. I felt bad for them.

"Now, everyone in the field knows my real name, including you. I swear. My dad does that on purpose to embarrass me. It's Melba—my name is Melba—okay? He could have just called me Mel, though." He kicked the dirt and the redness returned to his face.

"A name—is a name," I whispered.

"Well, guess you don't hear of many guys named

Melba."

"I can't say I ever have, but you didn't have a say in the name your mother gave you, right? My first name is Meryl. But at school I'm called by my middle name, Jean."

"Why? Meryl's a nice name. 'Course, there's nothin' wrong with Jean either."

"I changed my name after we moved here. Meryl had too many memories and—other bad things attached to it."

"Bad things? What other bad things?"

"Oh…you know, my mother's death and…and stuff."

"I may change my name someday after I'm out on my own, maybe," Mel growled through clenched teeth.

Mel and I picked alongside one another the rest of that day and every day for the remainder of the week. He was polite, witty, and fun. Another plus to having Mel as a picking buddy all week was Tara and her mother were in St. Louis again visiting her dad and school shopping. Being with Mel made the week fly by. It was the first time I'd ever wanted a week in the cotton field to last longer. Friday came way too soon.

"The next time I see you will probably be at school. Polly and I usually meet at the east door every morning. I know you'll be busy that first day getting enrolled and stuff though," I said as I climbed down from the wagon after emptying my sack.

"Nice meetin' and workin' with you this week, Jean. See you Monday at school."

Mel shouldered his mother's sack to empty it while she herded his little sisters to their car. His dad waited impatiently as Mrs. Bertram figured their totals for the day.

Flashing him a smile, I walked to the end of the field row to wait for Daddy. Mel gave me a wave as they drove by that reminded me of how Hutch used to do. His dad was yelling profanities at his family.

"What a beast," Daddy said as he watched them pull onto the road.

"Mel's dad?"

"Is that the boy's name you were so friendly with? Yeah—his dad. Evidently, his wife and young'uns didn't pick enough cotton to suit him."

"Their last name is Tarkington. We met earlier this week when he killed a giant cotton spider for me."

"A cotton spider? They won't hurt you."

"No, but this one was so big that I could have hurt myself trying to get away from it."

"Playin' the damsel in distress, huh?"

"I wasn't playing. Do spiders have hearts? If so, it would have probably died of a heart attack when I screamed if Mel hadn't stomped it into the dirt first."

"Last I heard, almost everythin' has a heart of some kind. I never heard of a spider havin' a heart attack though," Daddy grinned.

"Mel is starting school here Monday. He's also a senior."

"When I heard his dad yellin' for Melba, I thought he was callin' for one of the little girls. I was surprised when that boy answered him. Melba—I sure hope that kid can handle himself. He's bound to have his share of fights with a name like Melba."

"His grandfathers were named Melton and Bartholomew. Mel's mother took both names and came up with Mel-ba. He hates it, but what can he do? He tells everyone his name is just 'Mel'."

"Well, I hope 'just Mel has a good left hook. That's a terrible name to saddle your boy with. I don't care what his grandpa's names was," Daddy decided.

I had most of my school clothes already, but I still loved our Saturday trips to town. Tomorrow would be the last one before school started. The memory of how my season of hard work went up in smoke last year briefly overshadowed the moment. I gave a sigh of relief to know the Boones were tucked far into the hills of Kentucky—away from my bounty of new clothes.

A happy thought soon replaced the bad one. Come Monday, I'd have more than just meeting up with Polly and Darla again to look forward to. I'd be passing Mel in the halls all day long. He sure was handsome.

## Chapter Sixty-Eight

WE RARELY EVER left Caruthersville without swinging by the levee to see how high the Mississippi River had risen. Our Saturday's shopping trip had been no exception.

"River's up. Guess it's from all that meltin' snow and ice storms they been havin' up North. I remember weather in Michigan bein' fierce, and it only gets worse the further north you go," Daddy remarked, pulling as close to the river bank as possible.

"Y'all sure didn't live in Michigan very long, did you?"

"No, Mom, you didn't raise no fool. The first mornin' I woke up to the radio antenna stickin' out of the snow banked on the hood of my car, it didn't take me long to decide 'em lake-effect snows wasn't for me."

"Lake-effect snows?" Grandma asked.

"Yeah, the winds from Lake Michigan made the snows even meaner." Daddy always complained about Michigan weather.

Grandma had never been farther north than St. Louis. I could imagine she envisioned *up North* to be a continuous uphill slope that allowed the melted snow and ice to run down and gather into the only part of the Mississippi River she was familiar with—the river bank at Caruthersville, Missouri.

The water sloshed over the rocky banks and rejoined the river's southern flow. As we drove away I noticed a few planks, a severed tree limb, and one old boot, floating down the swift current. What stories they could have told, had they had a voice. Would possibly someone in New Orleans be standing at the river's edge to witness the same debris before it washed into the ocean? Also, I wondered whose *up North* eyes had seen it before mine?

A row of run-down shanties suspended on poles to escape high waters during floods stood to our left as we'd inched away from the river. The splintered steps and banisters surely posed a challenge to those who climbed them. Red and multi-colored curtains, some torn, some draped carelessly, covered the dingy windows. Several broken panes were planked over, likely to keep out the cold and inquisitive eyes such as ours, who snailed by on their way back to Main Street. Daddy's pace was as though he was looking for something—or someone.

"I'm surprised the law lets them houses of sin still stand. Hurry on by Larson. I don't want nobody seein' us lookin' at 'em."

"Mom, there's a lot of pot holes here in the road. I can't go fast. Don't look at 'em. Who's gonna see you lookin' anyhow?"

So those were the whorehouses I'd heard whispers about. I'd seen those shanties before, but assumed they were fishing cottages. I wished Daddy would have driven even slower, so I could've looked longer and harder. I'd only heard talk of whorehouses before.

Yes, Grandma could have looked away. However, curiosity overruled her ability to do so—mine too. Leave it to Daddy to add a little flavor to a normally dull situation. I wondered how familiar he was with that red-light district but wasn't going to ask.

NO DOUBT PASSERSBY questioned the smile on my face Monday morning during my walk to school as I was remembering how Daddy could bring excitement to a mundane Saturday trip to town without even trying.

The sound of grinding gears and smell of exhaust fumes erased my thoughts and snapped me back to reality as several buses lined up next to the school yard. I searched for Polly's and Darla's buses in the circled drive and was about to give up when I saw Mel making his way down the steps of a bus. Upon reaching the last step, he hesitated and turned to help—Polly. Yes, it was Polly who Mel was assisting off the bus. I blinked again.

A collage of emotions raced through my mind. However, not any of the pieces fit into my moment. I felt sheer happiness to see Polly. A surge of passion warmed my heart and head to see Mel. Then—a sting of jealousy left me numb. Mel acted as though he didn't know Polly when I mentioned her to him in the cotton patch last week. They were certainly acquainted now.

"Hey Jean, I've missed you so much. I couldn't wait for school to start." Polly and I hugged. She momentarily ignored Mel, who was standing inches from her.

"Me either. I missed you, too," I managed.

"You know Mel. He said he'd picked cotton with you last week. Who would have thought he'd live on the same farm as us, but he makes friends with you first. We talked about you almost the whole way here."

I was about to come up with a response when Mel broke in. "It's good to see you again, Jean. I gotta' go to the office, now. Bye Polly. See you around, Jean." Mel disappeared, and I confronted Polly.

"You talked about me? What did you—Mel, find to say about me for that long?"

"He said you were nice and were a hard worker. He's going to save me a seat this afternoon, if he gets on the bus before I do. He's really sweet."

I had no right to be jealous or even read anything into mine and Mel's week together in the field. I couldn't blame Polly if she was attracted to him. He was sweet and—gorgeous. She was cute, smart, and thin. No wonder he liked her—I guessed. Polly didn't know her words were cutting me like a machete.

Today I was glad Polly and I had separate home rooms. I needed time to process. My excitement at getting to introduce Mel to Polly, Darla, and the others was crushed.

She was my best friend. And he was—what was he? He was just a guy, a real dreamboat guy, I'd met in a cotton patch. He was nice to me, and we talked and joked for an entire week. That was all. Who was I kidding? Had I not been the only girl in the cotton patch, for that matter, the only person his age, he probably wouldn't have given me the time of day. Picking with me was better than picking alone. I felt devastated.

I thought we had something in common. He was ashamed of his name, and I was ashamed of my weight. I made him aware of Polly when he hadn't given her a thought before. At least that was my impression.

Polly has a right to like Mel if she does. Is Mel is shallow like Wade and all the other boys I know? Well, not Hutch. He was anything but shallow. I slid into the desk next to Darla. We exchanged a quick hello before class began.

"All right class. I'm glad to see everyone back," Mr. Vondell said when there was a knock on our classroom door.

"Excuse me sir, the office said this is my home

room."

"Okay, what's your name?"

"Mel—Mel Tarkington," he said handing Mr. Vondell his admission slip.

"Okay, Melb…uh…Mel, welcome to our class. Pick an empty seat." Mr. Vondell was kind not to announce Mel's actual name to the class.

There was an empty chair next to me. But Mel took a seat by Brenda Bittle in the back of the room. I looked up as he walked by me, but he kept his eyes forward. Was I being unfair? Darla and I sat on the front row. Someone new, especially a guy, wouldn't want to sit on the front row. He was probably nervous since he walked in after class began. I'd give him the benefit of the doubt.

Darla stopped to ask Mr. Vondell a question after class. I was waiting for her in the hall when Mel straggled out of the room. As he passed me, I gave him a warm smile and said, "Hi, guess we're in the same home room."

If I'd had doubts that Mel only wanted to be chummy with me in an isolated cotton field, they were confirmed when he glanced both directions before mumbling a quick one word reply, then scurried down the hall. It was obvious he didn't want to be seen talking to me at school.

"Okay, I got the assignment straight with Mr. Vondell. Hey, that new guy, Mel, is a real looker. I overheard all of the girls talking about him," Darla babbled.

"Believe it or not, I spent all last week with him in Mr. Bertram's field. We talked and joked and had so much fun. He even said he was glad he'd already know someone when he got here to school. But today, he's acting like he'd never met me before. He barely spoke to me in the hall just now. Guess he doesn't want to be seen talking with the fat girl." The word stung, coming out of my own mouth.

"Maybe he's nervous about being in a new school. Don't jump to conclusions."

"Darla, he didn't act nervous a few minutes ago, he acted embarrassed."

"I'm sorry. Don't let it get to you. Some guys are just immature."

"Who's immature?" Polly asked as she approached and heard Darla's remark.

"Nobody in particular—just guys in general," I interrupted. I wasn't up for discussing Mel with Polly at this point.

"So are we going to circle the school during noon hour as usual?" Darla asked picking up on my vibe. We often strolled the sidewalk that circled the school during noon hour for something to do when Polly and I didn't have lunch money. After the other students had finished eating, they joined the parade. It was a good way to see who the latest couples were.

"I overheard Cilla say a list of graduation expenses would be posted in the library. Let's check it out later. I hope I've saved enough money," Polly said.

"Me too," I moaned.

"And it should tell us how soon we need to get our orders in," Darla added.

"Man, it's going to be a long day. I am suddenly not feeling very well."

"Why, Jean? You were fine when Mel and I ran into you this morning," Polly asked.

"Oh, so you've met Mel?" Darla quizzed Polly.

"Yeah, he rides my bus…"

"We better get moving or we're not going to make it to second hour before the last bell," I interrupted again before taking off.

"Hey, thought you were sick," Polly's voice faded from behind.

"Oh, you know me. I'm tough. I'll be okay. Come on."

## Chapter Sixty-Nine

THE MORNING WAS busy. I saw Mel in the distance a few more times during class changes, but he avoided eye contact.

"Looks like you girls will be walking around the school alone today after all. I have to help with the school newspaper. See you fifth period," Darla said after meeting up with us in the library to check the graduation expense list.

I was once again thankful Brother had already bought my class ring, when I saw the cost of everything. If he hadn't, I wouldn't have had a ring at all.

"I'm glad I didn't spend any money in town last Saturday. I barely have enough to order a year book, pay for the smaller package of invitations, the pictures, and cap and gown rental. I can't spend another cent of savings," I sighed.

"Me, either. If I hadn't saved all along, I wouldn't be getting those things, either. I have an idea though. We can use one invitation to invite the entire church. It will make them go farther. Luckily, I don't have many to mail. Postage won't be too much."

"Postage? Polly, I didn't even think about postage. I

wanted to send invitations to family in Illinois and Arkansas. I doubt they'll get to come, but I wanted to send them an invitation anyway. Maybe Daddy will give me postage money." I made a mental note to ask him soon. With the crops over, his feet could be itching to take off again.

The wind was brisk, but the noon sun gave enough warmth to make our walk around the school bearable.

"So what do you think of Mel?" I knew the question was coming. Polly posed it no sooner than we'd stepped beyond the hall's rear door.

"He's nice. He's sure quiet. Y'all have a lot in common. I think his dad moves him around more than your dad did you before he took his sharecropping job."

"I'd noticed him in the field a few times, but we'd never talked. When he got on the bus this morning, he took the seat behind me. After turning my neck until it hurt trying to talk to him, I invited him to join me in my seat. I don't think he'd have spoken to me at all if you hadn't mentioned me when y'all were together in the field last week."

"He said he'd noticed you when I asked him about you."

"But he'd never spoken," Polly repeated.

"Guess I gave him the nudge he needed."

"Guess you did. Are you feeling better now?" Polly scanned my face.

"I'm okay. The day's almost over anyway." I was

ready for it to be over. I needed some alone time for an attitude adjustment concerning Mel. Polly didn't seem real smitten by him. But she did seem interested.

I SAID GOODBYE to Darla and Polly in the hall at the end of day and gave them an excuse of needing to get something from my locker. I didn't want to see Mel again right then, especially if he might have been waiting for Polly to join him on the bus.

I was walking slower than usual on my way home. I'd let the Mel and Polly thing get to me. I didn't notice Daddy's car come up behind me until he stopped. "Climb in Baby. How was your first day back to school?"

"It was okay. It was busy," I said as I slid into the passenger seat.

"Baby, I wanted to tell you first. I'm leaving out tonight for Florida. I'll tell Mom when we get home."

"She doesn't usually fuss when you leave after the crops are over. We've learned to expect it, actually. She'll be okay."

"Well, she might do a little fussin' this time."

"Why?"

"I'm not goin' alone."

"Who's going with you?" I figured he was going to say one of his drinking buddies from the blacksmith shop. Now Grandma could get out of sorts about that.

"You remember them little houses we saw when we left the river the other day?"

"Yes," I answered with reservations.

"Well, a *lady* who lives in one of 'em little houses is goin' with me."

So, that was why Daddy was inching by those shanties. And that's why he dreaded Grandma. He was right. She would not be happy about his traveling companion. Just when I thought Daddy couldn't do anything new under the sun to shock me—he did.

"You mean one of the women from the whor…?"

"Now Meryl Jean, don't go judgin' people. Not until you know the facts. Y'all don't know this woman. Did you really think I wouldn't ever have any lady friends anymore?"

Grandma and I had discussed this. She tried to prepare me for when Daddy might marry again since he was only thirty-nine when Mama died. Surprisingly, I was okay with that. I'd be glad for someone else to take over worrying with and about him. However, this wasn't what she meant. So far, Daddy wasn't talking marriage here. Poor Grandma, I dreaded for her to be told.

"Daddy, why tell her? You've gone off every year after the crops were done. If you went with anyone, we never knew it? Why tell Grandma now?"

His silence said more than I wanted to hear. After a long pause, Daddy said, "Baby, I've known this woman for a while now. I think a lot of her, and I've been wantin' to bring her to meet y'all before now. But after your Grandma's reaction to 'em houses last Saturday, I decided I might need to give it more time. That's all changed now."

"How did you meet her? Wait—don't tell me." I was so distraught I wasn't thinking. He didn't say what had changed to have her meet us now. I guess we were about to find out.

"It's not like you think Baby. I hung out at the levee a lot while I was in jail in Caruthersville, jest to watch the river rise and fall—you know. Well, one day I was mindin' my own business when I heard someone cryin' over by the sea wall. I heard a man's voice sort of mumblin'. A few minutes later, the man left towards town. The woman was still cryin,' so I walked over to her to see if she was hurt or anythin'."

"Was she having an argument with the man?"

"No, actually, the man was one of the local preachers."

"A preacher, Daddy? A preacher?"

"Again, it's not what you think Baby. He was prayin' with her."

"Praying with her?"

"Yes, preachers don't just talk to their members sittin' on the pews in 'em churches. A few of 'em go a little out of their way to talk to people in other places. Baby, some of those women over there like the business they're in. But this woman don't. That preacher went out on a limb to go down there. I think a lot of the guy for that. There's probably some people in his congregation that wouldn't understand though."

"So, she told you all of this?"

"Yes, once I got close enough, I saw she was a woman I'd met before."

"Was she in jail, too? What did she do to get put in jail?"

"Baby, I didn't say she was in jail. I said I met her durin' my time in jail. Remember I made trustee? I could come and go as I pleased as long as I was back by six at night."

"Yes, I remember."

"I recognized her from goin' down around the levee a lot. I met her down there."

"Oh—Oh—Okay." I was slow to catch on, but what Daddy said finally clicked.

"Well anyhow, when I went to see why she was cryin' and I realized who she was, we talked a long while. Baby, she wants to get away from that life. There's a long story why she took it up to begin with, but I won't go into it now. I'll just say there's a lot of reasons why people get into the life they're in. Some good. Some bad. She's a good person wantin' to change."

"Well…"

"Baby, she wants to get away from there, and I'm helpin' her do it. Nobody knows her in Florida. It'll be easier if she don't have a finger pointin' at her 'round every corner. I'm gonna go pick her up now."

Daddy started to call out for Grandma when he saw her note on the table. She'd left our suppers covered on the stove and gone to Hayti with Jake and Effie. The husband of one of her church friends died suddenly. They were going to comfort her.

Daddy gobbled his supper and pitched his clothes into his car. "I'll—we'll be right back. If your Grandma gets home before I do, why don't you let me fill her in?"

I'd be glad to let him fill Grandma in. No worries there. After I washed our dishes, I knew I should've started my homework. But feeling I needed my quiet time more now than ever; I sought the porch swing.

How light-hearted I'd felt during my morning walk to school, compared to how heavy my heart felt now proved I couldn't predict anything. If being shattered by Mel's apparent phony friendship wasn't enough, now my dad had gone to Caruthersville to bring home a female traveling companion that could throw Grandma into a tizzy.

I didn't have any more control over things than a pile of leaves that were being whirled by the wind along the roadside. They were bound by the will of the wind with no more choice in the matter than I had at that moment.

I couldn't control how Mel felt, but I could control how I would feel about him and Polly. I definitely couldn't control any of Daddy's actions. But as he had said, I didn't have the right to judge a woman I'd never met, especially if she wanted to change her life. And I surely couldn't do anything about the storm that would soon be arriving from Hayti—even less about the one coming back from Caruthersville soon after. Those two winds could possibly become a perfect storm disaster.

I could try to handle things tomorrow better than I did today. I had no idea about God's plans for my future. I only knew—they were surely worth waiting for. The early moon was peaking from behind a cloud, reminding me of a love song Mama used to sing to me.

*The moon is bright, and it shines on me.*
*Right through the leaves of our willow tree.*
*Please let the moon that shines on me,*
*Shine on the one I love.*

I wondered if the same moon that was shining on me at that moment could also be shining on my potential love, wherever or whoever he was…what a sweet thought.

## Chapter Seventy

I WAS STILL swinging and singing when Jake and Effie arrived with Grandma. They were unusually quiet as she eased out of their back seat.

"My heart hurts for Sister Gray," Grandma said as she dropped into the swing beside me.

"It must have hit Jake and Effie pretty hard, too. I've never seem them so solemn," I said.

"I remember how I felt after Omar died. And he'd been sick for a spell. Sister Gray called her husband to supper. When he didn't come, she found him sittin' in his easy chair—dead with a heart attack. Poor thing. She didn't even know how long he'd been gone," Grandma sighed.

"That's so sad. I'm glad y'all went to be with her. They were the sweetest pair."

"Where's your Daddy? Hasn't he come home yet? I liked it better before the crops got done. Least we knew where he was," Grandma sighed again.

"He's been here and left again. He'll be back soon. He went to Caruthersville."

"Caruthersville? Why? We were just there Saturday."

"He went to pick up a friend. Daddy will explain

when he gets back. I just know he's planning to leave for Florida tonight, and he's taking this friend with him. His clothes are already in the car."

"Figured he'd get the ramblin' bug before long. Don't see why he can't wait 'till mornin' though and drive in the daylight. Someone's goin' with him?"

"Yes, he'll tell you all about it when…"

"A car's comin' now. It's him," Grandma confirmed as she strained to see Daddy's mystery passenger. She looked shocked, but held her tongue, as his female companion followed Daddy to the porch.

"Mom, can we go inside? It's chilly out here. I want to introduce you to, Ruby."

"Sure, y'all come on in. Can I get you somethin' to drink—maybe some coffee?"

"No Mom, we don't have time. Guess, Meryl told you I'm—we're bound for Florida tonight."

"She was tellin' me when y'all drove up. Why are you leavin' out tonight? Can't you wait 'til daylight to go?" Grandma looked at Daddy and then to the woman, then back to Daddy. Daddy eyed me.

"I only told her you were leaving for Florida tonight," I said sheepishly, not wanting him to think I'd betrayed his confidence.

"Okay…well…Mom, this is Ruby Struthers. She's ridin' to Florida with me. I wanted you and Meryl to meet her before we take off."

"Do you have family in Florida, Miss Struthers?

"No, my only family is here in Missouri and over 'round Ripley, Tennessee."

"You have business there—maybe a job?"

"No Ma'am…um…not really…I'm…uh…"

"Mom, Ruby's reason to go to Florida is not to take on somethin' new; she's gettin' away from somethin' old."

"Leavin' somethin' old?" Grandma looked puzzled.

"Yes Ma'am. I'll be lookin' for a job once I get there. But that's not the reason I'm goin'. Um…Larson's told me what a good Christian woman you are. I know you'll understand. I've lived a sinful life and want to change my ways. I thought maybe Florida, bein' so far from the Bootheel would be a good place to do that."

"We're all only sinners, saved by Grace. No sin's so bad God can't forgive it. But it's not a change of place—it's a change of the heart we need."

"Sometimes forgivin' ourselves is the hard part," Ruby confessed.

"Mom, I met Ruby while I was in jail."

"Oh my, you were in jail with Larson?" Grandma gasped.

"No…no…Ma'am, I…"

"Remember, I was the trustee. I could go hang out by the river any time I wanted. I met Ruby there—she—lived there," Daddy said.

"Oh…" Grandma said. Then a light bulb went off

over her head. "Oh…I…see."

"Mom, that's the ways Ruby's wantin' to change and get away from." Grandma was without words. I was quiet, too. Even my quick wit couldn't find anything to add.

"So…we're gonna go now. Y'all don't worry. We'll take turns drivin' if I get tired and sleepy." Daddy stood up. "Here's thirty dollars, Mom. I'll try to send more after I get a job and get settled. And Meryl, here's fifteen to put toward your graduation savins'. Next time I see you, you'll be graduated."

"You're about all your Daddy ever talks about. He's so proud of you," Ruby said as she stepped off the porch.

"Thank you. And Daddy this money will help a lot," I said, giving him a hug and Ruby a smile. Now I had money for postage.

"Y'all be careful, Son. Good to meet you, Ruby." Grandma hesitated then continued. "Ruby, God sees and forgives a sincere heart."

"Thank you, Mrs. Strom. Larson says you pray all the time. Can you call my name too when you pray?"

"I sure will. I'll pray for both of you," Grandma said giving them both hugs.

"Well, we better get movin'." Daddy, probably anticipating a mini sermon coming on, ushered Ruby to his car. They waved and Daddy did his usual horn honking as they drove away. We returned to the kitchen and sat quietly at the table.

"I'll say one thing for him, your Daddy's full of surprises," Grandma broke the silence.

"Yes, he is," I agreed.

"I was hopin' Larson would find him another woman. He's too young to live out his life without a woman in it. But…"

"She said she wanted to change her ways," I interrupted.

"She said that, and God didn't appoint me judge over people. That's His job."

"Daddy seemed proud to be the one helping her."

"Your Daddy has a good heart," she agreed.

"And you do pray for him every night, Grandma."

"This could be God's doin'. God ain't picky 'bout who He uses to get things done, as long as they get done. Yes, I pray for Larson all the time. Guess I thought he was the one who needed changin'—still do. I wasn't expectin' God to use Larson to help someone else to change. But again, I can't tell God how to run His business."

"I've always known God listens when you pray, Grandma."

"God hears anyone's sincere prayers. If Ruby's serious—He'll help her."

Katty tapped on the screen door. Without waiting for an answer, she flung it open and burst in. Sadie tripped in behind her. They'd obviously been peeking through their window from next door.

"Mrs. Strom, I know I'm bein' nosey, but was that a woman Larson had with him? It looked like he was packed to leave."

"Yes, her name is Ruby Struthers. Larson met her when he was in jail."

"That woman was in jail with Larson, and now they're ridin' 'round together?" Katty jumped to our same conclusion.

"No, she wasn't in jail with him. She—lived in Caruthersville. Larson met her during the times he was in town and away from the jail."

"She lived down by the river past the sea wall," I said bluntly. Grandma shot me a look that meant maybe she hadn't intended to share that piece of information.

"You mean—you mean she's one of them women…?"

"Yes, Katty, but accordin' to her, she *was* one of *them* women. She's goin' with Larson to Florida—she said to change her lifestyle," Grandma interrupted.

"Change her…with Larson? Well, do tell." A faint smile swept Katty's face.

"I know—I hear you," Grandma conceded. "I know Larson's not a likely choice in that matter when he could use some changin' hisself, but oh well—it's Larson's and nobody else who's helpin' her right now."

"Well, you know that story you told us about God causin' a donkey to talk? Guess if God can do that, He can use Larson to do this," Katty snickered.

I was considering how I felt to have Daddy compared to a donkey. Grandma looked as though she may have been too. But, knowing Katty's simple but honest way of putting things, I allowed she meant no harm.

"Well, we gotta' go. I just had to know, or I don't think I could a slept tonight." Katty and Sadie rushed out almost as quickly as they raced in.

"She's probably in a hurry to fill Simp in," Grandma said.

"As close as we live, it's impossible to not see everything that goes on over here—or over there," I added.

"Especially if your nose is pressed against the window pane," Grandma said. We laughed. We might as well have laughed. Crying wouldn't help.

"I have homework. I should've gotten it earlier but couldn't get my mind wrapped around it with everything that happened today," I said once supper was over with.

"Guess I'll go work on my quilt pieces. No use frettin' anymore."

Knowing Grandma, she'd be praying silently for Daddy and his traveling companion while she worked.

## Chapter Seventy-One

POLLY AND MEL got off the bus together the next morning. I waited for them at the east door. Mel mumbled hello on the way to his locker.

"You two are hitting it off pretty well," I whispered to Polly. I'd decided to accept their relationship regardless of how it hurt.

"We're only friends. He sure didn't have much to say this morning."

"He was real talkative out in the cotton field, but he hardly speaks to me now."

"I've noticed. Wonder why?" Polly questioned.

"Guess he's like the other boys. I'm taboo when everyone's watching."

"Jean, Mel doesn't strike me like that."

"I didn't think so either. It's silly, but I thought we had a bond since we each had…"

"Had what?" Polly looked confused.

"Umm…nothing. It's nothing. We have to run now, or we'll be late for class."

Polly rushed in one direction, and I rushed in the other. I had to be more careful. If Mel's real name was ever revealed, I sure didn't want to be the one to reveal it. He was sitting in the back of the classroom next to Brenda Bittle again when I arrived. He looked troubled. I scooted in next to Darla. Mr. Vondell quietly counted heads.

"Okay, class. Put your books away. We're having a pop quiz." Groans were heard throughout the room. A pop quiz wasn't a great way to start a day. It sure wasn't how I wanted to start mine. I'd almost skipped studying last night with Daddy's leaving and everything. Now, I was glad I didn't.

Purposely dropping a pencil on the floor, I stole a glance at Mel. Though his head was down, I could see his furrowed brow. I wasn't sure if his level of concentration meant he was struggling with the questions or answering them with more detail. Why should I care? He clearly wasn't concerned for me.

The quiz took most of the hour. Mel laid his paper on Mr. Vondell's desk as he exited the room. After scanning my paper again, I turned it in and waited in the hall for Darla.

Whew—I hate pop-quizzes, don't you?" Darla moaned once she reached the hall.

"Yes, I do. Now, Mr. Vondell knows if we studied or not."

"Oh…I almost forgot, I won't be walking with you and Polly again during noon hour. We've got one more special layout for the school paper this month."

"It's okay. We understand."

"Wait, Polly can't walk with you either. I've recommended her to help with the illustrations. You'll be all alone—sorry," Darla sighed.

"I'll be all right. I'll find a quiet place to sit and read. Does Polly know this? She never mentioned it this morning."

"No, I still have to tell her. Bet she'll be glad though. She's a great illustrator."

"Yes, she is. If she doesn't do something with that talent after graduation, it'll be a crime. By the way, what's your plan after graduation?" I questioned.

"I've been accepted at Memphis University, where Coop's attending. And—we're getting married."

"Oh Darla, I always knew you two would get married. It must be wonderful to know exactly what you're going to do and when you're going to do it."

"What about you, Jean?"

"I don't know what I want to do yet. Grandma would be happy if I found someone, got married, and had two or three kids. Of course, Daddy thinks I could to be the first woman president. He'd vote for me, but he'd probably have to vote absentee ballot." We laughed.

"What's so funny?" Polly asked when she arrived. She laughed too when I told her about Daddy voting absentee ballot.

"Hey Polly, can you help us with illustrations for the school paper during noon hour?" Darla asked.

"Yes, I'd love to. Oh no, Jean, that'll leave you all alone."

"It's okay. Darla already told me. Go show off your talents. I'm proud of you."

I really didn't mind having an hour alone. I had a lot to think about. Did Daddy and Ruby make it safely to Florida? I'd shared with Darla what I thought Grandma and Daddy would want for me after graduation, but I needed to decide what I wanted. Had Hutch found someone to marry? What was Mel's problem—really? I had a lot to ponder.

The bell rang. A stream of kids headed for the cafeteria. A smaller group headed toward the Green Fly. Polly and Darla skirted off to the circulation room, and I darted out the south hall door to find a spot to sit, read, and think.

I'd just opened my book when Mel came through the door and ambled toward me. I looked to either side of me, wondering if I was really his target but to my surprise, he sat down and spoke first.

"What are you reading?" he asked casually. I couldn't believe after avoiding me all this time, he was concerned about the book I was reading.

"What are you doing?" I shot back.

"Sitting here—talking to you."

"Did Darla and Polly send you?"

"No, I looked for you after I saw them going into the circulation room together." He crossed his legs and picked at a blade of grass.

"So, what's wrong?" Something had to be wrong. Or why would Mel suddenly pair up with me?

"Nothing's wrong—well something's wrong, but that is not why I'm here."

"I knew it. So what's the something that's wrong?"

"We're moving again. Dad said we can't make it through the winter around here. He wants to go to Florida and work in the orange groves."

"Florida—really? My Dad and…umm…my Dad left for Florida yesterday, too."

"So, he's gone again?"

"Yeah…well…we expected it."

"Jean, I hate having to move again. I like what I've seen of Muddy Ox School so far. People here are really nice; like you said they'd be. Actually, better than any school I've ever gone to."

"I'm sorry you're moving Mel. I understand. If I didn't have Grandma, my Dad would be dragging me around all over the country too."

"I wish I had a Grandma to always be there for me. Well, I do have one, but my Dad wouldn't let me live with her. He needs my wages to help run the family."

"What's he going to do when you finally get out on your own?"

"Disown me—I guess. Without me, he'd be forced to do something other than follow the crops."

"So you'll have to start another new school. I dread

that for you."

"I'm going to drop out of school, Jean. Maybe one day, I'll join the service and get my GED. Who knows? Anyway, I didn't want to just leave without letting you know what happened. I'm going to tell Polly on our bus ride home."

"Do you like Polly?"

"As a girlfriend? No, she's just a friend."

"Oh, I—I guess—I thought you liked her."

"I do—as a friend," he confirmed. I believed him.

"I have another question?" If he was leaving, what did I have to lose?

"Yes?"

"If you knew this would be your last day, why in the world did you struggle with that test in Mr. Vondell's class this morning?" I now revealed I'd been watching him.

"Oh… that…" as though he'd expected a different question. "I really don't know. I studied. I knew it. I wanted to do well on the test. I'm not leaving as a failure, Jean—I'm just leaving."

If she'd heard his answer, he'd have been another guy after Grandma's own heart.

"Again, I'm sorry. I wish you could stay and graduate with me—and our class."

"Well, I've learned not to count on too much of anything. That's for sure. I guess I knew this'd happen. But I can't go through with starting another school, liking it, and getting uprooted again." This was the Mel I knew that week in the cotton patch—open, honest and genuine. The façade was gone. I was more attracted to him now than ever—even if he had treated me like the plague since school started.

"So how about you? Of all the things we covered the week we worked together; your future plans weren't among them? What do you…?

The bell saved me. The last thing I wanted to discuss was my future plans—especially with Mel. Especially since I didn't know what they were.

He stood and helped me to my feet. I felt so special when Mel held the door for me, then walked me to my next class. Of course, eyes followed us, but we didn't care.

That he didn't care was most important to me.

## Chapter Seventy-Two

MEL HELD MY hand as we walked with Polly to the bus. She looked puzzled but didn't ask. He lingered, after Polly boarded. My face flushed as he pulled me close. For that moment, it was as though we were suspended within the eye of our own private whirlwind while time swirled around us. His soft lips brushed my forehead and cheek before kissing me tenderly. At that moment, I only saw *his* eyes. Other eyes didn't matter.

"Good-bye, Meryl Jean—for now," He whispered as he released me and joined Polly on the bus."

I wanted to beg him to stay but knew it was impossible. *"For now."* I took that as he also hoped our paths would cross again one day—maybe. I imagined Polly had not been able to believe her eyes. She'd have trouble believing her ears, once she heard he was leaving again. Their bus was the last to leave so our farewell scene wasn't played out for the entire student body, only the few on their bus. Again, I didn't care. I only cared that Mel had confessed his feelings for me.

When we met Darla at the east door the next morning without Mel, Polly and I had long faces. I filled them in on everything Mel had told me the day before and about his regrets for leaving. I was surprised when Polly said she'd given him my address—at his request. Darla was confused.

"So, which one of you was his girlfriend?" Darla asked.

"We were only friends," Polly replied.

"We were only friends, too," I sighed.

If Mel had stayed, I was confident we could have been more. But for now, I was happy being a special friend to *just Mel*. Yes, it took his going away to give him the courage to open up to me. I didn't hold that against him. Life was hard at our age, especially in high school, when you're trying to find and define yourself. More than most, I understood how hard it was to trust your peers. I was only glad he'd stepped forward when he did. Had he not, my memories of him would be tarnished. Now, they glistened.

Mel, Hutch, and even Wade, had their time and place in my young life. They were gone but their good and bad memories would remain—for always.

THE REST OF my last year at Muddy Ox School flew by. Graduation Day was nearing, and excitement hovered in the halls. May 13, 1964, was one day away.

"You got a graduation card in the mail from your Daddy today," Grandma announced as I reached home that afternoon.

"A card from Daddy is a sure sign he's not coming to my graduation, or he wouldn't have wasted a stamp."

"Look at the return address," Grandma said solemnly.

It was from Mr. and Mrs. Larson Strom. "They got married?" I had mixed feelings. Ruby nor anyone else could ever replace Mama. But after her death, when Daddy did unpredictable things, I assumed responsibility like a parent felt responsible for their child. His new wife could fill that position, with my blessings. Just having another person in his world, gave me less cause to be anxious about him. If they could make it work, this could be great news.

"I hope both of them did some changin' before they did this. Marriage needs at least one strong, sensible person in it. It's likely to crumble for sure with two weak ones tryin' to hold it together," Grandma said.

"Wow! Daddy sent me a hundred dollars." I held it high. He must have felt real guilty about not coming.

"Let me see," Grandma was also shocked.

"He had Ruby write a note about how sorry he was they couldn't make it—some excuse about car problems. We know Daddy can usually take a piece of baling-wire and a screwdriver and fix most anything wrong with a car. It's not like he hasn't known about graduation for months. The money helps but it doesn't replace Daddy's eyes seeing me graduate."

"Well, I'm sorry he's not comin'. But I wouldn't miss it for nothin'. I'll be there."

"I know you will, Grandma. You've always been there for me."

"Well, you've been here for me, too." We were close to tears and the ceremony wasn't until the next day."

"Grandma, I need to ask you something, speaking of me being here for you?"

"Okay?"

"What are you going to do if I leave to find a job somewhere, or in the future, if I get married, or—maybe—go to college?"

"I know you're 'bout grown, and the day'll come when you won't—can't be here. Simp and Katty already offered when that time comes, I can spend nights at their house again, like before."

"So, if I wanted to go to college, you'd be okay with it?"

"Meryl, I wanted you to get your diploma. I hope someday you'll meet a good man, marry, and have a family. Until then, if you have to go away to find work, I'll understand. But if you go to college, you're on your own. I don't know much about college. But I never signed for my boys to go to no Army, and I ain't a signin' for you to go to no college. Besides, you don't have the money for no college."

"You're right about that. College is expensive. I don't have a clear vision of college myself. I guess we'll deal with all of that when and if it happens."

Grandma could have given me a solid out and said no to college altogether, but she didn't. She explained that if one of her sons lost his life in the service she wouldn't feel like she sent him to his death. That was why she couldn't sign for them to go. If I went to college and got into trouble, away from her watchful eyes, she didn't want to think she helped me go wrong. I clearly understood any decision I made about college—or for that matter anything else, would be mine to live with. Man, growing up was hard—and scary.

## Chapter Seventy-Three

THE GYM WAS packed. I sat Grandma by Mrs. McCrady before taking my place in line. I was so nervous I feared my diploma might slip through my wet palms once it was handed to me. As I looked at the faces of my classmates, some of them probably for the last time as they filed back to their seats, a somber feeling consumed me. Graduation Day was supposed to be joyous. Why did this almost feel like a funeral?

Had his father not needed to rely on child labor to provide for his family, Mel would have been in this line today. He possibly could have been my escort. Surely being able to graduate would have been worth divulging his actual name. If I'd agreed to marry and go with Hutch, I wouldn't be here at all—thus crushing my dream. I so hoped both those guys got their GED; if not for the chance of a better job—for their own self-gratification.

Of all the times Daddy had been absent in my life. To miss my graduation was so far, his worse possible choice. High School Graduation only happens once in a lifetime and he's missing mine.

"Meryl Jean Strom." My name was finally called, and

I walked toward center stage. Before I reached Principal Gaffin, Mrs. Tyree stepped forward holding an envelope and a book.

She began. "On the final day of school last year, I asked my class to each write a poem. Some entries were quite good and enlightening—others were very amusing." She paused for laughter before going on. "Without their knowledge, I took the liberty of entering the most outstanding poems into a National Poetry Contest. Today, I am proud to present Meryl Jean Strom the English award and this copy of the National High School Poetry Anthology Press for 1963-1964. Her poem, 'That Grandmother of Mine' was chosen for publication and is on page thirteen. If I may, I would like to read it at this time.

That Grandmother of Mine<br>
By Meryl Jean Strom

Once she was young, her complexion so fair,
And she wore a bright blue ribbon in her coal black hair.
And when she would smile, you could see the shine,
In those beautiful brown eyes of that Grandmother of mine.

Now, she is older, her complexion not so fair,
And there is no bright blue ribbon in her grey-streaked hair.

But yet when she smiles, you can still see the shine,
In those beautiful brown eyes of that Grandmother of mine.

Now, I'm sure when Jesus calls her,
To Heaven bright and fair,
She'll have the sweetest smile,
And the most beautiful brown eyes
Found in Heaven anywhere."

The assembly rose to a standing ovation as I hugged and thanked Mrs. Tyree. I never felt so honored. I glanced toward Grandma but quickly looked away before the tears in her eyes brought tears to mine.

Principal Gaffin stepped forward with my diploma and another envelope. "Jean, in addition to your diploma, I would like to present you with a full, one-year scholarship to Southeast Missouri State University. Please join me in congratulating Meryl Jean Strom with this honor." Another ovation followed.

Grandma couldn't have had a broader smile as Mr. Gaffin presented me with my diploma. I didn't look at her after he gave me the scholarship letter.

Simp was there to take us home after the ceremony. That evening, Jake and Effie joined the Simpsons and us for cake and coffee. "I knew your mama well, Jean. She would have been so proud of you today." Effie couldn't have said anything more appropriate as she hugged me and gave me a card.

"Schoolin' was important to you, and you saw it through. We're proud of you girl," Katty added. Simp and Sadie joined her in giving me a group hug and another card.

"I'd need another word that means proud to explain how I'm feelin' right now. I don't have you a card, but I couldn't love you more just the same," Grandma said.

"Thank all of you. You have given the terms friend and neighbor a greater meaning. And Grandma, there's not a card or envelope big enough to hold what you've given me these last six years. I'm rich, getting to live with you and learn from you."

"Well, let's eat. I held my mouth right for sure makin' this cake," Katty laughed as she not only cut the cake but cut into the seriousness of the room, as well.

"I heard you got a scholarship for college, Jean." Effie did her usual probing.

"Yes, I did. I'm honored but a little scared at the same time."

"Why scared? Ain't it somethin' you worked for and wanted?" Simp questioned.

"Grandma and I have talked about this. We need to talk about it some more."

No one said anymore concerning my future plans, and I was grateful. I opened the cards after we ate and thanked them again. I added Jake and Effie's twenty-five dollars and Katty and Simp's fifteen along with

Daddy's one hundred to my 'what's next' fund.

After my graduation party was over, the guests cleared. Grandma and I found ourselves as alone once more as the day after Daddy first left me. The May roses were exceptionally beautiful and fragrant that evening as we swung quietly.

"Meryl, I said I wouldn't sign for you to go to college, but that don't mean you can't go on your own."

"I know Grandma. But honestly—I'm really am scared."

"You, Meryl Jean Strom, scared? That don't sound like you."

"Well, college is a big step. What if I start and can't finish? Also, I'm not positive teaching is what I want to do for the rest of my life? I have to think about this."

"You're the only one who knows where your heart lies. I'm sure you're smart enough to figure it out."

"Grandma, that's the problem. After twelve years of school, I don't feel smart enough to figure anything out. I'm not sure I know anything. Do you want to really know how I feel right now?"

"Yes, I do."

"For five years, my name has been on a roll at Muddy Ox School. They expected me, had a place for me—wanted me. My name is not on their list anymore. I almost feel abandoned again. Is that silly?"

"I guess I can see how you might feel that way. But you asked me, and I'm goin' to tell you that yes—that's silly. After I married Omar, a plate was not set on my mother's table for me any longer. After Omar died, his plate stays in the cupboard. Life's like that. The school might not have your name on its list, but I'll promise you, Meryl Jean Strom's name is on somebody's list.

If not at a college, it could be at a work place, if not there, some special somebody has your name written on his heart—even if he don't know it yet. I know I'm always tellin' you Bible scriptures, but this one is the most important one you need to hear right now. *'Be still and know that I am God'.* Meryl, if you don't know which direction to go—stand still and see where God leads you."

After we went to bed that night, Grandma's words rang over and over in my head.

*"Meryl if you don't know which direction to go—stand still and see where God leads you."*

## Chapter Seventy-Four

I WALKED TO school for the last time the next morning. As I'd suspected, I found Mrs. Tyree cleaning out her desk. Luckily, she was alone. I so needed to talk with her.

"Jean, what a surprise. Wait, is something wrong?" She asked after reading my face.

"Mrs. Tyree, I'm scared."

"Scared how? Why? Scared of what?" She stopped cleaning, and we sat.

"I guess I'm afraid of failure and of the unknown. I remember this feeling when Daddy brought me here after Mama died. But that was just it—Daddy brought me here. I didn't have a choice. What I do now is all on me—my choosing."

"Hmm…up until now, I've only seen a confident, determined, and brave Jean Strom. I've never seen this Jean. Does your Grandma have anything to do with this?"

"Truthfully, Mrs. Tyree, my high school diploma was important to Grandma, but college is not. She isn't completely forbidding me to go, but she isn't encouraging me either. In her day, marriage was a girl's main option. Muddy Ox is Grandma's universe. College or a life elsewhere is almost inconceivable for her."

"I'm an educator, Jean. I've taught you eighth grade and four years of high school English. I recognized your potential from the beginning. That potential was there long before I met you, and it's always going to be alive and well inside you."

"Yes, but that potential, a hundred and forty dollars, and the one year scholarship are all I have. What happens when the money and the scholarship are gone? Southeast Missouri State University is the closest college to Muddy Ox. But Cape Girardeau might as well be Cape Canaveral as far as Grandma's concerned. I don't know where to begin. I don't know anyone there or how I'd get there. Daddy didn't even come home to see me graduate. He's not likely to come and take me to college."

"You were awarded a full, one year scholarship. Your room, board, tuition, and books are covered for an entire year. Don't worry about the rest. There are part-time jobs available for other expenses. Your performance in the cotton field is proof of your work ethic. Getting a job should be easy. There are also more scholarships. You can do this, Jean. I'll help you."

"But…"

"Let's address the other 'buts' as they come along. You said your Grandmother isn't completely against college. I'm almost sure she'll come around eventually.

And think about how proud your Mother would be to see her daughter as a college graduate. You've handled bigger challenges than this, and you can handle this, too. I believe in you, Jean."

I FELT LIGHTER walking home than I did walking to the school that day. Mrs. Tyree helped to lift the weight of indecisiveness concerning the scholarship. She even offered to drive me to Cape and get me settled in. That was another load lifted.

What she said about Mama really meant a lot. My mother helped to shape the potential Mrs. Tyree saw in me. She would only be ashamed if I wasted that potential. Mama would be proud to know I received a college scholarship and made it work. It suddenly occurred to me that with the counsel and caring of my high school English teacher, I had crossed off a whole new list of 'nevers'.

A note from Grandma was on the kitchen table when I got home. She was at Effie's working on quilts. Dropping into the swing, I pictured my future as a quilt. No one but Grandma chose the pieces, colors, or shapes for her quilt. I could do the same with my 'life quilt'.

I determined at that moment when I got a job, I'd be the best worker I could be. And—whomever I decided to spend the rest of my life with had better be ready to succeed. I wouldn't have it any other way. My only plan now—was to succeed.

Suddenly a whirlwind swirled by the edge of the porch. It wavered from one side of the lane to the other as if beckoning me. Its path steadied and disappeared beyond the end of the gravel road. I'd been wavering like that little wind. My path was leading away from Muddy Ox and Grandma to new horizons. Like that whirlwind, I couldn't—wouldn't look back. I had to keep going.

That very moment, I decided I'd tackle college like I did the cotton field—one day, one sting, one row, one whirlwind, and one season at a time.

A soft breeze kissed the leaves of the old willow tree in the edge of our yard and carried a bird's sweet song along with it. I joined her with a song of my own.

I hear a bird, as it sings to me

A beautiful song for my love and me.

Please let the bird that sings to me,

Sing to the one—I love.

What a sweet thought…

Psalms 46:10…Be still and know that I am God.

## Special thanks to:

The SKYWriters workshop: Bobbie Falin, John Bowers, Kimberly Bartley and Gerry Brown. You were instrumental in helping me by reading, critiquing, advising and encouraging me during this endeavor. You all are priceless.

Extra, extra thanks again to Bobbie Falin. Your patience was golden. The words give up are just not in your vocabulary.

Thanks to Rick Ashby for your advice, foresight and keen eye from the very beginning.

All my beta readers—you know who you are. This story would not have been what it is without all of your extra sets of eyes. Thank you.

And…to my family and friends who have left a handprint on this story, and to Zacchaeus for being so patient with me during the three years it's taken to get this book finished—love you guys.

Most of all, thanks to all of you who are fans of my books. I have been overwhelmed and humbled by your outpouring of love and your continued interest in my work.

## About the Author

*Noel Barton* spent her teen years in the Bootheel of Missouri.

She now resides in Bowling Green, Kentucky. She is a mother, grandmother, widowed (twice), best friend to her little dog Zacchaeus and a retired travel counselor. Being a devout Christian, she credits God for her writing ability. *Meryl Jean Another Whirlwind* is her second novel. Although, not an autobiography, many aspects of her books are pulled from personal experiences. It is her wish that those reading her novels will find peace to cross off some the 'never's in their lives. And she hopes that during their nostalgic journey down memory lane, her readers can see how her stories could remind them of some of the Whirlwinds in their own lives.

www.ingramcontent.com/pod-product-compliance
Lightning Source LLC
Chambersburg PA
CBHW052006070526
44584CB00016B/1641